Delia Falconer is the award-winning
The Service of Clouds, The Lost Thoughts
a personal history of her hometown, where she still lives with
her family. In 2018, she was the winner of the Walkley-Pascall
award for Arts Criticism.

SIGNS AND WONDERS

SIGNS AND WONDERS

Delia Falconer

SCRIBNER

SCRIBNER

First published in Australia in 2021 by Scribner, an imprint of
Simon & Schuster Australia
Suite 19A, Level 1, Building C, 450 Miller Street, Cammeray, NSW 2062

Sydney New York London Toronto New Delhi
Visit our website at www.simonandschuster.com.au

SCRIBNER and design are registered trademarks of The Gale Group, Inc.,
used under licence by Simon & Schuster Inc.

10 9 8 7 6 5 4 3 2 1

© Delia Falconer 2021

All rights reserved. No part of this publication may be reproduced,
stored in a retrieval system, or transmitted in any form or by
any means, electronic, mechanical, photocopying, recording or
otherwise, without prior permission of the publisher.

A catalogue record for this
book is available from the
National Library of Australia

9781760857820 (paperback)
9781760857837 (ebook)

Cover design by Daniel New
Typeset in 12.5/17 pt Adobe Garamond Pro by Midland Typesetters, Australia
Printed and bound in Australia by Griffin Press

The paper this book is printed on is certified against the
Forest Stewardship Council® Standards. Griffin Press holds
chain of custody certification SGSHK-COC-005088. FSC®
promotes environmentally responsible, socially beneficial
and economically viable management of the world's forests

I want to photograph the considerable ceremonies of our present . . . I want to gather them, like somebody's grandmother putting up preserves, because they will have been so beautiful.
—Diana Arbus, grant application to the Guggenheim Foundation, 1963

Here, at the edge of extinction, is the place to begin, when the worlds that one loves . . . are being trashed.
—Deborah Bird-Rose

Contents

Introduction	1
Signs and Wonders	9
Coal: An Unnatural History	29
Terror from the Air: Fire Diary 2019–20	47
Birds	75
How It Feels Now (After 'Hysterical Realism')	85
Gum Trees	119
The Opposite of Glamour	125
Coronavirus Time: Diary	147
The Disappearing Paragraph	155
Good Neighbours	173
The Weight of Things	201
Covid Walking: Diary	225
Everything is Illuminated	251
Selected Bibliography	275
Author's Note	289

Introduction

A few years ago, I found a bird's nest on the footpath, a beautiful thing of loosely woven she-oak needles lined with pale grey fur. I held it cupped in my hand as I continued onto the train from our inner-city suburb and walked through the long pedestrian tunnel to the edge of Sydney's central business district. The joyful attention it attracted surprised me. 'That's a little noisy miner's nest you've got there,' a woman told me as she passed. 'Lovely,' another called out. But when I reached the university and showed it to my student, a man my own age, his face fell. This meant a bird had lost its home, he said. Did I know, he asked, that when the Harbour Bridge was first built crows made their nests on its high trusses? But when they went out to search for food, the architecture was so repetitive that even these clever birds couldn't find their way back to their chicks.

I smiled a little to myself at my student's tragic cast of mind. Recent high winds had blown down this nest – a small drama innocent, as far as I knew, of any human interference. Yet I was all too familiar myself with a sense of wonder that flipped over quickly into apprehension about our impact on the natural world. Were the still evenings of a gloriously prolonged summer reason to rejoice or evidence of disrupted climate patterns? Was it great good fortune, while driving in a remote part of the country, to have seen a koala bundling along by the roadside with her joey on her back, or an indicator of distress? Over the last few years, these trains of thought have multiplied. Is what I am witnessing normal or abnormal? A good or a bad sign? And above all is it due, somehow, *to us*?

These days, the most beautiful things, whose perennial loveliness once sustained us, carry the weight of an apprehension that has come upon us with terrifying speed. Could it have only been 2014 that I first heard the word 'Anthropocene,' which denotes the astonishing concept that we've entered a new human-made geological epoch: that our signature will persist, stamped into the earth's strata, for longer than it's possible to imagine? Though the term is contentious, there's a broad scientific consensus that our activities have acquired the geological force to push the atmosphere, geology, hydrology and other processes of this twelve-thousand-year epoch out of their predictable patterns and variability. Around the same time I watched, with dismay, in a fuggy Canberra lecture room, as Australian environmental historian Tom Griffiths projected twenty-four graphs of the 'Great Acceleration,' which tracked the trajectory of human activities and their tolls on the planet's systems, such as carbon dioxide in the atmosphere and ocean acidification. They had been rising steadily since the industrial revolution. But around 1950, every single graph began to surge toward the vertical and head off-scale.

The International Geosphere-Biosphere Programme had only plotted these trends until 2010. I dread to think how they will look, once they are updated to include the last decade. And yet,

Introduction

as devastating as they are likely to be, these graphs may already be losing their power to predict the future, at least a future in which change is consistent. Our fossil fuel addiction may already have moved us beyond even the small comfort of the linear or gradual and into a chaotic territory of unpredictable feedback loops and tipping points. Some scientists have suggested the hundred years to follow 2100 will be the 'century of hell,' perhaps even if we manage to keep global heating below 2 degrees Celsius.

Such knowledge brings its own vertigo as we try to reconcile such dire warnings with our ongoing daily life. We find ourselves authors of a story we may not be able to escape, and which is increasingly difficult to look at objectively. In the words of French philosopher Bruno Latour, there is now 'no distant place anymore.'

*

And yet the world seems more beautiful than ever to me these days, more intensely lovely, as if these qualities were also undergoing an exponential feedback effect. It is often *sublimely* beautiful, in the classical sense of exciting emotions and thoughts beyond the ordinary. On any given day, a fleeting cabinet of wonders passes through my phone: ancient tardigrades (or 'water bears') under intense 3D magnification, like pouchy little taxidermist's armatures come to life, which can survive freezing, radiation or the blast of a supernova; the warped green beams of the Aurora Australis; the flight of a hummingbird caught in slow motion; a dinosaur tail the size of a sparrow's, with chestnut feathers, preserved in amber. More recently, there has been the disconcerting vision of some of the world's most polluted cities – Delhi, Bangkok, Bogota, São Paolo – their skies transformed in the midst of the human suffering of pandemic lockdowns from smog to a lambent blue. It's as if our feeds have become our prosthetic heightened senses, allowing us to see – even if only casually – the uncanny beauty in everything.

As we grapple with the awe-inspiring concept that we are now making the world's systems pitch and wobble even the most humble things seem radiant with this knowledge. How can we comprehend that the fate of species that preceded us by millions of years is now tied to ours – or, in the case of creatures like the nautilus and horseshoe crab, even preceded the coal we burn – which now seem more precariously precious? How can our daily lives be changing the movement of the Gulf Stream, causing heated subterranean gasses in Russia's Arctic to blow 'like a bottle of champagne,' or melting the permafrost so that it has started to spit out the more than ten million mammoths thought to lie within it, causing a 'gold rush' of ice ivory? How can we even imagine these shifts we are causing will last for many thousands of years into the future, like the light of stars? It is one thing to experience what the Japanese call *mono no aware*, melancholy at the passing of things, like the brief blooming of the cherry blossom, but it is of another order entirely to think of the grand overturning of the stability of time and place as we know them.

To confront the epic scale of these events can feel, paradoxically, as if we have been plunged back in time, out of a scientific era and into an age of myth and wonder. For as they come under more threat, we are also learning more almost daily about the fantastic complexity of our ecosystems and the miraculous self-balancing of our Earth's fragile atmosphere, which, as writer Lyall Watson notes, serves the same function for the planet as the fur on a fox or the shell of a snail but is 'a strange and beautiful anomaly' maintained by living beings. Sometimes it seems, as if in a fairy tale, that as science discovers more about the world's intricate agency, we are seeing everything we intuited as children now coming true: that a solitary tree in a paddock feels lonely, that the winds are alive, that animals talk, that fish feel pain.

'All things counter, original, spare, strange,' wrote Victorian poet Gerard Manley Hopkins in his celebration of pied beauty. 'Whatever is fickle, freckled (who knows how?)' As my student intuited, in the face of such enormity, even a humble bird's nest can become an almost unbearably poignant and vivid object.

'I have a similar feeling now as around 9/11,' my publisher said to me, as we began to talk about my writing this book. 'Like a whale breaching, there's something almost wonderful, while also awful, about seeing everything up in the air before it comes crashing down.' I've been living with this sensation of eerie suspension for almost a decade. As we teeter on the edge of ordinariness that threatens to drop away into the unimaginable, every day brings these apprehensions of beauty and terror, of deep past and rushing future. I know from the conversations I've had with friends and strangers that I'm not alone.

But do we even have the emotional repertoire to take in such enormity, to hold all these dimensions in our minds at once? Can the stories we are used to telling still sustain themselves, or us? Can feelings forged in a more stable age help us to try to look after our world or carry us into an unthinkable future? These are the questions that have occupied me as I have walked my children to school, prepared lectures, or taken my evening walk to the point below our apartment and back, going through all the motions of an ordinary life that now feel provisional and increasingly unreal.

Over the last few years my conviction has grown that we're experiencing a 'Great Acceleration' of feeling that is tracking parallel to the speeding up of our world's systems. Thinking back over twenty years of work as an essayist and reviewer, I've realised that the books and films I was reading and watching were also changing, too rapidly for me to see at the time, to anticipate looming catastrophe indirectly, like the shadow of an eclipse thrown onto a piece of paper. Because I've spent much of my life reading and writing, I'm most sensitive to shifts in the atmosphere of my own small literary ecotone, which I write about in these pages. At the same time, it's been shocking to realise that my own life spans most of the period in which our impact on the world has been most catastrophic, and so I've tried to use it, in this book, as a measure.

Here in Australia, deep time and survival both seem closer than in many other parts of our planet. In its complicated history, which has in turn shaped me, Indigenous Australians' cultural memories encompass the postglacial coastal inundation at the end of the last ice age twenty thousand years ago, sea rise of 120 metres dividing the mainland from Tasmania and inundating most of the coastal shelf, and survival through the continuing violence of colonisation. You can't grow up here without an understanding that humans and Country have already been long entwined; nor without knowing that drastic environmental changes are often uneven, and unfair, in who they affect. While I'm lucky enough to work mostly from home in a beautiful part of my city, where these effects are for the most part unobtrusive, elsewhere – in part because of my generational cohort's taste for global travel – they're already taking lives. And yet, for all this inherited knowledge, my old and fragile country is likely to bear the brunt of global

Introduction

changes first. These essays are dispatches from the present but also the near future.

It has surprised me writing these essays, how often my thoughts have kept circling back, like my publisher's, to the attacks in 2001 on New York's Twin Towers. While I don't want to exaggerate their place in world history, they do seem to have marked that year, in the West at least, as a turning point, when things began to wrench from their usual dimensions, to quicken and go off-scale. Over these last two decades – at the same time as the stricken earth has been putting on some of its most epic displays – I can't help thinking our culture has also been becoming brighter and more baroque, like a firework show unleashing its biggest rockets and most glittering cascades in its final moments.

I've also written this book with complicated feelings. In 2011 my partner and I had twins, a boy and a girl, who have filled our hearts and who have already lived, as my son points out, through two of the biggest events of their parents' five-plus-decade lives: Australia's first megafires in the summer of 2019–2020 and a global pandemic. Their lifetimes are now the queasy yardstick for everything I feel and read. In 2018, some scientists were saying that we had a critical window of just twelve years to save the planet. (Our twins would be nineteen.) In 2019, others revised the critical window down to eighteen months. (They would be just ten.) By the time you read this, that window will have closed. Looking at my children, I'm reminded of the American writer George Saunders's story of being on a plane that had just struck a flock of geese. As black smoke began to enter the cabin, the young boy beside him, travelling alone, asked, 'Sir, is this supposed to be happening?' It's hard to know what to say.

There are other books that will lay out the actions we need to take to stave off, or at least slow, the destruction unfolding;

although we mostly know already what these are. Instead, from my own small piece of turf on Australia's east coast, I have tried to take the temperature of this moment, to reduce it to my own human scale and at the same time to catch the terrific grandeur of its unfolding, which is becoming harder and harder to ignore. I have tried to let these essays follow the moods and surges of our new era of 'signs and wonders.' I write this book in the small hope that putting them precisely into words might also be useful. Whether it will be a record or a requiem remains to be seen.

Signs and Wonders

I have lived near the harbour for twenty years. In autumn I watch for fish fry in the water and the swifts that wheel like tiny warplanes above the naval dockyards. In summer, migratory koels call out from the trees in my local park with a grinding yearning. There have been surprises over the years: a fairy penguin off the end of the point and, once, a large stingray gliding up the middle of the canal on a high tide. But mostly I am looking for familiar creatures: the microbats that flit at dusk over the water or the flying foxes that land heavily in the Moreton Bay figs, though their numbers have declined and their squabbling in the tree outside our apartment no longer keeps us awake at night.

Walking to Mrs Macquarie's Chair in the Domain, I like to scan the small bay in Woolloomooloo for fish. But one day, in 2018, there was nothing to see in the flat green water, not even the usual mullet that nose around the marina's floating pontoons or the ubiquitous smooth toadfish with fins like tiny propellers. A few years earlier, I would have put this down to the seasonal variation of schools in the Harbour – but this time it felt different. I found myself wondering if there were no longer any fish to see.

What if they were disappearing, I wondered, like the small frogs that were such a common sight after rain when I was a child, or the greengrocer cicadas we used to catch in the school playground? In 2014, the World Wildlife Fund had released a widely circulated report, which concluded that we had killed off more than half of the world's wildlife over the last half-century – not only exotic animals but common creatures like giraffes, bats and even insects. That afternoon in Woolloomooloo I realised I had been ticking off checklists of animals on my walks to counter a growing sense of loss.

These days everything seems to carry a terrible symbolic weight, of potential catastrophic absence. Swimming at Nielsen Park, in Sydney Harbour, an ancient river valley filled by melting Ice Age waters that stabilised seven thousand years ago, I've found myself wondering how high the water will rise again when the ice caps melt. 'Every bird I see these days, every bee,' my children's godmother R says, 'I wonder if it's the last.' 'Are wombats endangered? Are echidnas?' my son asks, as we drive through the city's urban fringes.

And yet, within the span of one's own experience, it's hard to measure causes and effects, let alone grasp quite how quickly things are turning. As the world becomes more unstable in the grip of vast and all-pervasive change, it's difficult to discern exact chronologies, relationships, and meaning. In this unfolding context, even small things take on terrifying and uncertain connotations.

It is as if, I found myself thinking as I scoured the water for fish that day, we're entering a new era of signs and wonders.

———

Signs and Wonders

In ancient Rome, priests and officials called augurs would look for omens of the future in the weather, the flight of birds, and the entrails or movements of animals, especially those encountered out of place. Back in the 1980s, when I learned about them in Latin classes, it was easy to feel a smug sense of distance. But now we are scrutinising the same things, not to divine the gods' will but as signs of our own actions.

Surely some of the most iconic images of the last decades must be Chris Jordan's 2009 photographs of dead albatross chicks on a remote beach in Midway Atoll National Wildlife Refuge in the Hawaiian Archipelago. The atoll lies in the north Pacific Ocean, more than 2000 kilometres from the nearest continent. And yet in these pictures, which went viral, the birds' rib cages have collapsed to reveal, within the organic shapes of decomposing feather and bone, stomach cavities filled with an astonishing array of bright pen lids, buttons, and discarded bottle tops. In 2019, writer Cameron Muir described watching scientists pump the stomachs of shearwater chicks emerging from their burrows for the first time on Australia's tiny, world-heritage-listed Lord Howe Island, in the Tasman Sea between our east coast and New Zealand. The objects they discovered – as many as 276 per bird – confirmed the catastrophic spread of ocean plastics. Some studies suggest ninety per cent of seabirds have now ingested some of the material, which they mistake for food, while even a few pieces can cause significant health problems. Muir recorded the audible crunching of the belly of one young chick that had to be euthanised. Yet, he wrote, as seabirds decline faster than any other group of birds, in the world's shadow places, plastic production is likely to triple over the next thirty years.

Recently, whale stomachs have also been going viral. Forensic videos online show scientists pulling garbage, piece by piece, from the creatures' vast interiors, like the Roman *haruspices*, who would inspect the entrails of sheep for divine omens. In one necroscopy, filmed at night, of a 4.7-metre-long curvier beaked whale, found dead of starvation in the Philippines, a man reaches into the young animal's insides to unfurl large pieces of plastic, which look like obscene intestinal tissue in the artificial light. In her book *Fathoms*, Australian writer Rebecca Giggs records the story of a sperm whale that washed up in 2012 in Andalusia, Spain, having swallowed a flattened greenhouse that had once housed tomatoes for export to Britain, including its ropes, hosepipes, burlap, tarps, a spray canister, and flowerpots.

Then there are the deaths of animals on a scale that possesses the quality of epic portent of ancient plagues. Wikipedia's rudimentary page on mass mortality events (sudden die-offs of living creatures, truncated to a business-like 'MME') begins in 1904 with the death of 1.5 million migrating birds in Minnesota. Yet after this single attribution to a natural cause (a snowstorm), the remaining deaths – among them, 'George River Caribou (1984)', 'Harbour Seals (1988)', 'Birds (2010)', 'Birds (2011)', and 'Fish (2011)' – are either unexplained or attributable to human activities, which include hydro projects, unlicensed fireworks discharge, chemical poisoning, and oil spills.

Since at least 2015 scientists have been attributing some of these mass mortality events to global heating. In 2016, on a work trip in Buenos Aires, I opened my laptop to news that a mass bleaching event caused by unusually warm water temperatures had killed around thirty per cent of the Great Barrier Reef: a 2000-kilometre-long system built by billions of coral polyps. That I was on the other side of the world in a city that was itself experiencing unseasonal autumn humidity that locals were blaming on the loss of forests in the country's north, where day-biting mosquitoes carried the epidemic zika virus, made the sense of end times more urgent. In November 2018, an extreme heatwave killed an estimated 23,000 spectacled flying foxes in Far North Queensland – almost a third of this species of native pollinators, which first appeared on the continent's fossil records fifty million years ago – which essentially 'boiled' because they are unable to regulate their body temperature once the external temperature exceeds 40 degrees Celsius. That same summer, up to a million native fish, including bream, silver perch and decades-old Murray cod, perished in the lower Darling River in far west New South Wales in three separate mass death events. Footage of former state MP Jeremy Buckingham gagging and then vomiting on camera as he held the rotting corpse of a huge cod taken from the mass floating in the Menindee Weir pool seemed like a moment of visceral augury.

For the ancients, alterations in the flights of birds, their songs, or feeding habits, or any other unusual activity such as a wolf, horse, or dog in an unexpected location, all required interpretation. Today, we are witnessing such change on a global scale. In 2017, a tally of 4000 species from around the world showed that roughly half were on the move in response to changing climate conditions. Others are simply – and confoundingly – disappearing. In 2018, newspapers began reporting an apparent 'insect apocalypse,' after German entomologists described a drop in biomass in their nets, over 27 years of collecting, of 75 per cent. This confirmed an anecdotal sense of decline. In his 2016 book, *The Moth Snowstorm*, author Michael McCarthy had described how many of the insects whose presence we had taken for granted, even if this was as simple as moths flickering in a car's headlights 'like snowflakes in a blizzard' on childhood drives, were no longer a familiar part of our daily lives.

While it makes intuitive sense that these disappearances and deaths must also be signs of drastic changes caused by human activity, direct links can be elusive. In the northern hemisphere spring of 2018 – calving season – an estimated 200,000 critically endangered saiga antelope were found dead in Kazakhstan. Many had stood grazing normally a moment before they collapsed, in one scientist's words, as if 'a switch had been turned on.' This single event wiped out 60 per cent of the total global population. It was only after performing post mortems on 32 animals that scientists were able to determine that the cause of death was the bacterium *Pasteurella multocida*, which an unusual heatwave and 80 per cent humidity had caused to pass from the antelopes' tonsils, where it resided harmlessly, into their bloodstream, to cause haemorrhagic septicaemia. A panel from the Australian Academy of Science would subsequently attribute the Darling River fish kills to a combination of drought and over-extraction of water for irrigation by those managing the Murray-Darling river system, though WaterNSW and the Department of Primary Industries – who blamed the deaths on drought and algal blooms – have taken no real action since to prevent further die-offs. Anomalously warm sea temperatures are now also mooted as the cause of the 2013 die-off of hundreds of millions of sea stars along the west coast of North America from Alaska to Mexico, by making them vulnerable to a bacterial infection in which, as if in a horror film, infected starfish lose their limbs, collapse in upon themselves, and liquefy. It's hard not to wonder as Covid-19 now appears to be showing us, if we are not more gullible than the ancients, in ignoring these dire omens and imagining we might remain untouched by the effects of profound systemic disturbance.

Scientists are trained to approach data with caution and to avoid colourful or emotional language. Yet when these cautious people express their own shock, it feels as if the earth has suddenly fallen away beneath your feet. Over the last few years, some have begun to speak openly about their 'ecological grief.' 'Something inside me feels like it has snapped,' Australian climate scientist Dr Joëlle Gergis wrote recently, 'as if some essential thread of hope has failed.' In Australia, researchers who observed a drop in the night-flying bogong moth population were moved to describe it frankly as 'astonishing.' For thousands of years, an estimated two billion bogong moths have made their thousand-kilometre migration from grasslands in Queensland and northern New South Wales to estivate in caves in cracks and boulders in the Alpine region. It was only as recently as 2018 that scientists worked out that they were using the earth's magnetic field to navigate, the only insects in the world to do so. Yet in summer that same year, when they searched in the moths' usual hiding places, researchers counted only several individuals, or none. 'They haven't declined. They've gone,' ecologist Dr Ken Green told *The Guardian*. 'We have done mountains from down to the Victorian border all the way to Canberra. We have checked every cave we know.'

The cognitive dissonance such a disappearance produces is profound, even for those of us who have lived for decades in cities where we only registered the edge of these mighty migrations as lost moths blundered through open windows or swarmed around sports oval floodlights on hot nights. The last great influx of bogongs into Sydney I can remember was in October 2007. As I walked home from lunch with my cousin in the city, dark clusters of the insects crowded around the cool granite entryways of the buildings near Circular Quay, while those ousted from their resting places fluttered helplessly on the hot footpaths. When I moved back to Sydney from Melbourne in 2001, the bogongs had been so ubiquitous that, as I prepared to bite into a toasted focaccia at a hole-in-the-wall café near my apartment, I noticed just in time the antennae of an insect that had self-immolated in the melted cheese. These moments feel like a mere eyeblink ago and at the same time irretrievable.

And yet, as these portents unfold, there is still a queasy uncertainty about cascades and tipping points. Some scientists have criticised the 2018 UN Intergovernmental Panel on Climate Change (IPCC) report, which gave us a scant twelve years to limit climate change catastrophe by phasing out fossil fuels, for underestimating key dangers. So I find myself wondering as I open my freezer: is the bucket of fist-sized, cauliflower-shaped hail, which I collected with my children a couple of years ago as a 'once-in-a-lifetime' hailstorm battered Sydney and its north coast just before Christmas, another sign of disorder, or a souvenir of a joyful chance event?

And then there are the wonders. At the same time as global disarrangement is giving birth to signs of distress, it is throwing up phenomena of spectacular and haunting strangeness. Beautiful and uncanny marvels pass daily through our virtual atmosphere – through Facebook and Twitter and Instagram – trailing the weird incandescence that must once have attached itself to Halley's Comet or the northern lights. I became so fascinated by their eerie charisma, appearing one after the other in my feed, that I began to record them. Although they are less urgent than obvious signals of disaster, these wonders are perhaps more pernicious as they turn a dying world into a modern cabinet of curiosities.

Most miraculous, surely, are the images of long-extinct animals that are emerging after tens of thousands of years from thawing permafrost in the Arctic, which is warming faster than any region on earth. In 2018, gold miners in Canada's Yukon unearthed a prehistoric wolf cub, its fur, skin, and muscles perfectly preserved. Seven weeks old when it died 50,000 years ago, when today's forest was treeless tundra, the cub is the only one of its kind so far to appear; and yet, laid out on surgical gauze, with its thick honey-coloured fur, creased muzzle, and long, closed eyelids, it could be the Instagram photo of someone's sleeping puppy. That same year, from the Batagaika crater in Yakutia, Siberia, a Pleistocene era Lenskaya, or Lena horse, two months old when it perished, emerged after 30–40,000 years in the permafrost, along with a month-old cave lion cub, eyes not yet open, its head resting on its paw. Posted and re-posted, these images are forensic and yet, at the same time, shot in perfectly lit close-up – 'Little hooves,' 'Amazing detail,' enthuses one site of the foal's tiny feet and muzzle – they're also eerily beguiling.

In 2018, then the world's fourth-hottest year on record, other ancient things made themselves known over the northern hemisphere summer. Severe drought in Europe, in which rainfall in some places was three per cent of the usual quota, caused rivers in Germany to disgorge unexploded bombs from the Second World War. Archaeologists in Norway recovered thousands of objects including a wool tunic and broken tools going back as far as 2000 years from the scree-covered edges of Oppland's melting glaciers, while an eight-year-old girl found a 1500-year-old sword in one of Sweden's droughty lakes. In 2019, the revelations from the lost 'Viking Highway' continued, some announced on Twitter by 'Secrets of the Ice,' an account run by a scientist based in Norway, whose finds that August included a medieval packhorse, which died wearing custom snowshoes.

Over the 2018 summer, in the United Kingdom, the footprints of vanished Roman mansions, airfields, Victorian grand homes, and prehistoric settlements manifested in grassed fields and parks. Straw-yellow, or lush emerald green on lighter green, these weird patterns were 'parch marks': ghostly scars of human activity that revealed themselves as the land dried and grasses died off. In one haunting image, taken above farmland in Eynsham, Oxfordshire, a 'harvest' of darkly outlined Neolithic barrow graves, paths and walls sprawls across two vast fields, the inscrutable ceremonial structures of a lost society dwarfing a modern farmhouse tucked into its tiny patch of garden. The green circles, lines, and smooth-edged squares made the yellowing fields look like the entries in the pages of Leonardo da Vinci's notebooks, as if a giant hand had made busy calculations across the earth itself.

There was actual writing, too in the form of the dozen 'hunger stones' that emerged from the drought-stricken Elbe River, near Děčín, in the Czech Republic, which recorded low water levels caused by 'megadroughts' dating as far back as 1417. The inscriptions, in German, are also warnings to future generations. *'Wenn du mich siehst, dann wiene,'* one from 1616 read: 'If you see me, weep.'

'If you see me, weep' seems like pertinent advice for living in the Anthropocene, in which, among other portents, 'once-in-a-hundred-year' events are becoming increasingly frequent. It is hard, in the middle of this growing instability, to shake the feeling, which the Eynsham parch marks produce so unnervingly, that parts of the earth are trying to communicate with us in some way.

In the Batagaika crater, a 'megaslump' in the Siberian wilderness a kilometre long and almost 800 metres wide, the sound of running water and chunks of frozen ice thumping down the cliffs from the unstable rim announce the rapid melting of ground that has been frozen for thousands of years. 'As you stand inside the slump on soft piles of soil,' one ecologist told the *Siberian Times*, 'you hear it "talking to you", with the cracking sound of ice and a non-stop monotonous gurgling of little springs and rivers of water.' Recently, scientists have observed that icebergs are melting more loudly and emitting 'excruciating' sounds, which reminded a UNFCCC (United Nations Framework Convention on Climate Change) representative of 'animals in pain.' Instead of depending on satellite imagery to monitor melting icebergs, scientists are currently experimenting with recording the noises the ice makes where it meets ocean water. As the pockets of air between ancient snowflakes, trapped and compressed as layers of snow, meet seawater, they make continuous explosions. 'These tiny air bubbles are singing songs,' a lead author in the study said, 'and these songs are the songs of the changing climate.'

These awe-inspiring events remind me of Edgar Allan Poe's story 'A Descent into the Maelstrom,' in which a sailor who has survived the mighty power of a whirlpool speaks of being surrounded by a 'general burst of terrific grandeur.' Yet the fishermen who rescue the seaman, whose hair has turned white and nerves have become 'unstrung' in the course of a single day, don't believe his story. Not so long ago, it would also have been all too easy for us to dismiss such observations of the earth's 'singing' and 'writing' as instances of the uncanny, defined famously by Sigmund Freud in 1919 as a dread and creeping horror that occurs when the hidden or secret seems to become visible and something once very familiar acquires an eerie quality of animation. Such instances, Freud wrote, 'force upon one the idea of something fateful and inescapable, when otherwise we should have spoken only of "chance".' Yet for Freud, the uncanny wasn't 'real' but rather a result of not having fully banished animism from our modern souls. A belief in the return of the dead or the animation of the inanimate was related to infantile impulses toward wish fulfilment that adults should normally overcome.

But what if the earth – as Bruno Latour suggests – really *is* calling out to us? We've altered it so much, entangled it so much with our own existence, that rather than being the distant, objective foundation of our lives, the philosopher writes, it is now unstable and 'trembling.' Once we begin to recognise that our human activity is implicated everywhere, the world reveals itself to be, in his memorably ringing phrase, 'an active local, limited, sensitive fragile, quaking and easily tickled envelope.'

Latour argues that the sheer speed of this change makes it harder to claim an objective point of view, or to even speak any more about the 'laws' of nature; habits he believes (like the apparent level-headedness of the fishermen in Poe's story) have sucked the very 'eventfulness' out of the immense turbulence underway around us.

If the earth *is* trying to tell us something, then the apparent 'wonders' in our feeds are signals of deep distress. Take Russian deep-sea fisherman Roman Fedortsov's popular Twitter account featuring photographs of spectacularly bizarre bycatch, including living 'relics' such as the eel-like frilled shark or gelatinous black seadevil, which have been trawled up from the Mesopelagic or 'twilight' zone of the Norwegian and Barents Seas. We have explored less than 0.05 per cent of this zone, whose creatures scientists believe may 'pump' carbon from the surface to the sea bed, but fishing nations are nevertheless exploiting its immense masses of pelagic shrimp as feed for farm-raised fish. As we penetrate further into a dying ocean, and strip away the conditions of their existence, these survivors of life that preceded human existence (for 80 million years, in the case of the frilled shark and around 130 million years for the anglerfish family) appear now at their most vivid and strange.

One reason these fish are so 'ugly' – disturbingly shapeless, with faces contorted into almost human grimaces – is because they are designed to live in high-pressure environments. Their fat cells 'melt' as they are hauled to the surface turning them into ghastly distorting mirrors of our own human activities. Similarly, global heating is the terrifying expression of our dependence on fossil fuels as the ghosts of 650-million-year-old forests return to life to split the permafrost and churn methane into the atmosphere, heating it further in turn. Yet none of the numerous aggregator sites and online newspapers, which re-post Fedortsov's images in sections dedicated to the weird or curious, link these pictures to the expanding bottom trawl fishing industry, which presents a major threat to global deep-sea biodiversity. Instead, the fish appear exclusively as objects of idle entertainment, even amusement. 'Something about this reminds me of *The Shape of Water*,' jokes an anonymous writer in response to a CBS photo gallery of 'crazy-looking fish' from the Russian's feed. 'This looks like my sister,' an Instagram user says of another.

These days the infantile impulse toward wish fulfilment Freud described seems to lie not in entertaining the uncanny but our determination to treat these 'wonders,' isolated in their own strangeness and stripped of their complexity, as amusements. In *The New Yorker*'s 2018 piece on the English parch marks, after a paragraph paying lip service to the weird awfulness of the unusual hot weather, the writer quickly shifted his attention to the bonanza these marks represented for aerial archaeologists. 'It's a bit like kids in a candy shop,' one told the author, who went on to speak to other excited beneficiaries of these 'freak conditions.' Meanwhile, some sites like the Australian edition of the UK's *Daily Mail*, mocked Jeremy Buckingham's vomiting, triggered by the stench of a dying river system, as a 'bizarre moment.' Having already amassed 2000 views, the story was consigned to the newspaper's bank of comic stories, joining accounts of a father who threw up eight times a day and the regurgitating vultures that overran a couple's Florida holiday home.

Even when these wonders appear in a more critical context, they retain their powers of bewitchment. The Twitter account 'Secrets of the Ice' often retweets tweets about global heating but it is its excited 'finds', such as a mammoth's surprisingly dainty hind leg stood on tippy-toe from the museums of Yakutsk, which are constantly retweeted. Another Twitter account, 'Lego Lost at Sea,' has since 2014 been tracking the 5 million pieces of Lego that fell into the ocean when a giant wave washed 62 shipping containers off the *Tokio Express* in 1997, as they turn up on the beaches of Cornwall, as well as recording other plastic and linking to reports on plastic pollution. Nevertheless, the images of these little figurines, flattened into two-dimensional collages by the camera, are so beautiful and addictive that I often retweet them myself. It's easy to forget that they represent our literal haunting by petroleum-based plastic pollution, which is predicted to outnumber fish in the oceans by 2050. Ironically, some of the 'Lego Lost at Sea' finds (which often take the form of miniature sea creatures) have become collectors' items, photographed against natural backgrounds like beaches, to be tweeted and retweeted again.

Our huge appetite for such images makes me suspicious of the hope of some environmental writers, like George Monbiot and Caspar Henderson, that an increased sense of 'wonder' will help save the world by countering the sanitising numbness of scientific language. It seems to me that the web is constantly inviting us to marvel – and yet our wonder rarely translates into action. Could wonder itself be a kind of self-administered anaesthetic; a means of telling ourselves that what we're witnessing is rare, rather than the inevitable result of an ongoing disaster whose full dimensions we can't quite make out? At the same time, we've become so quickly habituated to such sights, separated from their terrifying contexts, that it's hard to know if we're even in the territory of the 'uncanny' anymore. As Zadie Smith has written about our changing seasons, the unfamiliar has become so pervasive that, barring obvious disasters, it is now our 'new normal.'

These objects may mesmerise us. But where is our urgency, our terror, our justified outrage?

According to Latour, the truly weird achievement of so-called modernity is its belief in a purely *inanimate* world, which can be acted on as dumb matter by science or economics. And yet even if we are prepared to hear the world 'talking' to us, it is also hard to know how to feel in the face of these overwhelming 'signs and wonders.' We are not equipped, Latour admits, 'with the mental and emotional repertoire to deal with such a vast scale of events' or the new 'emotions,' which the earth, pushed past its limits by us, is expressing.

Even with so many signs in plain view, to acknowledge the scale of this planetary distress can seem unhinged, as if one is embracing the mutterings of Nostradamus or the paranoia of a doomsday cult. 'I have absolutely no belief that we're going to be threatened by rising water or warming anytime soon,' a father at my children's school tells me. 'I think things are going to be pretty much the same, 40 or 50 years in the future, when we'll be sweating over the same small worries.' And yet . . . 'Have you started to feel guilty about having children?' a colleague at work asks me. Yes, I answer. But she and I keep our voices hushed whispers beneath the fluorescent lights.

In spite of my great fondness for Freud, I have to admit that he has a lot to answer for, in making us keep our voices low. Freud ascribed the feeling of 'uncanniness' (when 'something we have hitherto regarded as imaginary appears before us in reality') to a hangover from our 'primitive forefathers' – a reaction we need to overcome in order to be modern. This enduringly narrow conception of the rational as excluding beliefs relegated to the 'past' or 'nature', means, as Latour argues, that while we may be prepared to address individual symptoms of a stressed ecosystem – to save a bird colony or our local stand of old-growth forest – listening with urgency to the multiple signs of a world in distress, or ascribing it some kind of agency, can easily be dismissed as irrational or flaky.

Yet I had forgotten until returning to it, that Freud makes a distinction in his essay between experiences of the uncanny in real life, which in his experience were rare, and their appearance in fiction, which he generally found more affecting. These days, the ratio seems to be reversed. Amitav Ghosh opens *The Great Derangement* by recalling the moment on 17 March, 1978, when he was caught in the middle of the first tornado to hit Delhi in its recorded meteorological history, going on to argue that we are more likely to confront the weird signs of damaged nature in our everyday reality than in fiction, which often avoids such events as sensational and contrived. At the same time, scientists such as Robert Larter of the British Antarctic Survey are beginning to borrow terms which derive from fairy tale and folklore, like 'sleeping giants,' to describe increasingly fragile polar ice sheets, with their capacity, once melting becomes irreversible, for global devastation.

Yet I have to confess that seeing a world possessing agency has never seemed that strange to me. That's partly due to my own nature and partly because I came of age with some small sense of how Indigenous cosmologies already offer a powerful rebuff to our deafness to the earth. Reading both Freud and Latour, I'm struck by the thought that the knowledge of a world whose many elements have their own interconnected stories to tell has never been lost by the Indigenous cultures that Western modernity hasn't entirely colonised.

Instead of importing Latour's notions, we can learn as much, if not more, from Indigenous Australians' rich and ongoing understanding of 'Country,' which encompasses not just geographical landscape but all living things, seasons, stories, and ancestral law, in which people and animals and phenomena like the sun and moon are conscious moral agents, dispersing knowledge across a sentient cosmos. Indigenous writers like Bunurong author Bruce Pascoe, Tagalaka filmmaker Victor Steffenson, and D'harawal weather knowledge holder Fran Bodkin have written about the long histories of Indigenous land care, meteorology and astronomy, which involve reading relationships and signs within cycles accrued over thousands of years. Aboriginal people look after Country and it looks after them: Northern Territory

Yarralin man Daly Pulkara explained to late American-Australian ethnographer Deborah Bird-Rose that in his culture 'quiet country' shows the care of generations to those who know how to see it, while uncared for 'wild' country is disturbing.

In her last work, on flying foxes living on the edge of extinction, Bird-Rose wrote about building a bridge between extinction studies – with its emphasis on the complexity of relationships in the ecosphere – and the Northern Territory Yolgnu concept of *bir'yun*, or 'shimmering,' in which the world is composed of complex, multi-species 'relations and pulses'. This concept is embodied in the fine crosshatching of Yolgnu painting, giving it a brilliance and motion, and in their dance and song. 'These waves of ancestral power that shimmer and grab,' she writes, 'are also exactly the relationships that bring us forth and sustain us.' This is an entirely different sense of wonder to the way we often understand it in the West, as something we view or each add to our own personal imaginative storehouse. Instead, 'shimmer' is a kind of knot, or connection, existing in and outside the human world. Compared to this way of hearing and talking to the world, which has survived the last ice melt, even Latour's analysis begins to look shallow.

Meanwhile, as Western science advances – but also, in some ways, catches up with Indigenous knowledge – so much of what it once viewed as fanciful about the earth's intelligence continues to become real. At this moment, when they are most under assault, we are beginning to understand the extraordinary interconnections of nature's systems. Scientists have discovered, for example, that trees communicate and share food via mycorrhizal networks, which they've jokingly dubbed the 'Wood Wide Web'. Even our own bodies, it turns out, are only roughly half human, the other half made up of about 160 different bacterial genomes.

Developmental biologists like Scott F. Gilbert are even suggesting that we consider ourselves as 'holobionts': combinations of host and microbial community. Next to this, economic models of 'management' and sustainability seem more and more like magical thinking: what use will our seed banks be without companion species of plants or pollinators, whose relationships have developed over millions of years?

The challenge ahead is not only to recognise that it is rational to hear the uncanny messages from our present but also to allow ourselves to feel fear, awe, and rage equivalent to its 'terrific grandeur.' In the staggeringly tiny window left to us to act urgently, I'd like to think that it's possible to see the world not, as anthropologist and writer Michael Taussig puts it, as 'the dead, soulless object of European modernity but as something roused into life through the wounds and war conducted against it.' But some days I just can't get past the grief.

So where do these thoughts leave me, on a bright afternoon when the flocks of corellas call out from the park below my study window? How should I have answered my daughter when she asked me on the way home from school, 'Is it true the world's going to die soon?' Everything dies, eventually, I told her, but hopefully not soon. For the moment this was enough, and she and her brother ran on ahead, past the corner shop, and through the lane between high terrace houses.

As I sit at my desk, an email comes through from my neighbour about the renovation works around the apartment block next to ours. Just by the way, she signs off, have I noticed the dearth of insects? At this time of year we would usually expect an invasion of spiders and moths through our unscreened windows.

Is it because they've dug up the whole garden, or is this a sign of the insect apocalypse? 'I actually miss the huntsmen and even the thrilling and terrifying spider wasp,' she writes. 'Our little biosphere, gone.'

Coal: An Unnatural History

When we arrive at Parliament House, Canberra, the woman at the information desk hands our twins the *Children's Trail* brochure, inviting them to look for 'Shawn the Prawn' in the Marble Foyer's black limestone. At first glance, the large circles and curves of Belgian Granitello Nero in the white floor make a bold statement among the busy green-and-pink marble columns of this building, which was built in the grand-scale 1980s. But as we bend to look at them more closely, a cloudy riot of small white calcifications dapples the stone grey. These are the remains of marine creatures from the Carboniferous period, which sank into the sand, 345 million years ago, when the land we now call Belgium was part of the sea floor.

The Carboniferous period is sometimes called the 'Golden Age of Sharks' and the 'Age of the Crinoids.' But it takes its name from the rich coal-bearing deposits geologists observed in the soft hills of England as they developed the science of stratigraphy.

It is, primarily, the Age of Coal.

In 1768 Lieutenant James Cook set off from England to the 'unknown southern land' in command of the Royal Navy research vessel HM *Bark Endeavour*. The first ship to reach the east coast of Australia, it began its life in the coal and whaling port of Whitby as a merchant collier, *The Earl of Pembroke*. Cook knew Whitby well because, at seventeen, before he joined the navy, he had found his first job there with a coal merchant. He would undertake each of his three subsequent journeys to the Pacific in a repurposed 'Whitby Cat.'

Any history of modern Australia, it strikes me, should start with these facts.

My children find Shawn the Prawn at the base of the staircase that leads to the House of Representatives Chamber. The white, curved shape stands out instantly, bent in upon itself, caught in an extremity of motion. Its chelae, or enlarged front legs, grasp the base of its segmented abdomen, which ends in a faint tail fan. Its antennae sweep down and away from its head, as if pushed into a long curve by a current.

A black eye and distinct beaky sharpness define its ghostly face.

Around the same time as the Granitello Nero began to form, I will read later, when Europe was still part of the ancient supercontinent Pangaea, the first great wave of plant life left Panthalassa, the ocean that surrounded it, to colonise the land. The land mass was low and swampy. There were no seasons. There were so many plants that the air of the Carboniferous was more saturated with oxygen than it is today. The vast forests included giant club mosses, tree ferns, trees with leaves like long straps, and lanky Sigillaria, their scaled trunks dividing into two branches, each 'arm' of this truncated candelabra sporting an alert, grass-like tuft.

In the southern hemisphere, glaciers grew, then shrank. As the seas rose, they flooded the world's dense tropical forests or buried them under soil. As the glaciers reformed, the seas receded, and the tropical forests regrew. Over time, as mud or acidic water protected their fallen vegetation from decay, the swamp forests' buried layers compressed and grew hotter. They cooked, first into peat and then, over millions of years, into coal.

The striations in coal are the markers of each separate engulfment. A history of coal describes the process of burial and retreat as 'a very slow minuet between the coastal forests and the seas.'

Coal miners in Bedworth, North Warwickshire, believed the 'rushing, soughing' sounds of the Seven Whistlers heralded the death of a miner. Strange, mysterious noises heard in the night sometimes resembled the distant singing of a flock of birds, and at other times the smothered wailings of children chanting a funeral dirge. Pennsylvania coal miners gave the crumbs left in a lunch pail to the supernatural powers.

A stone expert writes that the black Granitello Nero in the Parliament House floor has a gentle history, largely unaffected by the deformation and change that created other stones. Made up of mineral calcite, it derives its black colour from finely divided carbon. In the foyer's symbolic scheme, it represents the significance of the ocean to the Australian continent.

When the area that would be called Canberra was first settled by Europeans early in the nineteenth century it was known as the 'Limestone Plains'. The establishment of large pastoral properties would have, as the Parliament House website notes, with some restraint, 'a major impact' on the Nugunnawal and Ngambri peoples.

The true marbles on the foyer's columns, the stone expert continues – the Cipollino from Italy and Atlantide Rosa from Portugal – also have their origins in shallow Carboniferous seas. These calcareous sedimentary rocks were once, like the Granitello Nero, full of fossils, but deep burial and deformation fused them indistinguishably into the rock mass. What we see when we look at their folded and twisting layers is the violence of their formation. They were chosen by the architects, the author notes with no discernible change of tone, to 'represent European Arrival in Australia.'

When you catch a prawn in your hand in a river, it will lie as if dead until it doubles up to suddenly kink itself back off your palm into the water.

Looking at Shawn the Prawn's bent shape, full of intention, I'm reminded instantly of the ultrasounds of my pregnancies: the anxious miracle of bone and flesh emerging through the screen's pixilated fuzz into flexes and jerks. It is astonishing how presence, and even character, assert themselves so adamantly within the expected poses.

The spotted darkness behind the fossil looks like a constellation, the scratches of white like shooting stars. I imagine a person wearing a ceremonial mask, bent double, toes pointed, as they tumble through infinite space. Or a straight-legged space alien, holding its knees, as it falls into a piked dive's irresistible momentum.

Coal is a combustible rock. Marco Polo described the coal he saw in China in the thirteenth century as 'black stones . . . which burn like logs.'

The early Welsh used it to cremate their dead but it was the Romans who began to burn it as fuel in their forts. When they left, the English kindled it to drive off serpents.

Not long after Cook's landing, coal was found south of Sydney by the survivors of the wrecked *Sydney Cove*, who picked it up on a beach to make a fire. The place would come to be known as Coalcliff. To the city's north, a party of escaping convicts stumbled upon the 'fine burning' material by a creek, but it was only officially discovered at the mouth of the Hunter River, when the search party noticed coal 'lying so near the waterside as to be conveniently shipped.' Newcastle would take its name from the coal town in England and become a prison within a prison. Convicts who had offended in Sydney Town were sent to work in its mines.

In 1801, the Crown took exclusive possession of the colony's coal. It levied a duty on any shipped by private vessels, historian Ian Hoskins writes, to offset the costs of punishment and exile. By 1824, coal was being exported from Australia, as ballast, to Bombay, Batavia and Mauritius and, by the 1840s, it had replaced the labour of humans, horses and windmills. By the middle of the century, coal gas, from coal roasted in a vacuum, was illuminating the streets of every capital. Today, only Indonesia exports more coal than Australia to the rest of the world.

Indigenous Australians' use of coal is rarely conceded in its official histories. The Awabakal people of the north coast Hunter region, used coal to waterproof canoes, repel insects, and cook fish, shellfish and abalone. Their word for coal was 'nikkin' and Lake Macquarie was called 'Nik-kin-ba,' the place of coals.

When we lived in Melbourne, twenty years ago, friends of a friend there were still living off Victorian English coal wealth. The mother joined an ancient Christian sect, her children became religious mystics. Abandoned among the heavy antiques, my friend said, the father would run about the house at night, making soft hooting noises.

For the Victorians, and even the Edwardians, coal was still a source of wonder and other, less fathomable, feelings.

In a 1913 article in the *Sydney Mail* titled 'A Piece of Coal,' the Australian writer Mabel Forrest recalls her first sight of coal as a child in a hotel fireplace. She recounts how, in her soft hand, she held the black coffin-shaped morsel of light and energy, which imprisoned the sunshine of centuries before. And now, she writes, looking out over the modern city, having come across the stolen lump in a tin matchbox, she feels regret for the vanished illusions of her childhood and the path of sacrifice she has taken.

A woman's life, she concludes, is like the earth that stores the coal, all its accumulated years of love and tenderness fuel for a man's brief burning hour of passion.

The coal-powered steam engine, according to one history of coal, allowed a break with the seasons and the topography of local landscapes. Lacking the autonomy of a river, coal does not dry up or flood a factory. A steam engine, unlike a river, can run faster or slower at the boss's discretion. 'The conquest of human labour went hand in hand with the liberation from uncontrollable ecological processes.'

In 1850, Dickens's journal *Household Words* published Richard Henry Horne's 'The True Story of a Coal Fire,' in which a dissipated young man, Flashley, is sent north from London to stay with a family in remote coal country. Bored by stories of miners and the smutty face that nature wears in this district, he is beginning to fall asleep before the coal fire, when a dwarfed black figure with shining eyes emerges from the shadows. The Coal-spirit bears him away, first to an antediluvian swamp of enormous sombre shrubs and trees whose leaves make marks like seals' tracks in the mud; and then on, over several chapters and editions, into the depths of a working coal mine, onto a collier, a coal-barge, and, finally, a coal wagon. All these stages of coal, the demon tells Flashley before he releases him, fuel the civilisation of future generations. When coal is ignited, the gases of the primeval forests are released and can begin to help new forests grow again. The story has been described as the '*Christmas Carol* of Coal.'

On each double page of the *Children's Trail* booklet – although the 'mouth' of the real fossil has a sinister, more beak-like downturn – a smiling cartoon Shawn the Prawn stands on the tip of his tail fan and explains different parts and functions of the house. In the pictures, he wears a crown and holds a camera, an artist's palette, and a mace.

How do we know he's male, I wonder.

Why not 'Dawn the Prawn'?

At the beginning of the twentieth century, attempts were made to mine coal from almost a kilometre beneath the harbour of my hometown, Sydney. Three hundred miners worked each of three daily shifts in tunnels that ran, from a large shell midden in Balmain, beneath the water. The fact of the mine was a demonstration for many of our modernity. 'Sydney is the only capital city in the world,' a newspaper boasted, 'which has a coal mine underneath it.' Old miners would tell author Ruth Park, when she wrote her history of the city, of hearing the clunk of ships' anchors hitting the seabed above their heads.

Miners described the Birthday Head tunnel as a living tomb. In order to allay public safety concerns, the colliery invited a male voice choir to descend into the mine and their singing was broadcast live from below the sea floor across the continent.

Jules Verne, one newspaper reported, could not have conceived of something more bizarre.

In the nineteenth century, coal was considered lucky.

Burglars carried coal in the belief that it would prevent them from being caught. Sailors believed a piece of coal found on a beach would save them from drowning.

Young women would place a piece of coal under their pillows in the hope of dreaming of their future husbands.

In England, the Mines and Collieries Act of 1842 would ban women, girls, and boys under ten from working in the mines. Pit ponies were introduced to replace them. By the beginning of the next century there were 70,000 working below the ground. Horses that worked the shaft mines stayed underground for life. 'Often a man must choose between forcing an exhausted horse and being sent home on the dole,' one miner wrote. 'He must choose whether the horse shall suffer or his wife and children.'

Coal gas, which was formed by roasting coal, lit Victorian-era Sydney. I grew up playing near the large gas tanks on Sydney's lower north shore, which still stand, viewable through the coastal angophoras, whose sensuous trunks seem to emanate pink light. In the playground chalky shell grit crunched beneath my feet, which I would later realise was from the old Balls Head middens. Sites like the gasworks, a study has found, are 'invariably contaminated' by heavy metal and cyanide residue from the purifying process. The wastes form a 'black odorous ooze and iron cyanide complexes . . . recognisable by their intense Prussian blue colour.'

The harbour below the old coal loader opposite, in Sydney's Waverton, I read, was once a 'canoe highway' for the Cammeraygal and Wallemudegal.

When she was living in the old shale oil town of Katoomba, a writer friend tells me, she was always finding lumps of coal beneath the house, which she believed was haunted. As if, she says with light wonder in her voice, it was constantly manifesting.

So much coal was used by ships in the nineteenth century, according to writer David Farrier, that rough pavements of clinker, or coal-burning residue, run beneath the ocean, connecting its major ports. More clinker surrounds those ports, from the cleaning of boilers. 'Unlike the road network on land, which will leave only fragmentary clues about its extent,' he writes, 'a future geologist will be able to reconstruct much of the major shipping network from these clinker roads beneath the sea.'

In Victorian literature, coal was often envisaged as a black slave.
In England, it was generally agreed, the best age to train a boy as a chimney sweep was six. Propelling himself by knees, elbows and back, the child would inch up flues diagonally, and sometimes naked, like a caterpillar. The bags of soot boys dislodged were valuable and could be sold by the bushel.
In *The Water Babies*, the sweep, Tom, losing his way and seeing his face in the little white girl's bedroom, realises for the first time that he is 'dirty.'

The Titanic, the largest ship afloat when it was launched, burned 600 tonnes of coal a day, which had to be shovelled by hand. The work of a fireman was so hard that suicides were common. Over the four days of the ship's maiden voyage a hundred tonnes of ash a day were dumped into the ocean. When it struck an iceberg, the firemen were ordered to remain with the boilers, up to their waists in icy water, to vent as much steam as they could, in case the vast cylinders exploded. Only a few would survive.

When our twins were born, a friend, a Titanic enthusiast, gave them a lump of certified coal recovered from the engine room within the wreck. It was a precious gift but, superstitiously, I hid it in a drawer.

Many ghost sightings over the last centuries, novelist Jeannette Winterson suggests, can be attributed to hallucinations caused by coal gas fires.

Britain's long history of industrial mining, according to academic Steven Connor, gave it invaluable experience in protecting against dangerous gases during the First World War, when the Germans began to use chemical warfare.

As my children head back down to the information desk to have their guides stamped with the purple image of Shawn the Prawn, I wonder: Do our leaders ever feel the presence of this small spectral traveller across hundreds of millions of years? Are the two chambers of Parliament aware of this fossil as they make decisions that are pushing the world past its miraculously precise life-sustaining systems?

'We live in the shadow of an eclipse,' writes David Farrier, 'that will endure perhaps ten millions of years before sound, shape and colour return in full to the land and to the oceans.'

*

I will discover, when we get home, that 'Shawn' isn't a prawn at all: it is actually a piece of coral. But 'Shawn the Coral' doesn't rhyme, Parliament House's Twitter account announces, 'so we'll keep on calling him a prawn for the sake of brevity.'

Australia's coal, I will also discover, didn't form during the Carboniferous period, like the northern hemisphere's, when Shawn was enfolded in gentle sediment. Instead, its bituminous, or black, coal mostly formed in the following Permian Period: the age of amphibians, fish, and sail-backed lizards.

During the Carboniferous, as Gondwana drifted south from the equator, more than half of the landmass on its outer margin that would become Australia was covered by a permanent ice cap; bituminous coal would only form here when the weather was warmer, and its large sedimentary basins were covered by meandering rivers, marshes, bogs and swamps. This phase is believed to have occurred in two pulses of major sea level change: the first when the ice cap melted, flooding what would become the Sydney and Western Australian basins, the second forming large, inward-draining flood plains. Lignite, or brown coal, would form even later, during the Paleogene period, the era of diversifying mammals, which began 65 million years ago.

Australia's 'coal reserves' are the fourth largest in the world. Unlike other countries, we obtain the larger part of our coal through open cut mining. Black coal contains less moisture and more carbon than lignite, releasing more energy when it is heated, and so Australia continues to export it as 'cleaner' coal.

The fossils in the black limestone in Parliament House's Grand Foyer are, in fact, remnants of the Carboniferous period's early coral gardens. They are crinoids, corals, sponges, bryozoans or moss animals, and brachiopods, also known as sea lilies.

The most common colonial corals, which extracted calcium carbonate from seawater to form their skeletons, took the form of vertical five-sided tubes; because they look like honeycombs when cut horizontally, quarrymen call them 'nests of bees.' The lively specks and streaks in the stone are fragments of crinoid stems, whose flowerlike heads with mouths, called calyxes, have not survived. The skeletons of bryozoans resemble lace, my guidebook tells me, while quarrymen would refer to the star shapes of the bisected sponges, with their dark centres, as 'footprints of the wolf.'

Yet no matter how hard I look at the photograph of the crustacean-shaped fossil in the passport-sized *Children's Trail* booklet on my desk, I cannot determine which of these creatures has given 'Shawn' its distinctive form.

Here or online, I can't find any source that will tell me.

Captain Cook would discover the Great Barrier Reef by running into it in 1770, in the repurposed *Earl of Pembroke*. The reef where the old Whitby Cat was stranded for a day, as the crew heaved almost fifty tonnes of ballast over the ship's side 'with the utmost expedition,' would be called the Endeavour Reef. When the boat was floated and repaired, the crew retrieved all of the *Endeavour*'s anchors except one they could not free from the seabed, which would be recovered by divers in 1971. It is now in the James Cook Museum in Cooktown in tropical Far North Queensland.

In the first floor gallery, upstairs from Shawn the Prawn, opposite a copy of the Magna Carta, you will find the Yirrkala Bark Petition, presented by the Yolgnu people of the Northern Territory in 1963 to protest the granting of mining leases to a private company to mine bauxite on their traditional land. The petitioners feared that 'their needs and interests will be completely ignored as they have been ignored in the past.' The petition was unsuccessful and mining leases were held valid, but this was the first formal assertion of native title.

A historian notes that there was always a 'close connection between the coal mining industry and the federal and various state governments.'

Most of our electricity plants run on brown coal, so Australia's 'coal rush' would only begin in the last decade of the twentieth century, when we began to export bituminous coal to Asia, to Taiwan and Korea for their steel mills, and to China. A banker has described this rush as 'a wild west resource stampede.'

The rush continues. Nine new coal mines are proposed for Australia's vast Galilee Basin, which stretches across Queensland. Together, they will produce 330 million tonnes of coal a year, which will be carried over the Great Barrier Reef by boat. If the Galilee Basin projects were considered as a country, it would be the world's seventh-largest CO_2 emitter.

Of these, Adani's Carmichael mine alone will drain billions of litres of groundwater a year from the Lake Eyre Basin springs. Since it received Commonwealth approval in 2014 two studies have been unable to identify which of Australia's two major underground aquifers feed into these springs.

In New South Wales, the industry is proposing twenty-three new coal mines; or, the equivalent of fifteen Adani mines, which would exceed the country's existing rail and port capacities.

The first time I visited Hobart I was struck by the way the air smelled of coal fires. It smelled like history, I thought – though it wasn't historical at all.

In 2016, the Great Barrier Reef suffered its worst mass bleaching event. A quarter of the organism, which is large enough to be seen from outer space, died. Stressed by the unprecedented water temperatures, its corals expelled the billions of tiny algae from their tissues, which fed them and gave them their colour. This would happen again in 2017 and in 2020.

The primary cause of rising sea temperatures is the release of stored carbon dioxide into the atmosphere as fossil fuels are burned.

In the decades to come, one scientist says, the reef will probably contain some corals, but they will not be growing or functioning.

Does it matter that children, visiting the seat of our parliament, are encouraged to believe in the existence of 'Shawn' as a prawn, and that nowhere in the small *Children's Trail* booklet is there any contradiction?

Kurnell, in Sydney's Botany Bay – where Captain Cook landed and first made contact with the Gweagal people – was dominated for the first half of last century by the giant Caltex oil refinery and bounded by national parkland, Captain Cook and Sir Joseph Banks Drives. Since it closed in 2014 it has become a bulk storage terminal for imported petroleum products.

The Permian period, in which most of Australia's coals formed, ended 252 million years ago, when global heating caused the world's third mass extinction event. The Permian Extinction is the single greatest calamity ever to befall life on earth, even more cataclysmic than the asteroid impact which caused the extinction of the dinosaurs 65 million years ago. In this 'Great Dying,' ninety-five per cent of marine species and seventy per cent of terrestrial animals, even microbes, were made extinct.

Recent research suggests that massive Siberian volcanoes erupting over centuries unleashed sulphur dioxide and carbon dioxide into the atmosphere, while the heated magma ignited coal deposits, releasing more carbon dioxide and methane, causing temperatures to rise. In the 'toxic hellscape' that ensued, oceans acidified and acid rain fell, while bacteria feeding on dead bodies released toxic hydrogen sulphide gas. Warming oceans released more methane, which further accelerated heating.

'Scientists,' a newspaper report notes, 'are observing many of the same signs of dangerously rapid climate change today.'

So many ships pass through the Great Barrier Reef on the way to and from our coal ports that it has been dubbed 'the miners' highway.'

In 2015, while scanning the seabed off the Australian west coast with sonar for the missing plane MH370, searchers discovered the remains of two coal-carrying nineteenth-century sailing ships, at a depth of almost four kilometres. The wooden hull of one had rotted, leaving only its anchors and scattered haul of coal behind.

'Whereas when we are in London and see the prodigious fleets of ships which come constantly in with coals for this encreasing city,' wrote Daniel Defoe in 1724, upon visiting Whitehaven in northern England, 'we are apt to wonder whence they come and that they do not bring the whole country away; so on the contrary, when in this country, we see the prodigious heaps, I may say mountains of coals, which are dug up at every pitt, and how many of these pitts there are, we are filled with equal wonder to consider where the people live that can consume them.'

Australia's Prime Minister, Scott Morrison, is the federal member for Cook, which includes Cook's landing site at Kurnell.

In 2017, as Federal Treasurer, he brought a lump of coal into the House of Representatives. Morrison told the chamber that the Opposition's coal phobia would leave Australia struggling in the dark. His government would keep electricity prices low, he boasted, by committing to coal power.

The coal, which had been supplied by the Minerals Council of Australia, had been treated with a coat of lacquer to stop its black dust from coming off. Morrison waved it at the house and passed it to the laughing deputy leader.

'This is coal,' he said. 'Don't be afraid, don't be scared.'

Terror From The Air: Fire Diary 2019–20

I don't record in my diary exactly when the fires around Sydney start but by early November smoke from blazes to the north and west of the city has become a terrifying fact of life. We wake to pitchy air and yellow light one morning, bituminous brown another. In the bath at night, I hear the wind lift and the smell through the closed window turns sharp and resinous. Even on days of reprieve, hazy and with little odour, our mouths register the ash grit in the air.

Driving along Anzac Parade one afternoon in an unnaturally early twilight, the sun an orange ball, I see a plane rise from nearby Sydney Airport into low cloud which I realise, against its white side, is brown smoke. When I point it out to my daughter she refuses to look and keeps her head buried in the book she's reading. In the gloom, the flying foxes have risen from their camps early, and are using the road to navigate before they peel off into the Moreton Bay figs in the surrounding parkland.

One week, and then the next, the children's sports are cancelled. On bad days we drive them the five blocks to school. When the smoke is lighter, I walk to pick them up through a premature twilight, close and boxy with orange shadows, though this should be a time of long, clear evenings. The new leaves on the trees are the luminous green of old Ektachrome. I am surprised by weird cross-tunings of nostalgia: for my father's slides, for my childhood on a smoggy, still-industrial harbour.

I have, I realise, been unconscionably smug about our fresh air. Even though we are the world's second biggest coal exporter, even though we have the highest rate of animal extinction in the world, thick air pollution is something I have associated with developing countries: a visible marker of carelessness. Now, as dozens of bushfires burn, with the largest in the Blue Mountains to the north-west of the city, Sydney has the worst air quality in the world. Satellite images show smoke plumes streaming from the east coast out into the Tasman while their heat also transports to New Zealand, pushing its temperatures eight to ten degrees higher than the average for this time of year. By early January, the smoke from our fires will shroud their South Island in a yellow haze, turn its glaciers brown, and continue on to Brazil, Chile, Argentina, and Uruguay, twelve thousand kilometres away. A scientist tracking the plume will describe it as 'a swirling, braided river'. Looking at the photographs of the hazy skies in Wellington now, I find myself thinking that we are Chernobyl to New Zealand's Scandinavia. Institutional neglect, a government pandering to oligarchs, and the deliberate underfunding of infrastructure have brought us to this point.

I recall Indigenous author Tony Birch writing about the construction of Melbourne's Westgate Park in an old sand mine next to the degraded Birrarung (Yarra River), using tonnes of valuable soils extracted from engineering projects on Aboriginal Country elsewhere to mask the past ruination beneath his feet. 'When country is sifted and shifted,' he writes, 'cultural and scientific knowledge is destroyed.' What we're seeing in the devastating satellite images, I think, is also Country, moving from one continent to the next, in yet another phase of colonial destruction.

*

The state's fire season, as marked officially by the New South Wales Statutory Bush Fire Danger Period, usually begins on the first day of October. This season began in early August. Further north, in Queensland, fire season begins in August but in June the Queensland Fire and Emergency Service was already noting erratic fire activity in the state's east and south.

In October, in Armidale in northern New South Wales for a conference, I witnessed what appeared to be a local catastrophe, without realising it was only the beginning. When I arrived, fires had been burning in the region for weeks. A red sun in the late afternoon was enough of a novelty for my friend to pull her car off the road and take a photograph; behind us, a man pulled onto the shoulder to do the same thing. Renowned for its lush grazing, the area had been in unprecedented drought for three years. On a minibus tour, looping 350 kilometres north through Glen Innes, the old tin-mining town of Tingha and the Myall Creek massacre site, stands of heat-hardy eucalypts were brown and dead, sheets of pale purplish dust rose in the air above paddocks, and the mood onboard grew increasingly silent. From the plane back south I would see other, smaller fires burning on mountaintops: thin funnels of smoke rising from invisible flames, as if from cones of incense. A week later, almost all the territory we had driven through would be on fire.

Since early September, remnant rainforest in Queensland – mountaintop islands permanently wet for tens of thousands of years – has also been burning for the first time. Articles report that the songbirds in these forests have always lived there. In fact, recent fossil and genetic evidence suggests that they are the most ancient birds on the planet, living ancestors of the world's 4500 species of songbirds, which originated here 54 million years ago and spread globally as Australia floated slowly northwards. All the birdsong in the world began here. Listening to the dawn chorus, a biologist says, is like listening to what the world sounded like in the time of the dinosaurs. These are areas, another says, 'where fire is simply not meant to go.'

By mid-November, more than a million hectares of my state have already burned. The ABC records that beekeepers up north – some of the first people into the fire-ravaged forests to check on their hives – have had to seek counselling after hearing injured and dying animals crying out in pain. Older beekeepers would go in first, 'to make the sure the forest isn't screaming at them,' the report continued, before they would allow younger workers in.

Online, I watch people try to find an accurate description for the catastrophe unfolding around us. A writer friend, holidaying on an orange beach two hours north of Sydney, describes what she is witnessing as a 'live cremation.' Another speaks of Australia 'undergoing incineration.'

*

A burned koala looks like a stuffed specimen in a museum, faded and dusty, as if its life force has already departed. In online footage, rescuers find the animals slumped, heads on chests like old men, backs against the base of tree trunks, as if they have simply given up. Acute stress, a vet says, will often stun koalas into a 'state of helplessness' so that they will submit to their fate in silence. On numerous Facebook rescue groups, women from all over the world respond to carers' calls for crocheted and stitched nests and pouches, and I imagine the mail filling with the work of caring hands.

Realising our kinship with our wildlife family, environmental ethicist Freya Mathews will write months later, 'Australia has been weeping in a new way.' And yet, I will wonder. An academic friend in Melbourne points out that the first story to try to imagine the sufferings of a kangaroo was published in Australia in 1830 while I was traumatised as a child of the seventies by Ivan Smith's *The Death of a Wombat*, whose marsupial hero forged on through a bushfire with a ponderous 'waddle and crump' toward his death in the cooling river. While we now know more about them (wombats are the most likely creatures to survive a fire front by retreating into their long, complex burrows), have our attitudes toward our native wildlife really changed that much?

By late December, when almost the whole east of the country is on fire, from Queensland to Victoria's East Gippsland, news bulletins will fill with 'heart-warming new details' of koalas begging for water in the extreme heat that grips the country, offering clips of 'amazing encounters' in chirpy voices. Yet I read elsewhere that only koalas in extreme distress drink since eucalyptus leaves usually satisfy their need for moisture; desperation drives them to push past the stress of human contact. A cyclist in Adelaide will take footage of a koala that has climbed her rear bike wheel to drink from her water bottle. It is, she says, 'the best thing' that has ever happened to her on a ride.

But now, in late November, everyone's feelings are ragged. I fight on the phone with my 94-year-old mother. I am already familiar with uncharted territory, I realise, from my only childhood – with life lived beyond any rational comparison.

I take an evening walk around the local park with my neighbour, another writer. She tells me that her partner and best friend challenged her to cry on cue last night. 'I started to think about the burned koalas and I cried,' she says, 'and they said, "We're never going to trust you again!" Then we all started to laugh hysterically.' And now we're both laughing, madly.

A few nights later, driving back from a swim at Nielsen Park – choppy and hazy at high tide, where we have talked about our despair about the future as we backstroked at the net – she checks the NSW Rural Fire Service's Fires Near Me app again. A blue marker is for a fire burning steadily, yellow shows where new fires have started, orange is for 'Watch and Act,' and red is reserved for emergencies. Even as I look at the road, it's clear that the map on her screen is almost obscured beneath its hundreds of diamonds. 'At least the fires are all blue ones today!' she says, and we give way to dark laughter again.

The actor Sam Neill tweets that three hundred miles out of Sydney, flying in from New Zealand, he could smell the country burning – landing, it looked 'like the End of Days.'

But maybe this *is* the apocalypse. Maybe there are tipping points in language, too, when nothing can be metaphorical again.

At yet another climate demonstration at the Town Hall, I stand with a friend under the last flowers of a spindly jacaranda in the shade of the cathedral. We've never been to a rally that's so quiet. Masked protestors make their way precisely through small veins of space that open between people. As the speakers address the crowd, there is almost as much contempt for the Opposition Leader as there is for the Prime Minister.

In the papers this last month, the news that we may have already crossed our tipping points in terms of Arctic ice melt and permafrost feedback loops. The humidity in Sydney usually sets in in early November but it's December now, and it still hasn't come.

In spite of the smoke and the relentless devastation, my local council decides to go ahead with its early December Christmas concert and firework night in the park behind our house. The air is so particulate and the news so sombre that I won't let the twins go. Around six, I notice a small fall of ash outside our back window, like the thin under-feathers of small birds. It is followed by whole blackened gum leaves, as if they have been instantly carbonised before being sucked up into the higher air. The closest fires are around two hours' drive away.

When the fireworks start, my son, who has been fairly calm these last weeks, starts running around the room and kicking furniture. 'The fucking Prime Minister! The fucking fires!' he cries. In this instance it's the fucking Lord Mayor we need to blame, we tell him. He throws himself on the sofa. 'What can I do?' he howls. 'I'm just an eight-year-old kid!'

We talk to him about the power of writing letters to politicians, tell him we will help him, but our words feel hollow.

Even though I have kept the windows of my study closed, the computer keyboard beneath my fingers feels porous. I will find a thin powder of black carbon on my books and papers and along each windowsill.

*

16 December, 22.5 degrees at 2am. Unable to sleep, I keep checking the Fires Near Me app on my phone. There are a hundred markers on the state map. Ominous dark blots show where fires have already burned or are still burning. They have blazed through the catchment around our main dam to the south of the Blue Mountains, joined together, and are now out of control, approaching south-west Sydney. Large swathes of the state's south coast are also obscured by dark patches, while new ones are making obscene inroads into the green map of the Southern Highlands. Yellow and red diamonds keep appearing with their terrible warnings – seek shelter in place, too late to leave – but it is impossible to work out what has burned and what is still on fire as the edges of the dark blots spread. At 3.30, a bursting southerly, acrid with smoke, wakes me from a brief

sleep and I move around the house closing windows. In the morning, there is not much smoke in the lower air, though the sky looks pale and wintry.

The Gospers Mountain mega-blaze to the north of the Blue Mountains has crossed the Bells Line of Road and west into the World Heritage-listed Grose Valley. The images coming out of the small Mountains towns perched on the thin escarpment's northern edge look volcanic. In one photograph, people stand at a lookout, phones held to their chests, as enormous clouds of gritty brown smoke loom into the sky, lumpy as a sheep's fleece and underlit by flame.

The extreme heat continues. 17 December is the hottest day in the country's history, at an average 40.9 degrees Celsius, a record that will be broken again the next day.

A mega-blaze makes its own weather. Its intense, turbulent heat draws cooling air into its smoke as it rises to higher elevations so that it condenses, giving birth to pyrocumulus clouds. When these clouds gather enough energy to create lightning, they become pyrocumulonimbus, or flammagenitus, clouds, described by NASA as the 'fire-breathing dragons of clouds.' Unpredictable, with intense updrafts, the towering fire clouds pull embers up to terrific heights and carry them far downwind at speed to start new blazes. Their bulky, ash-filled plumes are more familiar from images of volcanic eruptions and nuclear explosions. It's now fairly certain that the first photograph of a pyrocumulonimbus was taken above Hiroshima after the detonation of the nuclear bomb 'Little Boy' though until recently this plume from the firestorm was mistaken for the initial mushroom cloud. In these clouds' downbursts, terrifying, tornado-like winds as fast as 270 kilometres an hour, can flatten trees. Their heat can be felt from two kilometres away.

The Gospers Mountain mega-blaze – the first in Australia's known history – is made up of five separate fires that have joined together. It's already destroyed an area seven times bigger than Singapore. 'You can see the tree line 100 metres in front of you and then suddenly you can't see the tree line,' a firefighter says. 'It's like a big black storm going past, but it's not a thunderstorm; it's a fire.'

On 20 December, footage goes viral of this fire climbing in moments up a 200-metre sandstone cliff face beneath the village of Blackheath in the Blue Mountains. One commentator describes it as looking like a 'lava waterfall,' another a 'waterfall of fire' – although the movement is skyward, rather than down.

Historian Mike Davis uses the term 'disaster algorithm' to describe such fire events, 'since none of the variables involved are natural.'

*

For thousands of years, historian Steven Connor writes, 'the air has been seen as inexhaustible, a pure gratuity'. It has been seen as an abode of the endless, free of history. But now, it seems, the air does have a history, and one in which we are implicated. 'Without ever being able to habituate ourselves to the air, or fully inhabit it,' he writes, 'we have nevertheless brought the air under occupation.'

One of the reasons this fire season has been so disastrous is that the ground is so dry. As we heat the climate, I read, hot air holds more moisture, so it takes longer for it to become saturated enough to rain.

Fire historian Steven Pyne believes that we have already entered a planetary fire age, 'the fire equivalent of an ice age.' For too long we have covertly burned lithic landscapes – deep once-living underground fossils – while suppressing natural, living fire, which did important ecological work. Now the natural fire and human-made realms are crossing over. 'Too much fossil biomass is burned to be absorbed within ancient ecological bounds. Fuels in the living landscape pile up and rearrange themselves. The climate is unhinged. When flame returns, as it must, it returns as wildfire.'

Fire is a driverless car barrelling down the road, he writes, which integrates whatever is around it. We are changing the road it drives down.

Philosopher Peter Sloterdijk: 'the air that, together and separately, we breathe can no longer be presupposed.'

*

You could argue that this catastrophic fire season began in April 2019, when our Prime Minister refused to meet with the 23 former fire chiefs and emergency leaders who tried to warn him that Australia needed more water bombers for the bigger, hotter, and faster bushfires that were imminent. Or in 2008, when an earlier conservative government ignored the Garnault Report on Climate Change, which predicted that unless Australia played its full proportional part in the global reduction of greenhouse gases it would face earlier and more dangerous fire seasons whose extremity would be 'directly observable by 2020.' Or in May 1987, when the month-long Great Dragon megafire, thought to be the world's first, ignited the pine forests of China's north east, before it headed into Russia, killing almost 200 people, initiating an era in which extraordinary firestorms that devastate huge areas have become a thousand times more likely. Or, as historian Tom Griffiths argues, when British settlers denied the sovereignty of the continent's Indigenous people, whose gentle burning, harnessing and curating of its natural fire cycles, was often noted by the early explorers. The pride the colonists came to take in fighting this country's extreme variations, he writes, has sedated the populace against recognising a volatility that is now global, unnatural, and one-way.

On 21 December, after the deaths of two firefighters, the Prime Minister cuts his holiday in Hawaii short by a day and returns. The fires have been going since September, he reasons, and still have a time to run yet, so he took some leave with his family. 'I don't think panicking is the way to manage anything,' he says. Besides, he tells a journalist, 'I don't hold a hose, mate, I don't sit in a control room.'

*

Unable to bear the brown days in Sydney, scared of what we're breathing in even with the windows closed, we decide to keep our booking on the south coast for our annual pre-Christmas get-together. Our friends in the Blue Mountains can't come; they're on fire watch, not only for the Gospers megafire to the north of the thin escarpment, but for the fires on its southern side. But on the fire maps, this part of the coast remains green and untouched. We are an hour north of the massive Currowan fire, which has been burning up the coast for a month from Durras, and has joined up with the huge Tianjara fire between the coast and Canberra. The property sits in rainforest but the land is drier than we have ever seen it and, even here, the thick smoke comes and goes. At the beach, ten minutes away, my daughter takes to snorkelling at once while my son is more tentative. We emerge from the water at the Gerringong rockpool with a bitter taste on our tongues. 'The world of fish is so quiet!' he announces.

Three other friends join us. We go through the motions of a holiday, but we are also, for much of the time, online. The asthmatics check the air quality app while we are all constantly on our phones, checking Fires Near Me as new red flame icons for uncontrolled fires edge closer. I set the radius for alerts at 25 kilometres, my Melbourne-born friend sets hers at forty, so that it pings constantly in alarm, and we argue. I know the topography of this place. I know that the fire will have to change direction, make its way through a major town and river and highway to reach us, or cross the river again to come up the long valley behind us. If it starts to move this way, I say, we will go. But my friend keeps talking about spot fires and the children are unsettled. I snap at her but my mind returns for the rest of the day to a compulsive image of a fire erupting, or being deliberately lit, on the tree-lined kilometre of hairpin road between us and the highway. Unable to sleep, I wake every couple of hours and check the app.

Another friend arrives, and we pick her up from the station in Gerringong. The smoke is light. We swim, we go to the petting zoo at the markets in the park, where the animals are cool in the deep shade at its corner. By the time we drive back up to the cabin, it's hot: 43.3 degrees. In the late afternoon, a southerly roars up the coast; it covers the car in dust, a large branch bounces off the Perspex car port. When it dies down, the sky is smoky again and an ominous orange-yellow. As we walk up to the road, light ash begins to fall.

At the cattle grid a kilometre uphill, the two householders are also standing in the open field staring out towards the south where a huge smoke plume is towering. They've lived here for thirty years and they have never seen anything like this, they say, and they are going to drive out and spend the night in town. Eerily, even though the plume is an hour's drive away, we can feel the effect of its updraft here as the air grows close and stuffy, as if it has already given the fire some of its oxygen reserves.

This is when we decide to leave. We settle the children in front of *Jumanji* as we pack the car. Washing up, I realise my hands are shaking. We leave my daughter's gingerbread train, stuck together with blue and white icing, on the kitchen table and drive back with our friend through the night.

*

On New Year's Eve morning, as Sydney is still preparing to go ahead with its evening fireworks, in spite of protests, the long-burning south coast explodes. Six hours' drive south, with no warning, fire razes the small town of Cobargo, and kills two people.

Two hours further south, across the Victorian border, a twenty-metre-high fire front roars up from the Gippsland forests, almost to the water, in the small beach town of Mallacoota, where it has been impossible to leave for days. The sky goes black, gas bottles explode; firefighters tell everyone to get into the sea and, circling them with their fire trucks on the beach, vow to hold the line. Only a wind change stops the blaze from going through the town centre. Inland, an hour's drive to the north of Cobargo, the Clyde Mountain fire races through the town of Mogo, reducing hundreds of houses to sheets of tin and rubble. As a 'tidal wave' of evacuees make their way to coastal Batemans Bay, the staff at Mogo Zoo manage to save hundreds of animals by encouraging the lions, tigers and orangutans into their night dens while they stand and defend the property with trucks and water pumps. The zoo director keeps small monkeys and red pandas safe in his own home.

In Conjola, the huge Currowan fire – whose plume we could see flexing its muscle from Foxground – has jumped a backburn and is racing east on unpredictable winds through the holiday towns at the end of a winding ribbon of bush road. Water pressure slows to a trickle as everyone in the panicked community turns every tap on. 'The behaviour of that fire was something I haven't seen in 36 years of attending bushfires,' one local will say. The air above it catches on fire as gas balls ignite 30 to 40 metres in the air. Houses erupt in the radiant heat from other burning houses. Locals drive their cars and boats into the lake to survive, alongside sheltering kangaroos. Within days, the same fire will also run through the holiday towns of Bendalong and Manyana, all the way to the sand dunes.

Our friends from the Blue Mountains, who have decided to take a quick break from the anxiety of watching his house, are caught five hours down the coast from Sydney in Narooma. Before the sky turned black, and they saw the glow from Cobargo in the west, my friend says, they could see separate white smoke puffs, which they would learn later were from the fires an hour to the north-east in Bateman's Bay, Malua Bay, and Rosedale, and, another hour further north still, in Conjola and Lake Conjola.

Up and down the coast, power and electricity go out. The Fires Near Me app crashes. Trapped but safe at the evacuation centre in the yacht club, our friends listen to the national broadcaster on the car radio as, hour after hour, the announcers patchwork together calls from people near the fire fronts and information from the emergency services. When we see them a few weeks later they will look ten years older.

My friend writes in a blog post that when they were able to walk along the beach the next day, the shoreline was full of crumpled black leaves, which looked 'like shards of silk; like widows' weeds.'

In the national capital, three hours inland, the smoke is so thick that its offices, universities and tourist attractions are closed. At Canberra Hospital it affects the MRI machines, which are unable to run. An obstetrician reports smoke in the birth suite as he delivers a baby. 'The couple was really anxious,' he says, 'and they said "Look, we're really worried about what the future will look like."'

Meanwhile, in Sydney, we've 'seen in the new year in style,' according to one news report. A million people gathered around the harbour to watch 100,000 fireworks explode over our 'iconic harbour,' culminating in a glittering gold-and-silver waterfall cascading from the Harbour Bridge.

*

On Facebook, the friend of a friend posts that their uncle's untouched block is in the line of fire: off the grid on the Murrumbidgee River, it is home to rare plant species, wedgetail eagles, and platypus. He apologises for mourning this small piece of pristine bush among many. My friend, author James Bradley, responds: 'The world is made up of lots of small places. We lose too many of them and we lose the world.'

My children's godmother J comes around for dinner. She is afraid that Gulaga, the mountain sacred to the Yuin people near Cobargo, is going to go up. 'Each time I used to go to the family holiday house at Cuttagee,' she says, 'I would first walk down to the very far end of the beach where I could see the whole mountain – and I used to always say, "Hello Gulaga."'

I worry about my own small, loved places. I watch the dark shadow on the app approaching Bundanon on the Shoalhaven River, an artist's property turned into a retreat where I have written over several summers. I think of the sugar gliders whose calls from the surrounding bush I first mistook for the yaps of small dogs, the goannas that hiss furiously from high up in the tree trunks when they are disturbed, the nightjars, soundless nocturnal fliers that you don't realise are near you until they sigh like weary, aging Casanovas. I think of the river in Bermagui – one of the most tranquil places I know, and as yet safe from the fires – where bellbirds call from the bush like tiny clockwork mechanisms.

It's looking more and more likely that we could lose the entirety of Australia's eastern coastal forests.

Mallacoota local Nick Ritar posts images online of dead birds he took on the town's main beach: 'every few metres there was another beautiful, iconic Australian bird,' he tells the ABC. 'A kookaburra, a rainbow lorikeet, a king parrot, a wood pigeon, a barn owl, a magpie, a New Holland honeyeater and it just went on and on.'

In his photos, the birds aren't visibly charred, though their colours have bleached to the colour of old macrame, and they are dusted with large flakes of carbonised leaf and bark. They lie on beds of cremated leaves, which are brown-black, blue-black, coal-black, pink-black, and a deep black that grabs and flattens light all at once. I remember that a friend studying eighteenth-century painting techniques told me bone black was collected from charred animal bones, ivory black from charred ivory.

In spite of all these reports, and all the images that are inescapable, I still can't fully imagine the fires. Like my childhood nightmares about infinity, which would always end in a crashing of fuzzy forms, I just can't conceive of the scale.

It is becoming clear that these fires, which feed on themselves, are no longer behaving in predictable ways. I think of Steven

Connor, on the destruction of the Twin Towers: 'The site was quickly named "Ground Zero," but what had occurred was not really grounded at all. Rather it was an airburst, a burst in the air, and the bursting out of air.'

*

When the Prime Minister visits devastated Cobargo, where yellow smoke still hangs over the ground, locals jeer and refuse to shake his hand. 'What about the people who are dead, Mr Prime Minister?' a woman leading a goat on a piece of rope yells. 'What about the people who have nowhere to live?' A young mother, still dazed, who has lost her home, withdraws her hand: 'I am only shaking your hand if you give more money to the RFS [Rural Fire Service],' she says. 'So many people have lost their homes.' He takes her hand anyway. An older man in an Akubra hat and khaki shorts puts his body between her and the Prime Minister, tries to hug and kiss her. 'It looks as if he's herding her,' someone comments online.

The Mallacoota fires rush up, across the state border, to the old whaling town of Eden. As they consume the other side of the wide bay, residents are told that they may not be safe if they gather on the wharf, although it is in the middle of town, on the water.

The Australian pyrogeographer David Bowman writes online that we may have to stop scheduling our major periods of travel into forests and parks during peak bushfire season: as we contemplate a future of catastrophes like this, 'maybe it's time to say goodbye to the typical summer Australian holiday.'

'We had to just put down our phones and turn off the television for a while,' my agent will say, when I meet her a couple of months later. 'At a certain point it just felt as if we were watching fire porn.'

*

There is a lot of criticism online of our Prime Minister's Pentecostalism. Is he doing nothing because his faith is founded on believing in the rapture, commentators ask, when the righteous will be teleported up to heaven? Why are the 'quiet' Australians, they ask, who were once great callers of bullshit, falling for this faux religion? But it doesn't seem to have occurred to anyone that his rise isn't coincidental or a matter of unfortunate historical timing; that he might be just the right figurehead for an era that feels increasingly unreal, a time of terrifying wonders.

Mid-January, and the smoke in the city is sickening again. It smells fresh: browner, darker, and heavier than anything we've experienced before. Probably from the Blue Mountains, it has a grain, as if it has burned the bush so quickly that it still holds the internal structure of the living trees.

I think of theorist McKenzie Wark: we are in a period, she writes, of metabolic rift. 'Labour pounds and wheedles rocks and soil, plants and animals, extracting the molecular flows out of which our shared life is made and remade. But those molecular flows do not return from whence they came.'

Our work has not freed us from class, colonies, gender, or sexuality, she writes. It has set carbon free instead.

Another climate demonstration. As I head out, my son shows me his concept art for a poster. The Prime Minister dangles a lump of coal from a fishing rod. 'Why are there no fish?' his speech bubble asks.

Caught up in the crowd at the Town Hall, I find myself accidentally standing on the speaker's platform, behind one of our state senators. There is something to be said for our democracy still, I suppose, that this can happen. But what moves me most is the eldest of the Red Brigade protestors – stern, red-dressed living statues, who have arrayed themselves in a descending line on the steps beside me. As she holds her palm with its Extinction Rebellion symbol to the crowd below, her beautiful, white-painted face is held in tension, determined to overcome her shyness.

I am buying knitting needles and wool in the dollar shop to make pouches for burned wildlife. As I reach for my wallet my N95 mask drops from my hand. 'A million dollars!' jokes the elderly Chinese man behind the counter.

'The moon is red . . . a red moon!' he exclaims.

*

My friends laugh, but I have long had a phobia about any books set on islands or in prisons, even if they are as bland as *The Swiss Family Robinson* or *Blue Lagoon*. There are others I find unbearable: dystopias like *1984* or *The Handmaid's Tale* or *The Road*.

I have always thought of them as novels of entrapment. Now I have the same sickly feeling every day.

The violent storms and monsoonal rains we expect in January are still failing to come. Even without thick smoke, the air smells wrong. It sounds wrong too: there have been few birds calling this summer, except for the baby currawongs in the trees outside our apartment windows, insistent on being fed. I'm only fully aware of this during a rare shower when our neighbourhood begins to sound homely again: as the cockatoos and lorikeets call out to each other through the short drizzle there is no question in my mind that the sound is joyful. Afterward, there are mosquitoes in the apartment and a small black prince cicada, which crawls onto my hand and brushes its forelegs daintily, before I release it. Even so, a faint trace of smokiness remains in the sky and there are still hints of it, as the breeze moves, through the open windows.

Towards the end of the month, I work on the Afterword for the ten-year reprint of my book, *Sydney*. I have worried for years over the changes underway in our environment but even I, with my tendency to gloom, have taken for granted that certain things would remain fundamental to my city for some time to come: the wet air with its fecund umami smell, the subtropical green, the hot days cooled in the afternoons by slamming southerly busters. Now it's clear we risk losing these too. Will it even make sense to write books about place in a world that is burning and de-seasoned, when 'record-breaking' events have become the new reality?

*

Terror From The Air: Fire Diary 2019–20

In the last week of January, when the fire authority declares it safe to travel, we head down, via the edge of the Snowy Mountains, to Merimbula. As we drive from Canberra through high pastureland, smoke from fires to the far north throws an odd purple cast across the landscape, and browns and thickens as we descend the hairpin turns through state forest. On the first night, we are in the same familiar fug of resinous brown smoke. But when it passes, the next day, it feels impossible to believe that such a catastrophic event ever happened: even though ribbons of charcoal fringe the beach at low tide and pieces of bark, as clearly defined as tiny flakes of slate, float on the clear water's surface as it rises.

In an effort to try to grasp the scale of the fires I drive half an hour south to Eden, and look across the bay at the brown, which extends into the coastal hills back as far as I can see. Even here, it is impossible to believe the flames could have towered so high a few weeks ago that the wooden wharf where I am could be no refuge. Yet, slowly, I realise, as I stand in front of the empty restaurants and cafes, that the air has almost no smell. There's no salty marine breeze, no scent of earth or hint of leaf and bush flower. Instead, there is the edge of something chemical; a negative smell, like opening a new fridge, with its faint odour of rubber seals and dead air. It's so disconcerting I jump back into the car and drive away.

In the street where we're staying in Merimbula, my children meet two other gentle and capable children their own age, a brother and sister, who have travelled from interstate to stay with their grandmother. My son announces that we will be travelling overseas for the first time to England and Rome (a trip that

Covid-19 will make impossible). The boy stares into the middle distance with a world-weary expression. He sighs and says, 'I used to travel.'

The inlet opposite our holiday apartment has its own pulse. White egrets browse among the oyster leases at low tide. Lorikeets and plovers cry. Yet fires still rumble, barely contained, behind this thin strip of coastal villages. Further up the lake, near the small airport, firefighting helicopters refuel and fly with their suspended buckets, back and forth, between water and forests.

We head to Bermagui, an hour up the coast, to a holiday house on the cliff above the sea. With the children's godmother J, who is staying with us, we visit her friends – oyster farmers – in next-door Barraga Bay, in a house surrounded by cabbage ferns and spotted gums. Even as we sit at their table, they are watching the wind on their weather apps for every change of direction. Someone told them, the husband says, that spotted gums are the least likely eucalypts to burn. Two days before a big fire hit their friends' property further inland, these trees dropped all their leaves. I joke lamely that if we see leaves falling, we'll know it's time to go. We have a quick swim at the beach, where the same dark cuff of ash stretches along the back of the sand, which is strewn with the white skeletons of cuttlefish.

'So when the world ends,' my daughter muses in the car, 'all the trees will drop their leaves.'

*

Driving back, via Canberra, we take the winding Kings Highway, which has just reopened. National park stretches in every direction, as far as the eye can see, charred beyond imagination. It feels devoid of life. De-souled.

A professor at the University of Sydney estimates that the fires have killed a billion animals across Australia. Historian Tom Griffiths notes that this is the first fire season in which we have counted animal casualties. What does this say about us?

In July 2020, Professor Chris Dickman and his team will revise up this first estimate of creatures killed or with few prospects of survival to three billion: 143 million mammals, 180 million birds, 51 million frogs, and 2.5 billion reptiles.

Driving back separately to Sydney, J sees an older man standing next to a van at the highway's edge just north of Batemans Bay, selling peaches. 'I thought you could do with some support,' she says, as she pulls in. He certainly could, he replies – his house burned down, along with a hundred of his trees. 'What else could I do? I had to buy all his fruit,' she tells us, when we see her back in Sydney, where she is still stewing and putting it in jars and bottles.

*

In *Voices from Chernobyl*, one of the soldiers responsible for settling a new layer of soil onto the irradiated city told author Svetlana Alexievich: 'We buried earth in the earth. Along with the beetles, spiders, and maggots, that whole separate nation. We buried a world.' And yet, growing up in Australia, with some small sense of Country, I know that the creatures carbonised and buried under more carbon are not a separate world. When we lose these dynamic, shifting, complex ecosystems we lose part of ourselves.

'How does a country adapt to its own murder?' asks Richard Flanagan in *The Guardian*, as our Prime Minister continues to argue that hazard reduction burns are more important than reducing greenhouse emissions. 'It's as if in the middle of the Blitz, Winston Churchill announced that rubble removal was more important than dealing with the Luftwaffe in fighting Hitler.'

Back in Sydney, a friend tells me over coffee that, even as the fires raged, a terrifying number of people in the country town she grew up in still wouldn't engage with the idea of global heating. 'How do you engage,' she asks, 'with a mentality of "Nah, I don't reckon"?'

In a novel for teenagers of the 1970s, *Displaced Person*, a boy finds his world going grey around him as he fades from the consciousness of others. Only the odd coloured item falls from the real world into his own. The novel terrified me as a child. Now it seems like an allegory for a world that can fade in moments, where the colour and iridescence of nature are provisional and will become increasingly rare.

I am afraid this summer is only the beginning. A great shedding of colour and life before we head into the grey.

*

The air has for a long time been the neglected element of politics, writes political scientist Marijn Nieuwenhuis. An exploration of the air reveals whose lives matter and whose do not, 'who belongs and who does not, who is deserving and who is not.'

Yet if these fires have shown us anything, it is surely that those of us who have smugly assumed our right to fresh air over others are not immune; that those who profit from fossil fuels, who have already shown themselves indifferent to the fate of poorer populations in the global south and small island nations in rising seas, are just as prepared to sacrifice the populations of whole countries in 'the West.'

We are at a critical tipping point, Tom Griffiths writes, at which we might need to think of swapping the term 'Anthropocene' for the 'Pyrocene.' The Anthropocene is frightening enough, suggesting that our own activities are pushing us out of the stable period that began at the end of the last ice age. The Pyrocene, the age of fire, 'goes further, by declaring the end of the much longer and older Pleistocene, the whole epoch of ice ages.' It truly marks the end of the age of humans and, when it comes, we will feel it in Australia first.

'Rather than catalogue what is burning,' writes fire historian Stephen Pyne, 'one might more aptly ask: *what isn't?*'

'I'm sick of looking at the Fires Near Me app,' my son says at the end of summer. But what this summer has shown – and what Covid-19 will also show – is that when ecological disaster hits, it consumes everything. There is nothing else to think or talk about.

*

In February, intense rains fall in New South Wales for three days then steady and continue falling for the rest of the week. They extinguish the state's fires and recoup a year's worth of inflow into the Warragamba Dam, while floods sweep the ash and soil into the sea. A friend swimming at Sydney's Malabar comes across a whole scorched tree in the water. A sandstone cliff subsides on the Blue Mountains trainline near Leura.

'Aussies have weathered nature's extremes before,' crows a denialist pundit in the *Daily Telegraph*, as storms and winds batter the coast.

In a federal advertising campaign, tourist operators and locals in small towns declare Australia is 'open for business' again.

In my city, the old swamps in Centennial Park refill, while the trees in gardens and parks that had turned into brown sticks mostly revive. The air returns to its lush silkiness. And yet I am left with the sense that all the aspects of this place that are most familiar to me are now provisional. I no longer trust them.

On 10 February, the Gospers megafire, which started on 26 October as lightning hit a single stringybark in the droughty Wollemi wilderness north of the Blue Mountains, is finally extinguished by flooding. It has blazed for 79 days and incinerated over a million hectares.

Birds

When I experienced a great loss in in my early forties – almost a year to the day after another – I went to see my mother in the family home. She wasn't a hugger or giver of advice, so instead we fed the birds. As she had when I was a child, she stood behind me in the kitchen with her shoulder propped against the back door, passing slices of apple and small balls of minced meat into my hand.

Each bird, apart from the snatching kookaburras, was touchingly gentle in the way it took food from my fingers. The white cockatoos ate daintily, one-legged. The lorikeets jumped onto the sloping ramp on both feet, like eager parachutists, to quarrel over the apple and press the juice from the pulp with stubby tongues. Lined up on the veranda rail, the magpies cocked their heads to observe me before accepting meat precisely in their blue-white beaks. They had a beautiful, carolling song, with a chorded quality in the falling registers. But the bright-eyed butcher birds had the most lovely song of all: a full-throated piping, which I've heard compared to the Queen of the Night's aria in Mozart's

Magic Flute. Over decades, a family of these little blue-grey birds, had come to stack their hooked meat-eaters' beaks with mince, which they flew to deliver to young somewhere in our neighbour's garden, though we had never bothered to try to work out where they lived. This afternoon, when my mother and I opened the door, they landed by our side as they always had, having spotted us from their watching places. For a brief moment, surrounded by these vital creatures, I felt as if I might still want to be alive.

Birds have always been small agents charged with carrying the burden of our feelings simply by following the logic of their own existence. The Irish imagined puffins as the souls of priests. The ancient Romans released an eagle when an emperor died in the belief it would 'conduct his soul aloft.' In the Abrahamic religions, doves are given powers of revelation. We have even been inclined, right up until the present, to imagine birds as the souls of our recently departed returned to us, if only for a moment. Even without being recruited into such labour, birds touch on our lives in small but significant ways. Once, in the botanical gardens of Melbourne, a boyfriend laughed until he almost cried at the mechanical, eager hopping of the tiny fairy wrens, a fact that only made me like him more. A friend tells the story of her uncle who ordered quail for the first time at a restaurant and cried when he saw it on his plate. 'She had a raven's heart, small and obdurate,' American author Don DeLillo writes of a nun in *Underworld*; it is my favourite description in any novel.

In Japan, where my partner and I tried to ease our sadness, the calls of crows were ubiquitous in every town. Like the low sounds of its deer, they had a subdued, almost exhausted quality, as hollow as the bells that are rattled to call the oldest spirits to its

Shinto temples. In 1975, when his first wife left him, Masahise Fukase began to photograph these birds, which he had seen from the window of a train. He would keep taking their pictures – on a hilltop tori at dusk, grouped on the budding branches of a bare tree, in flying silhouette – for ten years. *Ravens* would become one of the most famous books of modern photography, hailed as a 'masterpiece of mourning.' While some people see the birds in his photos as symbols of loneliness I see them as embodiments of pure intention. 'I work and photograph to stop everything,' Fukase said. As if fulfilling a prophecy, he would spend the last two decades of his life in a coma, after falling down the stairs at his favourite bar.

Yet for all our emotional investment in them, we've never treated birds particularly well. To train a falcon in Qatar, owners sew the young bird's eyes shut, unstitching and then restitching them for longer intervals, until it is entirely dependent on its keeper. In Asia the appetite for caged songbirds is so great that their calls are disappearing from its forests. Our careless acceptance that these extraordinary creatures are subject to our will is perhaps as damning as any direct mistreatment of them. This is symbolised for me by that fact that, in North America, owners of long pipelines add a putrid odorant to the natural gas they carry so that turkey vultures, circling over the deathly smell, will alert them to methane leaks. We are currently draining marshes globally three times faster than we are clearing forests. Migratory Red Knots fly 15,000 kilometres per year between Australia and their breeding grounds in the Arctic Tundra, but they're declining because of the industrial development of the Yellow Sea's tidal mudflats, where they stop to feed and rest. One of the details that most haunted me in the reports of Australia's megafires was the fact that many birds that survived the radiant heat would die of smoke inhalation because the continuous one-way airflow of their breathing systems and air sacs meant they couldn't cough to clear their lungs.

When we first moved into my childhood home, wattlebirds fed in the grevilleas, calling from the rockery with voices that sounded, as a poet once said to me, like the cork being pulled from a bottle of champagne. While their long forms ending in a slim, curved beak seemed the embodiment of alertness, they were the birds our cat caught most often. To see one, rescued but internally injured, vomit up its honey and grow limp was one of my first intimations as a child of the world's evils. Unable to bear the thought of their sleek, streaky bodies in the bare earth, my mother would bury them wrapped in tea towels. But it was the seventies and no one thought to keep the cat inside.

As my mother entered her nineties, her life contracted around her birds. Although experts were now advising that the lack of calcium could soften chicks' bones, I continued, against my conscience, to put through her weekly grocery order, which contained as much bird mince as food for herself. She had stopped feeding the cockatoos, which had chewed her windowsills and the struts of the back door, but when they heard us in the kitchen they would still plaster their chests like great white flowers against the window or poke their heads through the large holes they'd made over the years in the door's wire flyscreen. But it was only the butcher birds that ever entered through these gaps to wait for her by the sink, feathers fluffed calmly. Once or twice, one would come and find her in the dining room and quietly walk back ahead of her to be fed. When I came with the children, she would press food into their hands as she stood behind them at the door, leaning against the kitchen counter for support. So she continued to be one of the estimated thirty to sixty per cent of

Australian households that fed wild birds, a statistic that suggests that we need them far more than they need us.

Scientists began to think in the nineteenth century that birds might have evolved from dinosaurs, when the 150-million-year-old fossil skeleton of *Archaeopteryx* – which we now know was capable of short bursts of active flight – turned up in a German quarry. The Victorian biologist Thomas Henry Huxley observed the bony-tailed, feathered fossil's striking resemblance to small dinosaurs like *Compsognathus* and proposed that it was a transitional form between flightless reptiles and birds. Huxley's theory fell out of favour until the last decades of the twentieth century, when a new generation of palaeontologists returned to the similarities between the metabolisms and bird-like structures of dinosaur fossils and birds, and there is now a consensus that birds are avian dinosaurs. That the birds with which we share our lives are the descendants of the hollow-tailed, meat-eating theropods is a true wonder that never fails to thrill me.

Birds, like us, are survivors. They escaped the Cretaceous-Paleogene (or K-Pg) mass extinction event 65 million years ago: the fifth and last great dying in the history of our planet, until the Sixth Extinction taking place around us now. Scientists were able to work out, from unusually high deposits of rare Iridium (which mostly comes from outer space) in the Earth's crust that a ten-kilometre-wide asteroid hitting the area that is now Mexico's Yucatán Peninsula had killed off three quarters of the world's living creatures by causing forest fires and then a freezing 'nuclear winter,' which inhibited photosynthesis and rapidly acidified the oceans. Its blast was thousands of times more powerful than the combined force of all the nuclear weapons in the world today. The dust and debris it dispersed into the atmosphere eventually settled into a thin grey band of Iridium-rich clay, which came to be called the K-Pg boundary and, above it, no trace of a non-avian dinosaur can be found. In historical ironies whose obviousness would shame a novelist, it was geophysicists looking for petroleum in the 1970s who would first discover the existence of the Chicxulub crater. Walter Alvarez, who discovered the 'iridium anomaly,' was the son of physicist Luis Alvarez, a designer of America's nuclear bombs, with whom he posited the asteroid strike theory; Alvarez senior had followed in a plane behind the *Enola Gay* to measure the blast effect as it dropped 'Little Boy' on Hiroshima.

The ground-dwelling, beaked avian dinosaurs were able to scratch out a life for themselves in the ferny 'disaster flora' that replaced the obliterated forests; their intelligence, their feathery insulation, their ability to feed on the destroyed forests' seeds, and to digest the 'hard, persistent little morsels' as one writer puts it, would help them to survive, and later flourish. More incredibly, these dinosaurs were already recognisably bird-like, inside and out; capable of at least short horizontal flight like quails, the parts of their brains that controlled sight, flight and high-level memory as expanded as those of modern birds', while our early mammal ancestors – small, nocturnal, insectivorous, shrew-like mammals – were hiding in clefts and caves. It is now thought that the world's oldest modern bird, *Asteriornis maastrichtensis*, could probably fly and was combing the shallow beaches of today's Belgium, in the way of modern long-legged shore birds, 700,000 years before the K-Pg mass extinction.

Because of a wealth of new fossil evidence in China, we now also know that feathers are far more ancient than we once thought; they didn't evolve with birds 150 million years ago but are instead probably as old as dinosaurs themselves. In fact, many of the dinosaurs that we have been trained to think of as scaley, were at least partially feathered, including the fearsome *Tyrannosaurus Rex*, which may have used its primitive feathers, like a peacock, for display. Powerful electron microscopes have allowed scientists to determine that the long filaments covering 150-million-year-old *Sinosauropteryx*, the first feathered non-avian dinosaur discovered, in China, in 1996, were 'proto-feathers'; and even, looking at the melanosomes inside them, that they were ginger, running in a 'Mohican' pattern down its back and ending in a stripey white-and-ginger tail. Similar examination of the melanosomes of another Jurassic-era theropod found that it had a grey-and-dark plumage on its body, long white and black-spangled forelimbs, and a reddish-brown, fluffy crown.

Scientists are puzzled about what dinosaurs' feathers, which developed before the capacity of feathered flight, were 'for,' but I don't really care: the fact of them is startling enough, along with the imaginative readjustments we have to make in seeing the fearsome creatures of paleoart that we grew up with, locked in orgasmic conflict, as softly plumaged. Did their young call for them with the same open-mouthed yearning as baby birds, I wonder? Did they possess their own sense of beauty? If we imagine dinosaurs as being less alien and fluffier, does it make our own era's potential annihilation seem more real?

Over the last century folkorists and psychoanalysts have kept trying to account for birds' deep hold over our imaginations; as agents of death, prophets, ferriers of souls, omens, and symbols of renewal and productivity. Some attribute it to the power of flight and their ability to inhabit the heavens, others to the way eggs embody transformation. But could it be that the vestigial shrew-like part of ourselves has always recognised them instinctively as the emissaries of a deep past, much older than we are? 'We float on a bubble of space-time,' writes author Verlyn Klinkenberg, 'on the surface of an ocean of deep time.'

Recently, this deep past has begun to reassert itself as, even during Coronavirus lockdowns, burned fossil fuels continue to release carbon dioxide into the atmosphere, bringing its concentration in the air to levels not seen since the Pliocene three million years ago when the seas were 30 metres higher. To try to help us understand the literal profundity of this moment in the history of the earth, writers have been looking increasingly below its surface, far beyond the human realm, to its deepest, billions-of-years-old strata. In his astonishing *Underland*, English writer Robert Macfarlane travels physically far underground into caves, mines, and nuclear waste bunkers, to revive our ancient sense of awe as forces and substances once thought safely confined there begin to exert themselves aboveground, but also to convey the enormity of the long shadow we will cast into the future of a planet that has already seen periods of great transformation. In *Timefulness*, geologist Marcia Bjornerud argues that understanding the Earth through her discipline's vastly expanded time-scales can help us avoid the almost unthinkably grave consequences of our actions. We live in an era of time denial, she writes, while navigating towards the future with conceptions of the long patterns of planetary history as primitive as a fourteenth-century world map. And yet, she writes, 'as a daughter, mother, and widow, I struggle like everyone else to look Time honestly in the face.'

Yet here, I think, all around us on the surface of the planet, are our vivacious and inscrutable companions, feathered messengers from deep time, who still tell their own story of complex change.

At a writer's festival in northern New South Wales, I remember, a magpie lark landed between the chair and speaker on stage to let forth a cascade of liquid notes, 'as if, to say,' a droll friend sitting next to me said, 'I too have something to contribute!' while I found myself wondering, yet again, how something with such a small heart could be so alive.

To think about dinosaurs, as evolutionary biologist Steven Brusatte writes, is to confront the question of what lives and what dies. To think that dinosaurs were far more complex than we imagined, Klinkenberg muses, interrupts the chain of consequence we've been carrying in our heads, which assumes that deep time's purpose was to lead to us as the end point of evolution. The history of feathers and wings, in which the power of flight appears to have been discovered and lost at least three times, shows that evolution is not a tree, but a clumped bush. And yet, Klinkenberg writes, 'Because we come after, it's easy to suppose we must be the purpose of what came before.'

The same could be said of mothers. When the time came to choose the photographs for my mother's funeral, the images of her as a child in Mexico and Canada seemed as unreal as dispatches from the moon. The photographs of our mothers as young girls are so affecting, a friend wrote to me, because they show them living lives that were whole without us. Now my own children turn their heads away from pictures of me as a girl, because, they say, 'You don't look like you.' And yet, if our minds struggle to encompass the deep time of our mothers, I think, how can they hope to stretch across aeons?

On my last visit to my mother, I left her on her front step throwing meat to the two magpies which had learned to come around from the backyard, away from the other birds, and would follow her on stilted legs around the garden. When she pressed her emergency pendant the next morning, I missed her call; it was my partner, hearing her faint answers, who called the ambulance. Unconscious in the hospital, she died having never known that she had left her home. When I stopped back at the house afterwards, one of the butcher birds, which I had never seen around the front, was on the windowsill of her dark bedroom, break pressed against the glass, looking for her.

How It Feels Now
(After 'Hysterical Realism')

I.

On the morning of 12 September, 2001, I woke up in our terrace in Melbourne's Fitzroy to a message on the answering machine from my partner. 'Turn on the TV, hon. Interesting things have been happening in America overnight.' He was at work and so the communication was curt, almost comically so. But what could have prepared me, alone in our small lounge room, for the jerky mobile phone footage, the agitation in the reporters' voices, the cries of the crowd at the impacts of those impossibly low-flying planes?

The novels of Don DeLillo, the great writer of America as televised catastrophe, had primed my imagination for this moment, in which terrible spectacle, disbelief and horror repeated and multiplied on our screens, but it didn't occur to me to think of it as a literary event. Nevertheless, a mere week later, the book critic James Wood took the contemporary novel to task for its failings. In an article in *The Guardian* titled 'Tell Me, How Does it Feel?', he declared that turn-of-the-millennium novelists were incapable of engaging with a 'mutilation' like 9/11 because they were insufficiently serious. Since DeLillo's magisterial *Underworld* was published in 1997, Wood wrote, writers had become carried away by their social and documentary mission to capture the times and an entire 'writhing culture'. Their novels seethed with 'tentacular ambition' but it came at the expense of human feeling.

A year earlier, in a patronising review of Zadie Smith's debut *White Teeth*, Wood had christened this new type of novel – information-heavy, plotty and talkative – 'hysterical realism.' His complaint wasn't that these books, in all their 'glamorous congestion', lacked reality but rather that they offered us *too much* of it; they were too broad in their reach, too lavish with their details, and too excessive in their use of narrative conventions borrowed from a more modest realist tradition. Pursuing vitality at all costs, novels like Smith's, with its terrorist plots, transgenic mice, and multicultural North London setting, were, variously, 'perpetual-motion machines'; an 'endless web' of connections; and a 'caravanserai' of gaudy lights mistaken for habitation. By offering us only shiny caricature and spectacle, they ultimately evaded reality *and* lacked metaphysical depth.

Now, in the smouldering aftermath of the terrorist attacks on the World Trade Centre and Pentagon, Wood was moved to recycle his review. Novelists had become mere 'Frankfurt School entertainers,' he declared, who filled their books with mini essays on 'obscure and far-flung social knowledge.' Critics had overpraised writers like Smith (but also Salman Rushdie, Jonathan Franzen, David Foster Wallace, Tom Wolfe, Richard Powers and 'anyone in possession of a laptop') simply for 'knowing things': about 'the sonics of volcanoes! . . . how to make fish curry in Fiji! . . . terrorist cults in Kilburn! . . . the New physics!'.

How It Feels Now (After 'Hysterical Realism')

Now September 11 had showed that their 'preachy presentism' was no match for a culture that could always get up to something bigger. These books' 'trivia-tattoos' had already faded, while their busy smartness disqualified them from the deeper business of knowing a single human being.

Wood's polemic stung – and it would go on to be quoted for two decades. Writers would worry, publicly and privately, about the power of the novel to match an atmosphere of accelerated horror that seemed historically original, at least to those in the post-Gulf War western world. But it was Zadie Smith, having had time to contemplate Wood's first volley, who was able to summon up a response in *The Guardian* the next week. Hysterical realism, she wrote under the guise of being chastened, was a 'painfully accurate term for the sort of overblown, manic prose to be found in novels like my own *White Teeth* and a few others he was sweet enough to mention.' (Not all readers grasped Smith's sarcasm: her 'confession' would also go on to be quoted, verbatim, for years). Smith was not, she assured Wood, working on a 700-page generational saga set on an incorporated McDonald's island north of Tonga. Instead, she was 'sitting here in my pants, looking at a blank screen, finding nothing funny, scared out of my mind like everybody else.' Yet, even as she contemplated the possibility that she might have one of 'the most pointless jobs in the world,' Smith offered a sly defence of the novel as a supple, humorous and changing form, which might offer more immediate consolations, even if these were just laughter in the dark, or a refusal of cliché, than the gravitas Wood seemed to have in mind. (And, she suggested, Wood might be wrapping his own preachy presentism around the much older search for 'soul').

As a writer friend remarked to me the other day, only half-jokingly, Wood's piece now feels 'almost quaint.' Viewed from 2021, the terrorist attacks look like the first in a series of shocks to our senses and moral fibre that would unfold over the next decades: among them, the staged cruelties of ISIS, cages of children and civilians caught on grainy film waiting for immolation; photos of American soldiers abusing prisoners in Boschian tableaus at Abu Ghraib and later, refugee children sleeping under space blankets in US detention centres deliberately separated from their parents; not to mention the slower violence of Australia's own long-term detention of refugees where time, as well as isolation, amount to torture. Add to these the almost unthinkable catastrophes in which nature has met human folly: the 2011 Tohoku earthquake and tsunami, when a wave of dirty water would kill 10,000 people and cause three reactors at the Fukushima Daiichi Nuclear Power Plant to melt down; the loss of huge parts of the Arctic ice shelves; wildfires in areas of the world that had never burned before, culminating in the destruction of a fifth of Australia's forests and billions of animals over the summer of 2019–2020; and the global spread of Covid-19, which, as I write, has killed 3.5 million people. Add to these, again, the inkling that they were only the visible flares of threats so large that they are beyond our ability to comprehend or see fully, which philosopher Timothy Morton describes as 'hyperobjects,' and Wood's alarm seems both premature and excessive.

And yet. Wood's article has lodged itself firmly into my own feeling for this moment. For all his moral disappointment with the novel, he does seem, in retrospect, to have captured the tone of an emotional rearrangement just getting underway. Whenever I put fingers to keyboard to think about these uncertain times we're living through now, I find my own gut compass also points back to 2001 as (in writer Phillipa McGuinness's words) 'the year everything changed.'

II.

If you were an aristrocrat or an intellectual man in want of entertainment in 1880s Paris, you would take yourself on a Tuesday to La Salpêtrière, the domed mental asylum in the thirteenth arrondissement, whose sprawling wings had been built where a gunpowder factory once stood. There, in its floodlit amphitheatre, you could watch neurologist Jean-Martin Charcot present his hysterics. Hysteria encompassed a wide range of physical symptoms, from anxiety to fainting, paralysis and abdominal pain; but in his packed-out weekly lectures (or 'matinees') Charcot showed off women in the grips of the trances, paroxysms, back arches, and convulsive gestures of a *grande attaque*.

If you were lucky, you might have caught the teenager Louise Augustine Gleizes – who had up to 154 attacks a day that ended in seizures and faints when the doctor struck a tuning fork – before she escaped from the hospital dressed as a man, never to be seen again. Or you could watch Marie Blanche Wittman, the 'queen of the hysterics,' who would hold unnatural postures indefinitely or sleepwalk under hypnosis, her face running through the gamut of emotions. A young Freud would attend Charcot's salon. 'After some lectures I walk away as from Notre Dame,' he wrote, 'with a new perception of perfection.' Charcot was revolutionary in determining that hysteria was not an affliction of the womb but neurological in origin though Freud would later come to redefine hysteria's repertoire of physical symptoms as the cathartic 'conversion' of unbearable mental conflict. (Many of the women of La Salpêtrière were victims of sexual trauma, a fact one fears would only have enhanced the titillation for many in the audience.)

If you were unable to attend the lectures, you might peruse Albert Londe's pictures. The medical photographer had devised a nine-lens camera to capture successive images of the gowned patients, faces and bodies caught in obscenely orgasmic prostrations that look at once disconcertingly stagey and abandoned. These quasi-pornographic photos would fascinate the twentieth-century surrealists, who saw in them a kind of uninhibited, 'convulsive' poetry. For arts students like me in the last decades of that same century, they were inescapable: essayist and academic Wayne Koestenbaum remembers that he 'flipped out with intellectual glee' when he first saw them as an undergraduate. They were the 'Open Sesame', he writes, into gender theory, which reclaimed these spasmic poses as a wordless protest against a male-dominated symbolic order.

Although Charcot claimed that hysteria was more likely to affect men, it would lodge itself in the twentieth-century popular imagination as female affliction; and it was, after all, *women* in extremis the neurologist chose to display to an eager public. It is hard to find many clips online now, but the archetypal scenario of a man delivering a slap to the face of an unhinged woman (or sometimes, in slapstick comedy, a babbling, unmasculine man) to bring them back to their senses was prevalent enough to etch its weird libidinal violence on my childhood. By the end of the twentieth century slapping hysterics was such a cliché of disaster movies that the 1980 spoof film *Flying High!* could build a visual joke around it (which, one hopes, would be unlikely to make it onto screen today). As an out-of-control plane bucks in the sky, a male passenger slaps a panicking woman – 'Calm down, get a hold of yourself!' – only to be followed by another slapper, also a man, who pushes him out of the way . . . then a nun, then a Hare Krishna. As the camera pans along the queue of passengers in the aisle, each holds a different weapon.

All of these associations were present in Wood's coinage, which was calculated to convey the message that 'hysterical realist' novels – and maybe their authors, too – were excessive, emotionally incontinent, and, paradoxically, too self-conscious. At the same time – in Wood's reading – the authors' plotty pyrotechnics, pimped-up facts, and wild narrative gestures were avoidance tactics. Lesser book critics, he implied, may have encouraged the hyperrealists' extravagant writhings like misguided Charcots, but Wood, a literary Dr Freud, exhorted novelists to drop this posing in the name of 'real' feeling; though his article was unclear about what this would look like, beyond making a space for 'the aesthetic and the contemplative.' Novels that tell us how people actually feel about different things, he concluded, 'are commonly called novels about human beings.'

Even without a degree in psychiatry, it's hard not to look back in wonder at Wood's vehemence and wonder what unresolved conflicts of his own might have driven it. Why did he choose to label novels he found unruly and garrulous with a term loaded with the iconography of convulsing female bodies? Why did twenty-five-year-old Zadie Smith, a stunningly successful Anglo-Jamaican debut novelist, draw his first fire? My eighties Arts degree had also taught me that there was a long and tired tradition of associating a loss of cultural authority with the feminine. (Mid-twentieth-century modernists had blamed female consumers for a runaway and mindless mass culture. For Flaubert, only writing in drag as Madame Bovary – *'Madame Bovary, c'est moi'* – would allow him to explore the sickly romanticism of the bourgeoisie.) Certainly, there were a number of changes underway as the millennium turned that might have made a critic feel his literary authority was becoming surplus to requirements. If it was true, as Wood grumbled, that 'anyone with a laptop [was] thought to be brilliance on the move,' and if 'knowing things' was now the yardstick for judging a novel's value, then surely the literary ecology would have less use for a Cambridge-educated specialist able to explain the finer points of the aesthetic and contemplative.

Wood's anxiety was not unfounded: this was only the beginning of a period when a degree in literature, or even having written a book, would come to seem like the least desirable qualifications for talking on book shows or judging literary prizes, as cultural commentary was wrested from the hands of so-called 'elites.' (Australian academic Mark Davis has described this as the 'decline of the literary paradigm,' as market forces, rather than aesthetic values and artistic autonomy, began to dominate in publishing and, more generally, the struggle for cultural value). Other boundaries were dissolving, too, though this is only clear in retrospect. The distinction between 'literary,' 'middlebrow,' and 'genre' fiction was blurring, along with the once-firm demarcation between fiction and nonfiction. The twenty-first century would see the rise of generically every-which-way novels that mixed and matched horror and sci-fi with historical or literary fiction, as well as novels (W. G. Sebald's essay-novels like *The Emigrants* blazed the way) by writers like Rachel Cusk and Karl Ove Knausgaard, in which it would be hard to place a pin between the authors' real lives and their fictional reflections. Meanwhile, as 'literary fiction' was losing its allure, a new era of pay-per-view television was just beginning that was positively Tolstoyan in stretch and ambition. *The Sopranos*, whose first series appeared in 1999, would be followed by series like *The Wire*, *Six Feet Under* and *Breaking Bad*. Old hierarchies were crumbling, though it seemed a bit rich to blame authors.

If he had been less intent on prosecuting, Wood might have been able to stretch his sympathies to see that writers and critics were in the same wobbly boat; or to admire the nimbleness and invention of the 'hysterical realists' in trying to reinvent the novel for an era that no longer made such a distinction between 'high' and popular culture; or even to concede that interesting new voices, like Smith's, which were perfectly capable of explaining themselves without mediation or interpretation, were emerging from the shake-up of the pecking order. But instead, in the aftershock of 9/11, he tightened his grip on his own ideal vision of the novel that these end-of-the-millennium novelists were apparently failing.

Although he wasn't explicit about what exactly this longed-for book might look like, conceding that the old social realist novel could no longer 'trudge along,' it was a nineteenth-century French author Wood chose to invoke in his last paragraph as he looked forward to a new kind of literature worthy of the moment. Marie-Henri Beyle (who wrote as Stendhal) famously described the realist novel as 'a mirror carried along a high road,' reflecting blue sky and muddy puddles. While we might blame the man who holds the mirror for being immoral, or the mirror for showing us the mire, Stendhal wrote, we should instead blame the road that holds the puddle or the inspector of roads who lets the puddle form. (In other words, we shouldn't shoot the messenger for showing us what's wrong with our world but instead turn our attention to fixing it). But in his last flourish, Wood nudged the weight of Stendhal's quote, so that the mirror was no longer a metaphor for artistic artifice. Instead he hoped, he wrote, for a novel that would show 'that the human consciousness is the truest kind of Stendhalian mirror, reflecting hopelessly the newly dark lights of the age.' While it's hard to parse quite what he meant, Smith was onto something when she gently mocked Wood's longing for 'soul'. He seemed, in his metaphor, not to have much patience with the novel as a chameleonic artform but to be demanding fiction that was at once neat, limpid, and transcendent.

But was Wood's conviction that there was a more real 'real' that novelists should capture an overly worked-up response to 9/11? Smith suggested as much in her reply. After all, she wrote in her *Guardian* piece, seeming to accept the role of compliant patient, it wasn't clear what remedy Wood had in mind for the terrified author contemplating the failures of her art while smoking her way through a family-sized pouch of Golden Virginia:

> Be more human? I sit in front of my white screen and I'm not sure what to do with that one. Are jokes inhuman? Are footnotes? Long words? Technical terms? Intellectual allusions? If I put some kids in, will that help?

Perhaps Wood was calling for a 'suppression of ego,' she mused; for writers of sparse 'gasps' of prose like Kafka and Borges, who didn't suffer from the American and English instinct to 'cover the world in [their] shit immediately.'

And yet, Smith found herself thinking, this wasn't the time to be making lists or throwing around words like 'human' and 'civilised.' If she and her fellow novelists had anything in common, she wrote, it was simply trying hard to write in a way that wasn't full of generalisations or deadened by clichés. Besides, the novel wasn't an immutable fact of artistic life; it was a 'historically specific phenomenon that came and would go unless there are the writers who have the heart, the brain, and, crucially, the cojones to keep it alive.' If Wood was going to resort to gendered terms, Smith hinted, she was the more rational party with greater testicular fortitude. The title of her piece? 'This is How it Feels to Me.'

III.

How was I feeling in 2001? As the new year turned my partner and I had been homeowners for just over a year. In late 1999, we had bought into a row of two-up, two-down terraces in our suburb of bluestone-edged streets and old dunny lanes, where colourful wall-sized stencils were replacing the enigmatic graffiti ('Dog on wheels,' 'Ooh, it pinches,' 'More hairy women on TV') on the sides of houses.

Turning to the pages of my writing journal, I see that I began the year with a vivid dream that I had a dolphin's fin growing from my back. As I lay on a beach I had induced two small, scowling monkeys to fetch sunscreen in a bucket and rub it into this sensitive organ until they became bored and ran off. Immediately, a tidal wave swept over the sand to carry us all away. Over coffee in one of the many cafes on nearby Brunswick Street with 1950s tchotchkes on their polished Gaggias, my friend and I, two overeducated academics, workshopped the dream: was it a literalisation, we wondered, of 'spanking the monkey'?

My notebook also tells me that, as I walked the flat, permanently twilit streets between our house behind its row of ginkgo trees and my teaching job in the city, I worried over a novel I had recently given up on writing about French explorers to Australia (still unfinished); the usefulness of historical fiction; and the new novel I was working on about the American West, which I would not complete for another four years, and publish as *The Lost Thoughts of Soldiers*. Other worries loomed behind these ones. Would I regret my choice not to have children? Which door-to-door scammer would next take advantage of my mother, back in Sydney, who lived alone on her leafy North Shore street?

In notes I took on W. G. Sebald's essay-novel *The Rings of Saturn*, in which the narrator contemplates destruction as he walks around a ruined East Anglian landscape, I see that I wondered if critics were right to view the narrator's depression as simple neurosis; couldn't it be a legitimate malaise in the face of ongoing environmental ruin? Matters of ecological disaster were on my mind already then. And yet, at the same time, I am struck now by how ordinary and personal most of my worries were. My face, as Patrick White wrote of the young heroine in *The Tree of Man*, 'had not received the fist.' (Oh, but it would.)

In 2001 any catastrophes were in the distant future.

My worries had a horizon.

IV.

Wood was an astute and gifted critic so it was frustrating that he seemed uninterested in asking *why* some of America's most brilliant writers might have felt driven to fling their skeins of story beyond the novel's usual limits. Why had Jonathan Franzen piloted his huge family drama, *The Corrections*, which would sell over three million copies, between both American coasts and a small ex-Soviet republic, with excursions into the business of universities, celebrity chefs, internet start-ups, cruise ships, and big pharma? What was Richard Powers, whose novels Wood found particularly grating, aiming to achieve, as he interwove the stories of a chemical conglomerate and a woman with ovarian cancer in *Gain* or connected the stories of a prisoner of war in solitary confinement with workers' attempts to build a virtual reality machine in *Plowing the Dark*? What was DeLillo's rationale for his mighty *Underworld* – which Wood seemed to regard as hysterical realism's Patient Zero – in which he tied the story of a man's present-day hunt for the ball in a legendary 1951 baseball game home run to America's waste management systems, a nun's ministrations to New York's poor, an art installation of painted B52s in the Arizona desert, and the nuclear detonation of waste in Kazakhstan? Surely there was more to their ambition than mere *showing off*?

It wasn't as if the writers Wood had labelled sat comfortably together as a group either. Some, like Zadie Smith, seemed to be reviving the playful, riffing bagginess of the earliest English-language novels like *Tristram Shandy*. Others, like Franzen, who wrote earnestly about his aims in his essay 'Why Bother?' (which came to be known as 'The Harper's Essay'), were trying to recut the cloth of the social novel to fit modern lives when the 'social' now extended far beyond village or city limits. DeLillo – who would go on to write the novella *Falling Man* about September 11 – had spent his long career grappling to find story forms capable of tracking the increasing complexity of the corporate and political powers that shape our world; and, an even harder task, to catch the white noise of disaster and terror humming away around us that we repress. Salman Rushdie, on the other hand, was surely more of a classic 'magic realist' in his use of exaggeration and fusion of the supernatural and real, to upset, in his own words, the 'conjurers of power' in India's colonial history.

If anything did unite these writers, it was a sense that human life had become more interconnected but scattered, in ways that were harder to pin down using the novel's traditional forms; and this was before that other many-tentacled creature, the internet, came into its full powers, which would allow us to cast our lives even further and more quickly across time and space. (It was the rolling TV coverage of 9/11 I was glued to, I recall now, rather than my computer or hand-held device). Powers, with his deeply erudite fascination with developments in science around DNA and artificial intelligence and the way they could create new organisms, expressed his inclination, in interviews, to imagine novels as another type of 'sublime, transformable code,' like DNA or software. And while Wood criticised these authors for the flatness of their characters – as if they had simply been squashed by the heavy machinery of their novels – some, DeLillo especially, were interested in the question of whether the late twentieth century was actually giving shape to new types of human being. DeLillo's characters have always seemed to me to speak the primal scripts of an American unconscious; conspiracy in *Libra*, the deranged economic fantasies of the one per cent in *Cosmopolis* (both personal favourites). By the time he published *Point Omega* in 2010, DeLillo would wonder 'if human consciousness is reaching a point of exhaustion and that what comes next may be either a paroxysm or something enormously sublime and unenvisionable.'

The last decade of the twentieth century was not only becoming hyper-complex and speedy, it was also becoming phantasmatic. This wasn't an entirely new feeling. In 1848, Karl Marx and Friedrich Engels had written that 'all that is solid melts into air.' In the face of growing industrialisation, they saw that traditions were giving way, religious beliefs were fading, and communities were coming apart. The generations of modernist writers and artists who followed would also recognise the self-consuming speed of modern life as a kind of 'maelstrom.' Marx and Engels had hoped that the stripping away of the old ways would lead to revolution. And yet, 150 years later, it seemed that even those last solid foundations we had come to take for granted were disappearing. The old estates were not so much evaporating into steam but being transformed into real estate.

The ecstatic languages of economics and glamour were priming us to live in a bright and slippery parallel reality. So any author who set out to write about the conditions of life heading into the new millennium would surely need to 'know things' about a quickening global economy! . . . local currency pegged to the foreign currency market! . . . a credit-fuelled housing bubble! . . . the loss of old blue-collar jobs and the rise of precarious part-time work in service industries! As housing prices in global inner cities boomed, you could almost argue that the property market had become our new lingua franca. When my partner and I had been searching for a house in 1999, there had been a residual level of resistance to the transformation of the local by the inflated imaginary of the market. 'This loft could be in London or New York,' began one auctioneer as they warmed us up to bid. 'But it's just a shit box in the arse end of Fitzroy,' someone called out, 'so let's get on with it!' We had been able, just, to afford the loan for our small terrace on a part-time lecturer's and bookshop manager's salaries. But by 2001, endless reality TV shows about 'hot properties' and 'hot auctions' were not only driving up prices but we were being told constantly that we should be delighted by their acceleration. 'In good news for homeowners today . . .' news reports began, as they announced yet another fall in interest rates.

Like the planes landing eerily into their own sub-Saharan desert reflections in Werner Herzog's *Fata Morgana*, other once-solid things were receding into the neoliberal economy's heat mirage. My partner and I had enjoyed free educations – high school, undergraduate degrees, and PhDs – but the writers

I taught at university were now burdened by deferred student loans, introduced in 1989, for user-pays courses, which would be garnished from their incomes for years to come. We were also old enough to remember a time of big public institutions – banks, telephone companies, newspapers with the presses churning in their basements, post offices with polished brass chutes – before they were privatised, offshored, or sold to become upmarket apartments, hotels, and shops. Academic Bonnie Honig has suggested that these old 'public things,' from phones to energy companies, used to nourish our sense of being part of a democracy centred on a shared purpose. Now the imposing places of our childhood, which had imprinted us with their impressive smells and heft, had melted into an ever-shifting corporate dreamscape. Even place itself had become less distinct. Back in the early nineties, when we were living in Melbourne's North Carlton, our local sportsground had swapped its name from the park it inhabited to its telecommunications company sponsor. (Now part of a shifting universe of brands it would go on to be named after a labour hire firm and a paper company – or rather, a 'global leader in packaging and resource recovery'). This sense of living in an evanescent and provisional location wasn't only a Melbourne, or even an Australian, phenomenon. In Brooklyn, New York, I would marvel at how every shop whose signage announced ship chandlers, steam equipment and shoemakers, now housed a hairdresser, dress shop, or café.

No wonder writers like Smith, DeLillo, Powers and Franzen were so intent on filling their novels with the minutiae that Wood dismissed as 'trivia.' In a world becoming unanchored from any form of value beyond the market, their garrulous insistence on 'knowing things' now looks like an attempt to preserve the weight of a mercurial shared reality before it disappeared; and, for some of these writers at least, to document the blooming of a whole range of different realities that the market and internet were, paradoxically, liberating. At the same time, as more information became available online, the 'hysterical realists' had to look in more obscure places to find details of the real – the sonics of volcanoes, physics, garbage disposal in Kazakhstan – that were new or fresh.

The Global Financial Crisis of 2007 would show just how unstable and fantastical the ground had become beneath our feet, as banks that had bet on an American housing market they had constructed as unstoppable, lending riskily and at low rates, and then borrowing to enable more loans, saw house prices fall and borrowers default on payments. The world's financial system went into meltdown, with banks coming very close to crashing, until they were bailed out by public money.

In the face of a 'real' that was increasingly global, and at the whim of quicksilver global markets, Wood's call for writers to return to a more contained human novel of metaphysical truths looks from a twenty-first century viewpoint to be the most perverse kind of magical thinking. Was the realism he seemed to desire even the appropriate template for novelists trying to capture the disconcerting vitality of the times? To reach for ambitious forms, even if their novels were sometimes flailing and ungainly?

V.

When Wood's article came out in 2001, I had been grappling with the question of how to write a second historical novel to follow my 1997 debut. It wasn't just the present that was speeding up: history was also accelerating, in ways that made writing historical fiction tricky. It was harder to find unknown stories or historical byways that could carry the shock of the past. I'd learned this lesson the hard way. In 1999, I was a year into a novel about a soldier who had survived the Battle of Little Big Horn travelling with Buffalo Bill's Wild West Show through Europe, when Thomas Berger published *The Return of Little Big Man* (the sequel to his sixties blockbuster *Little Big Man*). It was also about a survivor of the Battle with the show on its European tour.

'Buffalo' Bill Cody's hugely popular tours to cities like Venice, Paris and London were then a lesser-known part of his legend, especially to those of us living outside America. The idea for my novel came about when I saw a startling (though now iconic) photograph of Cody and some of the show's Native American performers in a gondola in Venice. I was fascinated by the layers of displacement it embodied, especially for these men, who were able to free themselves temporarily from a reservation system and practise their formidable skills only by re-enacting their own defeat day after day. While I was nervous about writing into another country's history, I felt more confidence as the inheritor of a different colonial legacy, in telling a story where *everyone* was out of place. I had spent time in the archive of the Buffalo Bill Historical Museum in Cody, Wyoming, contemplating the large glass balls Annie Oakley had launched from a trap to show off her sharp shooting, and sifting through tickets and programs and autograph books containing the adamant pencilled signature of Hunkpapa Dakota chief and spiritual leader Sitting Bull, who, with Crazy Horse, had led the united Sioux people to victory at Little Bighorn in 1876.

But now here was Berger's book. And here, within its pages, with the dust rubbed off their wings, were the charged historical details I had painstakingly accumulated. To my dismay, these included the story of the death of Sitting Bull, who had toured for

How It Feels Now (After 'Hysterical Realism')

four months with the Show, booed by the crowds but mobbed by fans. When he left, Cody gave him a horse called 'Rico,' which had been trained to dance and fall to the arena floor as gunfire erupted. Rico was still with Sitting Bull in 1890 at the Standing Rock Indian Reservation in Dakota Territory, when Indian Police, working with the army to suppress the Ghost Dancing movement, shot the great chief in his cabin. Witnesses said that as Sitting Bull died, the horse, thinking he was back in the arena, danced, bowed, and cantered in a circle. Although this is not a novel I would try to write today, the moment struck me as appallingly emblematic of the tragic contradictions of America's staging of its past, and I had planned, until Berger's book came out, to place it toward the end of my story. As I gave up on my novel and put it away, I realised that I could no longer depend upon the raw aura of history – on the bracing shock of bringing facts to light – because so little was now obscure. Of course the positive effect of this change would be that writing would move on from white storytellers 'discovering' stories in archives to a wider range of writers telling their own stories. In the years since I've learned to question that first urge to plunder, synthesise and interpret – and that the Stendhalian mirror is perhaps more profitably and ethically turned back on the writer and their own expectations as the first subject of inquiry.

By 2001, a mere mouse-click could connect anyone to facts and photos that only a few years earlier would have required serious time in libraries and archives to bring to light. By then I had already realised that any new historical novel would probably need to incorporate the rapidly lengthening shadow of history itself; those questions of who got to tell it, and how. In 2005 I would return to my notes and write about the Battle of Little Bighorn in *The Lost Thoughts of Soldiers* but I would skirt the event itself. Instead, working on a small scale, I would move my story into a halfway space between novel and essay, to reflect, through the eyes of my character, Seventh Cavalry officer Captain Frederick Benteen – a 'failure' in the history books – on how history and modern celebrity were made.

VI.

As it turned out, the 'hysterical realist' novels Wood slammed in 2001 were among the last of their kind. After publishing *The Autograph Man* in 2002, about a Chinese-Jewish autograph collector hunting for a 1940s movie star's autograph – which Wood compared unfavourably to *White Teeth*, as a novel of 'wisps' – Zadie Smith would abandon the epic-comic novel to write more soberly realistic stories. She would also publish literary criticism more nuanced and cannier than Wood's. DeLillo would downsize to spare, hypnotic novellas tightly focused in place and time (a desert bunker, a cryopreservation facility, a New York apartment). Jonathan Franzen would take eight years to write his next novel *Freedom*, which, though lengthy and filled with information on birds and strip mining, was less bravura in its digressions than *The Corrections*. (He also earned a reputation as an out-of-touch reactionary for publishing essays that railed against the 'total electronic distraction' of the internet.) Richard Powers would release *The Overstory*, in 2018, a mighty environmental fiction depicting the lives of nine people with special knowledge of trees, who would come together in the fight for northern California's redwoods, though his work had never seemed to fit into the jokey-talky, know-it-all category that Wood so disliked. Writers are still publishing long, ambitious novels but they are more likely to be in the spirit of Modernist experiment, like Lucy Ellmann's single-sentence *Ducks, Newburyport,* deep dives into small social worlds like Sally Rooney's *Normal People,* or serious speculative fiction, like N. K. Jemisin's *The Fifth Season* (itself part of a trilogy) and Kim Stanley Robinson's *Ministry for the Future.*

But if 'hysterical realist' novels faded away after 2001, I don't think it was because their authors had taken Wood's scolding to heart. Instead, what these capacious, ambitious novels could no longer sustain was playfulness. The terrorist attacks on September 11 had been a revelation, at least to a certain section of the West, that not everyone was on the same page. As Rushdie had learned back in 1989, when the Supreme Leader of Iran placed a fatwa on his head for 'blasphemy' in *The Satanic Verses*, we had not all entered a global era – as I had been taught as a cultural studies student – of irony and textual knowingness. The 'internet superhighway' had not freed up information into a kind of smorgasbord of liberal enlightenment but created its own paths and cul-de-sacs where not everyone was godless or possessed by a spirit of sprightly relativity. Though not listed in Osama Bin Laden's 2002 'Letter to America,' in which he outlined al-Qaeda's motives for the suicide attacks on the World Trade Center and Pentagon, some have argued that their intent had been to wrench back a moral and symbolic order from a globalising 'West.' After 9/11 it would be harder for a novelist to assume that a majority of their readers 'felt the same way' or to believe they had the same licence to flit in and out of the lives of others. You would be hard-pressed after 9/11 to write lightly about a militant fundamentalist brotherhood in London (as Smith had in *White Teeth*), let alone give them the silly acronym KEVIN (Keepers of the Eternal and Victorious Islamic Nation). The second decade of the century would see increasingly fraught conversations about whether it was acceptable for writers to represent cultures or identities outside their own 'lane.'

Literary theorist Mathias Nilges has even suggested that around the turn of the millennium the novel entirely lost its last illusions of critical distance: its belief in its ability to stand back, like Charcot at La Salpêtrière, and give a full accounting of a sped-up, hyper-complex world. He argues that neoliberalism has now penetrated so far into our lives that no corner remains free from the market: not even fiction. To be fair, Nilges' argument is not so far removed from Wood's that the novel was no longer able to keep up with social reality because the culture could always get up to something bigger. Yet while Wood believed the novel could return to its job of seeing through the noise of the present to 'metaphysical' or human truths, Nilges argues that our era is characterised by the 'utter exhaustion of our ability to imagine the future as difference.'

Still, Wood was right, in a way. There *was* a sense of 'hysteria,' or nervous violence, in the air, and in those novels. Wood's article could not have had the same lasting impact if there wasn't. Looking back, it seems he got the symptomology right but came up with the wrong diagnosis. What if, rather than running away from the emotions of the present, novelists were trying to take the measure of a new feeling of helpless agitation? If we take Wood's charge of hysteria seriously and remember Freud's assertion that it was a malady in which extravagant gestures stood in for what could not be said, then perhaps we can discern another reason why these novels were so vivacious and awkward.

There was another crisis looming, which was yet to show itself fully, and which we weren't quite talking about. In 2016, in *The Great Derangement*, the Indian novelist Amitav Ghosh would criticise contemporary novelists for ignoring the simmering chaos of climate change. For a long time, he wrote, floods, hurricanes and fires have been seen as unworthy subject matter by serious novelists, who, in their desire to maintain the boundaries of good taste and believability, have left such sensational material to the writers of thrillers and disaster fiction. In doing so, Ghosh argued, they have been complicit in capitalism's 'great derangement.' Its death drive, as it pursues growth and profit at all costs, requires our collective denial of its unsustainable toll on the climate.

But hadn't the 'hysterical realist' novels of the late twentieth century been trying to register a new feeling of turbulence with their ungraceful narrative gestures, even if the nearness of ecological disaster wasn't yet quite so clear? Franzen's second novel, *Strong Motion* (1992), had even revolved around earthquakes, which its plot connected to an inheritance, big money, and secret drilling by a chemical company. (As if to prove Ghosh's point, reviewers criticised it as unwieldy and unconvincing). Other 'hysterical realist' novels registered social, political or emotional tremors that ran in 'tentacular' directions too big to capture with straightforward plots.

It seemed plain to me, even at the time, that 'hysterical realist' writers were trying to give shape to a sense that the world was no longer as we had once known it; that it was skewing away from what had once seemed solid, as if they sensed but could not quite see or articulate the urgent dimensions of a crisis yet to come. And, in fact, three years after making his case in *The Great Derangement*, Ghosh would write *Gun Island,* a sequel to *The Hungry Tide* that was more explicitly concerned with climate change, and which seemed to owe a small debt to those writers in its mix of mythology, SMS texts, dolphin biology, tragedy, and comedy.

It's true when we look back at them now that most 'hysterical realist' novels weren't addressing ecological catastrophe directly but they did seem to register the weather front of a shift of feeling; a sense that the world was changing and – more significantly – that it was hard to know quite what to feel. Some seemed unable to settle on the tragic or the comic. Franzen's novel began with the matriarch Enid responding to an unheard alarm and the novel would lurch between her efforts to bring her three children together for Christmas before their father succumbed to unacknowledged dementia, with tragi-comic turns involving a farcical Lithuanian start-up and the father's hallucinations, in which a talking turd critiqued civilisation's repression ('Me, personally, I am opposed to all strictures'). Smith mixed displacement, anger, and terrorism with wry humour. DeLillo's characters had been in a state of barely repressed hysteria for years. Tonally, these novels anticipated a twenty-first century that would be characterised by Twitter storms of outrage, public shaming, and meltwater pulses of crisis that would peak online and give way quickly to the next, interspersed with playful TikTok videos and comic memes; an emotional landscape distinctly different from the detached 'postmodern' irony that supposedly defined the late twentieth, though this was certainly not universally shared or enjoyed. This century's state of constant flux would buffet our appetites for books and films whose forms were built to take us on long-haul flights of feeling; no wonder some writers might choose to match the constant, intoxicating crests and climaxes of our feeds. Look back over the last two decades and you can see books and television drama have also been struggling with this dilemma: to go long and slow, or pack in as much drama and action as possible.

With the benefit of hindsight, it seems that 'hysterical realist' novels looked forward to the era in which we live now, in which our senses are constantly heightened (alert *and* alarmed) but it's hard to know quite what to do with the information they feed us. Academic Lauren Berlant coined a name for this hyper-alert state: 'crisis ordinariness.' There *were* metaphysical questions implied by their busy stories and hard-to-pin down tone, which have only become more urgent. In an era of epic planetary shifts and a hyper-accelerating culture, what is serious and what is not? Could this enormity and speed be causing feelings to oscillate so quickly that they were transforming into a kind of deadpan acclimatisation to crisis? This question has continued to play out in the slew of dramedies like *Six Feet Under*, *Dexter* or *Breaking Bad* where the extreme elements that were once annexed into forensic drama (grisly decapitation, a body dissolving in acid in a bathtub) switchback with hilarity or sweetness.

Just as Australian gum trees will go into a phase of 'panic growth' after a big fire, throwing out small branches all the way up their trunks in order to maximise their chance of getting light and air, could the multiple stories and characters, the verbal ticcing and posing, of the novels of the late nineties also be thought of as a perfectly sane response to stress? As well as trying to find a shape large enough to contain a new reality . . . weren't they also showing us exactly how it felt?

VII.

In my notebook for 2001 I see that I jotted down with approval the Frankfurt School theorist Theodore Adorno's observation that the only correct moral attitude for an intellectual to adopt was a feeling of alienation: of not feeling at home even in your own home. In 1962 Adorno's colleague Georg Lukács would accuse him and his fellow German intellectuals in exile of having a worldview so melancholy that they had taken up residence in the Hotel Grand Abyss – 'A beautiful hotel, equipped with every comfort, on the edge of an abyss, of nothingness, of absurdity [where] the daily contemplation of the abyss between excellent meals or artistic entertainments can only heighten the enjoyments of the subtle comforts offered.' Yet Adorno had good reason to be sombre, having been forced out of his job as a lecturer at the Institute for Social Research in Frankfurt as a 'non-Arayan' because his father was Jewish and into exile in America in 1934. The only certainty, as his colleague Max Horkheimer had written to him in 1932, was that 'the irrationality of society has reached a point where only the gloomiest predictions have any plausibility.'

I had loved Adorno's tone since I first came across him as a student, and in the right mood I can still consume the acerbic observations of mid-century America in *Minima Moralia* (1951), his 'Reflections from Damaged Life,' like poetry. Looking back now, I am struck by how modern his sense was of the moral imperative of feeling homeless in place; how fitting to this moment at the edge of a different sort of abyss of unfolding environmental chaos. Not for the first time I'm also fascinated by the way that one's subconscious, in the process of taking journal notes, can anticipate what the forebrain hasn't yet processed. I can see now that I was also feeling some kind of deep shift in 2001 that I couldn't yet see the shape of, as I wrote this quote in my writing journal.

Since then, many writers have been trying to name the new feelings that our precarious present demands. In *Rising*, her nonfiction book about rising sea levels, author Elizabeth Rush uses the word 'endsickness' to describe her physical responses, like motion sickness or vertigo, to small shifts in weather or familiar places, which alert her to the fact that she is 'living in a world that is moving in unusual ways to what I imagine as a kind of event horizon.' In 2014, artists Alicia Escott and Heidi Quante created the online 'Bureau of Linguistical Reality,' which invites participants to coin their own terms to replace a collective 'loss of words' in the face of a collapsing world. Entries include the self-explanatory 'pre-traumatic stress disorder'; 'shadowtime' (the parallel time scale of climate change shadowing our daily activities); and 'gelm' (a powerful and continuous feeling of foreboding or premonition related to human initiated incidents, which opens a gulf between us and our pleasures). In 2005, anthropologist Glenn Albrecht coined the most-used of these terms, 'solastalgia,' to describe the feeling of being out of place even when we are at home because our environment changes in ways we find distressing.

Feeling homesick in place, which seemed like a moral choice to Adorno, is now our inescapable condition. Though it might still be – perhaps more than ever – an ethical decision to recognise this feeling.

I didn't record any details of 9/11 in my journal. By September of 2011 I had stopped writing it because I had been – a thought that seems almost laughable now – too depressed.

VIII.

There are two ways of looking at the decline of 'hysterical realist' novels. One is to say that Wood was right, in a way: that these books, which looked like the apex predators of the literary scene, were more like lumbering megafauna, consuming everything in sight until they finally exhausted themselves. Yet when I look back at those busy novels, twitching and wriggling within their own skins, I don't see extinction, but transformation. They're not dying, but evolving.

If it had become too difficult, by century's end, for novelists to capture the whole heaving reality of their age – and perhaps Don DeLillo's *Underworld* in 1997 was the last great, heroic attempt – what could novelists do next? You could feel the nervous energy building in those restless 'hysterical realist' books, as they tried to outrun a sense of entrapment. It's not as if our times have gotten better, or less complex. Instead, we would be cursed, a decade into the millennium, by the uncanny knowledge that we might already be living out our end times; that standing back to get perspective on it all was harder than ever. The dream with which I began 2001, of an alert fin on my back that was vulnerable to the sun and shimmered with pinkish chromatophores like a squid's skin, now seems strangely prescient: an unconscious premonition that my own body was now implacably meshed with those of other creatures as the great seismic movements of the earth swept us away.

Some novelists have tried to solve this problem of how to write about a present so immense as to be almost unrepresentable by slowing time. Over six volumes of his autofictional 'My Struggle', Norwegian author Karl Ove Knausgaard described the minutiae of his life, in all its banality, as he agonised over the need to make great art; the fictional equivalent of 'slow cinema,' his sextet hacked out a place for the novel and its ability to represent the world through sheer will and effort alone. Others have been trying to find new sped-up forms to match the pace of a rapidly accelerating present. By far the most interesting attempt is Scottish novelist Ali Smith's 'Seasonal' quartet of loosely connected novels (*Autumn, Winter, Spring, Summer*), each of which she wrote over a period of six weeks. Smith has described the process of working from 2016 to 2020 on these novels, which range over time and fragments of folklore and modern art, while folding in as much up-to-the-moment contemporary detail as possible, as 'moving on sheet ice.'

But the novels that interest me most are those that are pushing the boundaries of the real even further. Instead of reducing the novel's scope to 'knowing a single human being' or homing in on simpler stories concentrated in place and time, they have been wildly expanding its sympathies and timescales. Although Wood might see more tricksiness or showing off, I see purpose and compassion in these newly ambitious novels.

In *Clade* and *Dyschronia*, Australian authors James Bradley and Jennifer Mills stretch the usual time and character limits of fiction to find ways of thinking about how precarious our present has become, to the point of almost exceeding what we can imagine. Beginning with a climate change researcher in Antarctica waiting to hear from his partner if their attempt to conceive through IVF has succeeded, Bradley's novel tells the story, in episodes, of the human members of a single 'clade' – that is, a group of organisms with a single ancestor – across a century, and through hurricanes, floods and plague, while always keeping its main focus on its fragmented family drama. He bookends his story with deep time, balancing the melting ice layers of Antarctica in its opening against outer space at its end, as the astronomer Noah detects some kind of 'language' in a far radio signal. 'Perhaps human beings arrived too late or too early and the heyday of galactic civilisation had already passed,' he thinks, 'or lay billions of years in the future.'

Mills also connects an unimaginable future with a near future very close to our own. Growing up in a small coastal town afflicted by climate change, where the sea has suddenly receded or, rather, 'pulled away, embarrassed, from the mess it has made,' her heroine Sam has suffered from migraines since a childhood car accident. These bend her sense of time and even seem to let her see glimpses of a grim future. Her 'gift' attracts people interested in exploiting it to 'develop' this poor post-industrial town, though the novel depicts her premonitions as a curse and hints that they may have been caused by toxicity (from industry, from climate change) in her environment. The hallucinatory quality of *Dyshcronia* mirrors the unreal quality of our own moment, in which we struggle to process the warnings of a nature in distress or to fathom that we may already be living in end times, our fate entangled with the planet's.

Over the last decade novelists have also been challenging Wood's contention that the realist novel about the present should be about human beings. British author Jon McGregor makes a very interesting tilt at writing outside of an entirely human perspective in *Reservoir 13*. A murder mystery that becomes increasingly less interested in solving the crime at its centre, it begins when a teenage girl disappears on a visit with her family to a small Northern English town to see one of the thirteen man-made dams perched eerily above it. As her body decays over a decade, we watch the local townspeople go about their business – while the animals also go about theirs. A woman winds her twin babies' mobiles, then the novel pans to badgers in the beech wood, which feed quickly to lay down fat for the winter, while the river runs towards the millpond weir. This haunting novel hints that more vital drama lies in the goings-on of a disturbed but still-surviving landscape than any conventional whodunnit.

How It Feels Now (After 'Hysterical Realism')

Just as radically, each of the ten linked stories in Ceridwen Dovey's *Only the Animals* is told by the soul of an animal killed by human actions around the world, beginning in late nineteenth century Australia (the explorer Mitchell's camel) to 2006 Beirut (a parrot left behind in a bombed apartment). They are especially discomfiting because of their biological veracity and the fact that each of their animal narrators seems to accept, with a certain humility, that killing it is a defining feature of our humanness. In *From the Wreck*, Jane Rawson stretches the novel's sympathies even further by introducing an octopus-like time-travelling alien intelligence into the story of a nineteenth-century shipwreck. Having seen its own oceanic planet exploited and wrecked by colonists, the alien takes the shape of a female passenger on a boat foundering on a reef off South Australia; for eight days it sustains a young male passenger, then disappears. Like an alien Orlando, it will manifest in other forms throughout that passenger's later life, occasionally allowing him glimpses of its own unique cephalopod-like intelligence. Interestingly, Rawson, who is also an environmentalist, originally began her work as a historical novel based on her great-great-grandfather's survival of the wreck of the SS *Admella*, only to find she wasn't able to sustain its realism. Introducing the alien intelligence allowed her to represent 'all the other species that humans just don't give a rat's arse about.'

Krissy Kneen's *An Uncertain Grace* moves through a century in its five parts, from the near future to a post-flood world, as its characters try to find the plasticity of mind and body to evolve and survive radical change – a potentially sexy task in the novel's watery and erotic universe. In one of its episodes, a sex offender agrees to have his consciousness fused with a jellyfish to reduce his sentence. As his fused senses link to the colony, he finds himself making:

a kind of connection I have never dreamed of making. I'm more than the sum of myself . . . The light touches my skin and I shiver. We're all shivering. We're walking towards the light and the electric charge of sunlight excites us.

It's striking how often – as if literalising Wood's horror of the 'tentacular' – cephalopods and jellyfish appear in contemporary novels as symbols of ways of being in the world as far removed as possible from the human. Cephalopods, with their chemo-tactile distributed intelligence (they have nine brains) and ability to 'see' through their skins, and jellyfish, creatures older than the dinosaurs and lacking a central nervous system, challenge our very definition of consciousness or the 'mirror' it might hold up to the world. This new generation of novels suggests that maybe we should stop fighting to distinguish ourselves from a planet worldlessly expressing its distress. Instead, if we open our imaginations up to other ways of seeing and feeling, we might share something tender and profound. It could even save us.

There *was* hysteria in the air in 2001 and Wood's article, in its affront and disappointment, let us see it. But the source of that agitation wasn't the novels or the ambitions of their writers. It was the wind shift of a world accelerating, in all its heedlessness and incantatory beauty. The novelists Wood castigated were taking the temperature of the moment by pushing their forms as far as they could and testing their limits. What Wood saw as a failure looks to me like the beginning of a revolution.

I'm seeing them everywhere I look now, the next generation of novels they gave birth to which ask us to expand our sympathies. By pushing into new territory, they're proving themselves precisely capable of expressing how the great planetary 'mutilations' underway around us feel. Perhaps, they suggest, the only way to understand our present is to understand that a too-narrow sense of time and history got us into this mess in the first place – and will no longer hold. From acceptance, they suggest, change might yet come.

Notice how calm they are, this new generation of books. Having acknowledged that life and feeling are moving out of the old order into a more precarious future and taking the novel with them, there's nothing 'hysterical' about them.

Gum Trees

The two gum trees outside my study window had grown so close together, each leaning out from the other at a slight angle, that they could have been a single tree dividing from the same roots. By day, their thin leaves filtered the light into dappled patterns that danced and shifted on my study walls as the sun moved. By night, they were white-trunked sentinels in silent counsel. Each Christmas our downstairs neighbours wound fairy lights around them and we drank martinis by their soft glow. Once, working late, I looked out my second-storey window to see one of the brushtail possums, which growl like horny old men, hunched at their base in the full moon's drench, contemplating the sky in perfect silence.

The lawn where the trees stood didn't belong to our apartment block and it wasn't really a lawn. In the way of this densely populated neighbourhood, where the early colonial estates were subdivided and re-subdivided, it was actually the rooftop of the underground parking garage for the apartments next door, which bends in a right angle around our building. I doubt anyone ever planted them. There is such a remnant wildness to our street – Moreton Bay figs grow out of the sheer sandstone cliff face on one side – that it seemed most likely the eucalypts had seeded themselves in the thin soil decades ago and struck root in this small no man's land.

So when the notice came that the trees were to be chopped down there was nothing we could do. The letter said that their roots were growing down into the garage roof. The council had agreed to their removal.

For weeks, I mourned the gums in advance of their disappearance. I found myself, instead of working, on the day bed in my study, for the pleasure of lying in the middle of the city in the play of bush light through their leaves; a 'fishing net of shadows,' as the late poet Martin Harrison described eucalyptus shade. It's this constant, gentle sifting I miss about the east coast Australian bush when I am overseas, the busy threading through of air and life. On some of those afternoons when I lay there, white cockatoos would swoop down to hang from the top branches and call out, as the novelist Ruth Park once wrote, 'in boys' voices.' I didn't have the heart to tell our children, then four, that the trees were slated to go, their companions each evening outside the dining room window as they had sat in their highchairs.

We don't like native trees much in Australia, perhaps because they stood in the way of the colonial will to clear and conquer, perhaps because they were so intransigently unlike the British trees of 'home.' Here in Sydney, they have the quite wonderful effect of making everything look tousled and off-kilter, as if the streets have been dug out of an older, ruined metropolis, to the chagrin of those who prefer neater designer landscapes. In Australian exploration teams, a chain dragged between two horses would clear all trees out of the surveyors' way, a method farmers still use to lay bare unloved bushland today, only with tractors. In the Victorian children's classic *Seven Little Australians*, the loveliest character, Judy, dies rescuing the baby called 'The General', crushed in his place beneath a falling tree limb. With their propensity to drop large branches, some eucalypts have been dubbed 'widow-makers.' During bushfires, we count their burning in hectares, but rarely concede in our news of the national figures a sense of loss. The antipathy seems to run nerve deep. Some people move to the New South Wales Blue Mountains, a local writer once told me at a party, imagining they will love the tranquillity, but they can't cope with the smell, a deep eucalypt-oil vapour mixed with dried leaf matter and the always-disintegrating sandstone of the valley walls.

Still, there are those of us who love Australian trees, for all their capriciousness and their tendency to shed great strips of bark as if one is witnessing a catastrophe in slow motion. For millennia, Indigenous Australian have used hollow trees as birthing rooms, scarred and marked them, or bent their tops together in their graveyards to form a living bower. Even colonists with a good eye could appreciate their beauty. Some critics deride the early European artists for not being able to come to grips with Australian gums, made oddly smooth and neat beneath their camel-hair brushes. This is unfair, I have always thought, since their pictures capture so uncannily the feeling of dusk's blue turn, when eucalypt leaves fade back into anonymous nothing while their trunks flare, in the lowering light, into glowing paleness.

It's only fairly recently that scientists have revealed to us trees' true complexity; their social networks, which share information, and may even 'think'; the 'mother' trees that feed their children, via their root systems, over their first decade; the forest communities pumping sugars to their fallen comrades on the ground.

(Though the human metaphors are our own for processes whose ancient intricacy still eludes us.) Biologist Tim Low writes that, because of the poor soils, Australia's trees are factories for sugar, attracting more bird pollinators than any others in the world. The banksia family are so old, he writes, that it's likely that honey-eating birds 'flitted past dinosaurs' in the Cretaceous forests to lap at their flowers. The rift valley between prehistoric Australia and Antarctica is probably where 'beak and flowers first met.'

Trees have also become newly precious, as we face their potential loss, not only from logging, deforestation, and fire, but new diseases, which have almost wiped out species like America's chestnuts. More than half of Europe's native trees face extinction, while a quarter of our eucalypts are on the International Union for Conservation's red list. In 2019, in northern New South Wales, as the catastrophic fire season was beginning to take hold, it was a shock to see whole stands of gum trees – our landscape's tough survivors – brown and dead. On a farm in the state's south, I saw a thin tree give up before my eyes, its roots losing their grip on the dry soil to keel over, silently, where it had stood upright a moment before. It was as startling as seeing a shooting star streak across the sky.

Anyone who has watched trees closely knows they're more than sap and wood. In Japan, one comes often across large trees in temple gardens marked as *yorishiro* – objects capable of housing *kami* or ancient spirits – by rope-and-paper girdles around their trunks. A Shinto shrine will lead up, through its gate, to a sacred grove in which one great tree has become a permanent home for a *kami* and is now a divine object or *shintai*. In my mind I keep a kind of Significant Tree register, filled with trees that please, and sometimes frighten, me. When I lived in the Blue Mountains, I used to take a shortcut across a park to my quiet suburban street. A huge grey-trunked gum stood at the top of the small track that ran up from the Three Sisters, and each time I would get halfway across the grass before having a compulsive sense of being watched. There was never anyone behind the tree when I turned around. In an essay on river red gums, writer Sophie Cunningham confesses to giving in to the urge to hug these buckled old trees with their frayed crowns twisting to the sky. Similarly, whenever I pass the river red gum in our local park, the lone survivor of the pre-colonial swampland, I stop to rest a hand against its bark.

Trees are more active, too, than one might think. Because of global heating, evergreens in America's east are heading toward the cooler north while oaks and maples head for the west in search of water. In Ecuador's rainforests, palm trees 'walk' up to twenty metres a year. As the soil beneath them erodes, they send down long roots into firmer ground and bend towards them, lifting their old roots into the air, and slowly cartwheel into a different spot. In his book *A Million Wild Acres*, the writer and farmer Eric Rolls tried to account for the peculiar beauty of the Pilliga 'Scrub', an intricate forest system in northern New South Wales that had survived brute treatment by generations of farmers and timber-getters. In the pine flowering season of 1973, he recalled, all the plants in the forest exploded at the same time, sending up dense rolling clouds of pollen that drifted into the shearing sheds until it became almost too dark to shear. 'If one is near a pine when all the cones burst together,' Rolls wrote in a passage memorable for its gruff poetry, 'one hears a crack like a pistol-shot. The branches recoil and the tree shivers. One does not expect to hear a tree move in passion.' I have not seen pine-cones burst in simultaneous ecstasies but I have watched cypress trees on Rome's old Appian Way ejaculate pollen from their flat crowns in golden drifts, which lingered, hazy and particulate, in the still air.

Perhaps the two gum trees outside the window trembled with passion in their own way. And yet, having grown up in a country where all wild trees were lumped together as 'the bush,' I never thought to discover exactly what type of eucalypt they were.

Two months after the letter, men arrived with chainsaws and a chipper. It is shockingly fast work to make two trees disappear. 'New trees step out of old: lemon and ochre splitting out of grey everywhere,' wrote poet Les Murray, of the gum forest on his property. But these trees, which had had only one another for company, would have no descendants.

Six years later, I still miss them. The sun radiates a steady heat through my window. As I sit at my computer, I feel spiritually out of whack. I have not seen a possum on the lawn since, although a smaller tree has been planted where the roots were grubbed out of the ground, and the marsupial family still ranges along the branches of the camphor laurel outside our loungeroom. But sometimes, just as one imagines one sees the face of a dead friend in a crowd, when I walk into my study, I expect to see the trees' soft lantern slide of shadows on the wall. To look out my window and see them still standing there.

The Opposite of Glamour

When the twins were about five, I found myself longing to reread John Steinbeck's *The Log from the Sea of Cortez*. I first read it as a teenager, studying one of Steinbeck's minor novellas at school. Anxious for their only child to succeed, my parents had also bought the author's other books in the cheap Pan editions, whose pastel covers featured naïve paintings constrained by circular borders, as if viewed through a telescope. I could still remember this edition clearly, on which a man in overalls stooped with some kind of instrument over a flat, sunset beach. The book is Steinbeck's account, a decade after the event, of his travels in 1940 with marine biologist Ed Ricketts, who would become the model for Doc in *Cannery Row*. Under the pretext of a loosely conceived scientific expedition, the men hire and equip a small purse seiner – a fishing boat – and set out from Monterey in northern California, for the Sea of Cortez, between the Baja California Peninsula and Mexico. Over six weeks, they amass a plenitude of creatures from the intertidal zone, collecting specimens for Rickett's marine biological business, but also for the sheer pleasure of gathering them and seeing how these small animals propel themselves and behave. It is from such close observation, surely, that Steinbeck conceived the metaphor for storytelling that would open *Cannery Row*:

> There are certain flatworms so delicate that they are almost impossible to catch whole for they will break and tatter under the touch. You must let them ooze and crawl of their own will onto a knife blade and lift them gently into your bottle of sea water. And perhaps that might be the best way to write this book – to open the page and let the stories crawl in by themselves.

In the end, I couldn't find the old edition of *The Log from the Sea of Cortez* at my mother's house so I bought a new copy and read it with a kind of hunger; for the wonders it catalogues, but also for the calm, certain joy of its writing.

Over the last half-decade I have also found myself picking up and putting aside the books I have collected about the French expedition of 1800–1803 to Australia, which are still waiting to play their part in a long-stalled novel. With ambitions to extend his empire's grand intellectual project of 'civilisation' into the southern hemisphere, Emperor Napoleon sent scientists, artists and sailors in two boats, the *Géographe* and the *Naturaliste*, to explore the coasts of 'New Holland.' The expedition's leader Captain Nicolas Baudin has always struck me as the story's tragic hero. A career merchant naval officer, ostracised by his ambitious young crew, Baudin died in 1804, on the way back home from the tough four-year stint, in Isle de France (now Mauritius), that ill-fated island of failure for expeditions to the great southern continent. (A year earlier, English navigator Captain Matthew

Flinders had been arrested on his way home from his exploratory expedition to Australia and would languish there in frustrated captivity until 1810.) In the official history he wrote, anthropologist François Péron would take credit for the voyage's many scientific discoveries, while blackening Baudin's name. Yet I find my interest always shifts from this human drama to the illustrations of Nicolas-Martin Petit and Charles-Alexandre Lesueur, two young assistant gunners tasked with illustrating Baudin's personal journal, who had become the expedition's official artists by default after its three government-appointed artists resigned at Isle de France on the voyage out.

Among the many delicate images these men made, I feel myself called by Lesueur's watercolour paintings of jellyfish. To look at them – ethereal, mysterious, yet weirdly adamant – is to feel that you are looking at the mystery of life itself. Some are faint and ghostly, floating scraps of bare existence. Others with brightly mottled orange bells and ruffs of tentacles resemble small monsters in eighteenth-century garb. Like Steinbeck's flatworms, they are compelling metaphors for the magic of artistic process: reanimations of dead creatures whose colours have faded within moments of collection, painted with a fine brush to live a second life on the skins of dead calves, which have themselves undergone a transformation into vellum. Lesueur's felicitously-named medusae are emissaries from a century of wonder. I was returning to these books, I realised, because I needed to immerse myself in their world of long-gone natural abundance; a place of astonishing throngs, untroubled by any sense of being imperilled.

Around the same time, I was walking through the Botanic Gardens with my children on a sunny-misty spring Sydney day. We stopped to watch an Indigenous heritage tour wrapping up. One of the objects the guides passed around and invited us to hold was a shell; chalky, as large as a saucer, and miraculously dense, even without the meat of the creature that once lived inside it. Oysters of such amazing size, they said, had once thrived in the harbour's estuaries. This was a shock. I had grown up assuming that the small Sydney rock oysters with rusty-coloured frills that you see today clustering around the sandstone walls and rocks of the harbour were the oysters mentioned in early colonial accounts of its bounty. That day I also had to revise my understanding of the city's lost middens – so numerous the invaders burned them to make quicklime that was in turn made into the 'shelly mortar' that binds the bricks of our colonial buildings – as mere garbage dumps. Created over thousands of years by Indigenous Sydney people, the guides told us, the mounds of discarded shells functioned as a kind of organic index. If the huge shells were at the top of the heap then they would not be taken from the area for a certain period, to preserve the supply. But the colonists, with no such system, ate and burned as they pleased (live oyster beds were also dredged to make lime) and such giants are no longer to be found.

Back home, I went online to look for more information about these lost shellfish. Instead, I found – unspooling, page after page – articles about oysters' worldwide decline. A newspaper report from 2011 described a scientific study which had found that wild oysters were already becoming 'functionally extinct.' Because 85 per cent of oyster reefs had disappeared around the world, due to overfishing, oysters were at 'less than ten per cent of their prior abundance in most bays and ecoregions.' (My hometown harbour's reefs, once as large as ten hectares, are now at an estimated one per cent of their original profusion). Other articles discussed how oysters, among other molluscs, including lobsters, are vulnerable to ocean acidification as increased levels of carbon dioxide in the sea threaten to dissolve their calcium-carbonate-based shells. Their own element consumes them. You can watch this sequential dissolution in a series of photographs of pteropod (or 'sea butterfly') shells: from one image to the next, their shells thin, their glassy transparency becomes etched and then fragments, until they become as ethereal as Lesueur's watercolours.

This has become a too-familiar story when we read about nature, which is now under tremendous stress, its wild populations shrinking even in its remotest corners. It's not hard to think of historical examples of decimation: passenger pigeons, American buffalo, the cod banks of the north Atlantic; while on Mauritius, where Baudin and Flinders both came to grief, the dodo had already been hunted to extinction by 1662. Yet these seem almost small-scale, minor premonitions, compared to the era we're now living through, in which species are declining at such a rate that the phenomenon has been named the 'sixth extinction': that is, the sixth mass extinction event since life on earth began 3.7 billion years ago. However, this time, instead of being caused by an ice age or volcano or meteor, the loss is caused by us.

In just the last five decades, less than my own lifetime, we have lost an estimated 68 per cent of species worldwide: mammals, birds, amphibians, reptiles and insects – an extinction rate which scientists estimate is 100 to 1000 times the natural rate without human involvement, and which is mostly due to clearing land for food. And yet it can be hard to see this decline when we measure it by the small scale of a human life; when such things are, for many of us, in the distance; and when we find ourselves forgetting creatures we haven't seen for some time, even if they were once ubiquitous.

When had I last been surrounded, I wondered, by an obvious abundance of wild creatures? Visiting the country around Tenterfield every Christmas with my family in the seventies, I have clear memories of seeing clusters of potoroos and wallabies in quiet conference around the water troughs in paddocks – pointed out by local farmers as 'pests.' Snorkelling on the Great Barrier Reef, I have experienced the out-of-body sensation of being suspended among fish in vertiginous strata, from the tiny fish I always think of as the 'heavenly hosts' hanging in the bright sunlit water near the surface, to the larger parrot fish, puppyish and social, grazing on the coral heads below. I remembered the cold brown bodies of small frogs plopping around my feet after rain in northern New South Wales when I was eight and the less romantic childhood sound of the wet bodies of moths and crickets hitting the car windscreen when driving through the bush at night. When I was twelve, on a family driving holiday in New Zealand's Bay of Islands, a passing truck kicked up a stone that shattered the rental car windscreen, which my father had to remove in order to be able to see to drive. It was a formative experience to hunch on the back seat for hours after night fell, my parka hood wrapped around my ears, trapped with dozens of fleshy flying creatures, their passage through the car frustrated by the back window, against which they fluttered, buzzed and pinged.

A great joy of returning from Melbourne to Sydney twenty years ago had been the dusk migration of its flying fox colonies over the eastern suburbs – 'windrowing,' as Les Murray puts it in his poem 'The Flying-Fox Dreaming' – as they homed in on the Moreton Bay figs' 'ripe tree beacons.' I remember reading somewhere that the kinds of animals we've witnessed, and lived around, make us different people: that is, humans who were surrounded by passenger pigeons are different people *for that*

The Opposite of Glamour

reason from those of us who no longer are. I like to think that these flying foxes are part of who I am.

And yet – a twenty-first-century question – how abundant is abundant? Since the flying foxes were moved on from their camp in Sydney's Botanic Gardens in 2012, they have seemed less prolific, now 'going on out continually over horizons,' as Murray puts it, in a reverse direction, from west to east. Watching them in 2021, I miss that terrific drama I wrote about in my book *Sydney* when they boiled up from the Gardens each sunset like dark ash from a fire. And yet I knew even then, a decade ago, that the population I was witnessing was itself already diminished, displaced into the city in the late 1980s by the destruction of habitat in the state's inland bush and the city's suburban outskirts. Some years ago, from the Mitchell Library's old handwritten catalogue card drawers, I ordered up a yellowing clippings file on flying foxes. A newspaper article from the middle of last century described vast clouds of them wheeling over farmers' sheds in central New South Wales, keen noses attracted to the scent of the honey they were decanting.

Still, it is hard to miss what you haven't seen. This problem of only being able to judge loss within our own lifespan has a name: 'shifting baseline syndrome'. Fisheries scientist Paul Daniel coined the term in 1995 when he noticed that each generation of scientists tends to use the status of fish stocks during its own lifetime as the baseline from which it conducts further studies. In his book *Wild Ones*, journalist Jon Mooallem writes about taking his very young daughter with him to see and write about America's endangered animals in order to extend the baseline in at least this one small human in the eye of a 'great storm of extinction'. Nevertheless, I feel for Mooallem's daughter: such knowledge is an ambiguous gift. Like her, I can't claim to have had the luxury of obliviousness during my childhood, as my mother was also preoccupied, presciently, with environmental damage and extinction. In the seventies, at Mooallem's daughter's age, I was addicted to Belgian nature documentary-maker Armand Denis's *Wildlife Magazine*, which, along with documenting life with animals in Africa, often showed the depredations of hunting and poaching. Even so, it has come as a terrible shock to learn that even the 'common' African animals I read about then, like giraffes and wild dogs, are now in serious trouble.

I'm not the first to observe that this knowledge means our encounters with the natural world now have a darker emotional texture. The ongoing crisis of global heating, with its delayed yet already tangible effects, means we're often suspicious of beauty itself, impermanent beyond the predictable cycles of life and death. When you are homesick in your very being, even pleasure is shadowed by preemptive sadness or loss.

It was while watching flying foxes from a friend's roof garden in Kings Cross, during the strangely endless summer of 2016, that I realised my solastalgia had become a permanent condition. One of the women I was with is a science writer; another works, with cautious hope, in the non-profit sector. The flying foxes moved across the sky with their odd stop-motion action, like footage from an old movie camera; some dipped close enough for us to see the blaze of fur on their chests, the same red-brown as the velvet inside a banksia pod. 'Something has crossed over for me this last year,' my science writer friend said. 'I no longer think things will be okay.' We each felt the same way. My friend who works with environmental organisations sighed and quoted the late comedian Spike Milligan: if we were all going to drown, she said, she wanted to at least be manning one of the lifeboats.

Although there is a strong agreement among scientists that human activity has pushed the earth out of the stable patterns of the Holocene, debate is far from settled about whether this constitutes a new geological epoch and, if so, where to plant the golden spike between the epochs – the industrial revolution, the dropping of the atom bomb, the beginning of the 'Great Acceleration' in the 1950s? And if, as seems increasingly likely, this period in which human activity dominates the earth's systems is officially ratified as an epoch by the International Commission on Stratigraphy, which oversees the official geologic time chart, it will almost inevitably be called the Anthropocene, since the name already has such popular traction. Nevertheless, 'Anthropocene' is a controversial term, particularly because it implies that all people are equally responsible for the earth's vast, accruing distress. Some academics have instead proposed the terms Capitalocene (to make it clear that our growth-addicted global markets drive the damage, with unequal effects on rich and poor); the Thermocene or Carbocene (emphasising CO_2 accumulation); the Phagocene (focusing on our rampant appetites for mass-produced goods); the Plantationocene (emphasising colonial history and racial inequality); and the Thanatocene (an age of deadly and more frequent wars).

More recently, two more terms have begun to assert themselves: the Pyrocene, defined by the increasingly out-of-control effects of human fire on the planet, including our binge-burning of fossil fuels; and the Homogenocene, named for the diminishment of biodiversity and increasing uniformity between the world's ecosystems and cultures because of global travel and trade; a process that has been ongoing since the voyages of Christopher Columbus. Given this accumulation of new names, the American scholar Steve Mentz has playfully suggested another term for our era: the 'Neologismscene.'

For me the name that rings most achingly is the Eremocene, or the Age of Loneliness. Coined by biologist and writer E. O. Wilson, it warns us of the existential and material isolation looming on the other side of the Anthropocene, if we don't act to protect the web of life with which we share our planet. Not only will the world be less rich without most of its wild creatures, but we face a future, which seems unbearable to me, in which we will be thrown back only upon ourselves as measure. As John Berger, and many writers since, have pointed out, humans have used animals to think with since we first began to paint their images on cave walls with our blood. They entered our lives, Berger writes, not as our subjects but as 'messengers and promises,' their presences magical, oracular, sacrificial. We study them when we are tiny and learning to become human: polar bears, alligators, elephants, apes, and pets fill our nursery shelves and picture books. They fill our language with metaphors: one is 'sly as a fox,' 'flash as a rat with a gold tooth,' 'bird-like' or 'leonine.' With their different life spans, they even help us measure time. I have always loved St Bede's description of human life as being like 'the swift flight of a sparrow through the mead-hall,' where the fire blazes, before it flies again into the winter. Of what lies before and ahead, Bede wrote, we are utterly ignorant. For the eighth-century monk, the future was unknowable, a matter of God's will. Today it's our will that matters, or our lack of it: we live with the awful knowledge that our actions are predetermining and foreshortening the future of life on earth as we know it.

It is a tragedy for the planet's wild creatures if they disappear: it is also a tragedy for us. If we lose all but our most domesticated companions, do we risk becoming something less than the humans we once were? Can we bear to live with just ourselves? Another way the Anthropocene era has been defined (by anthropologist Anna Tsing) is as an era without places of refuge for animals or people. Until well into last century, it was possible to live in or travel (at least as a free, white, wealthy man) to remote or hidden parts of the world. In *Ragtime*, E. L. Doctorow's novel of early 1900s America, the character Father joins an exploratory expedition to the Arctic where, with a depressingly familiar urge for destruction, the men net hundreds of birds, including auks so tiny they can be killed by the pressure of a thumb on their chests to stop their hearts. But still, for animals, even until late last century, there were some corners, too, where they could mostly escape us: pockets of the Amazon, Siberia, Indonesia, Papua New Guinea, the Congo. This is the case no longer, as resource extraction, forestry, roads, and human population penetrate these last bastions, with the help of more and more sophisticated technologies for wayfinding like GPS, along with their attendant side effects, of increased fire, feral animals, and disease. As Mooallem writes, wildlife has always been 'a reminder of all the mystery that exists outside my own experience.' What happens once we lose all these great wonders? If we can't value them, can we value anything at all?

Yet even if we try to be good citizens, to protect those last animal refugees from a once-abundant age, the responsibility is terrifying. In 2004, I heard the conservationist Willie Smits speak at the Australian Museum in Sydney. A Dutch microbiologist and conservationist who has made his life in Indonesia since 1985, Smits works with orangutans, which he described in his talk as being 'like us, but more peaceful.' Founding the Borneo Orangutan Society in 1991 to rescue and protect trafficked orangutans, Smits created the Wanariset research station as a temporary refuge from which rehabilitated orangutans could be released back into the wild. But in 2001, as Indonesian deforestation continued at a terrifying pace to obliterate this habitat, the charity bought 2000 acres of degraded rainforest in Kalimantan and set about replanting it as a more permanent home. (Smits has claimed, controversially, that his accelerated reforestation has established its own cloud-attracting microclimate, which has increased rainfall in the local area by 25 per cent). Because orangutans in the wild usually stay with their mothers until they are around ten years of age, Smits also had to set up 'forest schools,' in which human 'teachers' could train baby orangutans with the knowledge to survive. While the rehabilitated orangutans roam freely, most return to cages to sleep at night. But the work didn't stop there. Smits had to build special islands in the middle of the river for those rescued orangutans that had acquired human diseases or were disabled by maltreatment. To provide locals with income from the work of preservation, he planted a hundred-metre-wide ring of sugar palms around the sanctuary. He used satellite imagery to report palm oil companies breaking their permits by covertly clear-cutting virgin forests and Google Earth to encourage donors to 'adopt' (and monitor) hectares of the sanctuary. More recently, he has even founded a factory to process sugar palm into sugar and ethanol, to pump cash and energy back into the local community and save 200,000 trees each year being cut for fuel wood. I admire Smits's passion and yet I'm fascinated by the terrible authority he has had to take on: hasn't he had to become, in a sense, a kind of God, responsible for reimagining every element of this reduced new world?

At the same time, allowing animals to live in healthy numbers has never been a matter of sheer numbers, but of complex balance, as the Gadigals' middens remind us. Once that balance has been lost, our attempts to 'manage' animal populations can seem like hubris. In South Africa's Kruger National Park, scientists observed angry adolescent elephants terrorizing other animals because rangers, in attempts to 'thin' the population, had removed the dominant bulls. The loss of one species can cause rippling loss among other species that were dependent on it. Here in Australia, many of our native trees need to be pollinated at night; if we lose our flying foxes, these trees, which have co-evolved with them, will follow. The loss of one species can also lead to the 'hyperabundance' of other opportunistic creatures, like rodents.

Thinking about this makes me feel a little suspicious of my desire to return to moments of abundance where animals were thick on land, water and the sky. Am I identifying too much still with the colonial urge to measure and acquire? Perhaps, instead of 'abundance,' with its sense of the more-than-enough – which implies a party who judges the bounty ripe for the taking – it would be more accurate to say that I long for equilibrium, amplitude and complexity, whether I am there to see it or not. Some scientists have recently come to the similar conclusion that it's the evenness of distribution of species, rather than their numbers, that matters most for healthy ecosystems. And yet, for me, that's still not quite the point. The world has always seemed the most beautiful to me as it goes as much as possible about its own business, as oblivious as possible to my presence; eavesdropping on the small dramas of a reef while snorkelling off Queensland's Lady Elliot Island or watching the nocturnal activities of wombats in southern

New South Wales, I'm always struck by how these worlds seem so much more interesting and alive than anything than goes on in our cities.

Our ongoing grim state of affairs – the ghastly, forced closeness between the last remaining animals and human beings – seems to have been foretold by one of my favourite writers, Franz Kafka. In his two-page story, 'A Crossbreed (A Sport)', published in 1933, the unnamed narrator tells us that he has inherited a strange creature from his father: half-lamb and half-kitten, it is unique, the only one of its kind. When it is pressed against him, it is happiest. When he cries, the animal seems to cry too. And sometimes, he relates, it jumps up on the armchair beside him, plants its front legs on his shoulders, peers into his face, and puts its muzzle to his ear, 'as if it were saying something to me.' If he pretends to understand it, the creature capers about the room with joy until the narrator is forced to wonder if it in fact has 'the ambitions of a human being.' And yet, the narrator confesses, in the story's chilling last paragraph, he believes that the creature longs for the release of the butcher's knife – but because the animal is his legacy, he can't kill it. 'And so,' he concludes, 'it must wait until the breath voluntarily leaves its body, even though it sometimes gazes at me with a look of human understanding, challenging me to do the thing of which both of us are thinking.'

I find myself reading this tiny story as a parable of animals' fate, and ours, at the end of nature: a ghastly endgame (as its subtitle suggests) of false closeness, in which we have inherited, as a legacy of our own actions, increasingly rare animals that live entirely and abjectly as slaves to our whims, while we – their ambivalent masters – find that we can't live without them.

But what is the role of the writer, faced with a world whose frail and miraculous complexity is vanishing before our eyes? Leaving aside the question of whether art can have much real effect against the overwhelming threats we and other living beings face, it's possible that the very underpinnings of storytelling itself are also becoming endangered. The passage of seasons; the opposition between wild and domestic; the ideal of progress; and even the notion of futurity – all these traditional drivers of writerly machinery, which authors depend upon for momentum and feeling – seem increasingly hollow. Philosopher Freya Mathews goes further, suggesting that the present's great unravelling endangers the one story to which we all unwittingly belong: the intricate jigsaw of the biosphere. The narrative of the earth, of its 'symphonic energies' and metabolic processes that 'assure the inexhaustible regeneration of life' even out of death, she writes, is the 'proto-story that sets the stage for all the smaller stories we tell ourselves – the religions, myths, histories, ideologies, all the narratives by which we give meaning to our lives.'

And yet writers, of both fiction and nonfiction, have been practically turning themselves inside out over this decade trying to grapple with how to tell the story of this great, ongoing loss. In the first rank are books like journalist Elizabeth Kolbert's *The Sixth Extinction*, which try to simply string together local instances, observed on the ground, in ways that let us grasp the bigger picture. Other authors, like Rebecca Giggs, begin with a single threatened species and expand their stories outward. In *Fathoms*, she plunges into the world of whales, from their songs to the heavy metals in their blubber and the bone-eaters they sustain in the dark depths of the sea, to explore the ways in which they are so relentlessly enmeshed in our human presence. While they embody the 'gruesome afterlife' of our ravaging of the earth, Giggs writes, they also offer the possibility of a 'more fruitful variety of haunting,' in which we imagine what we might lose in the future if we don't change our ways. Other nonfiction writers have been reworking the once-cosy genre of nature writing to make it uncomfortable. In *Orison for a Curlew*, English writer Horatio Clare travels the world in search of the slender-billed curlew – a plentiful wonder of his childhood – only to find not a single one. In *Moby-Duck*, a personal favourite, Donovan Hohn subverts Ishmael's quest for the white whale by embarking on a search for a legendary shipping container of 28,000 rubber ducks that fell into North Pacific in 1992; a mission that takes him on a journey through ocean currents changed by global heating and the Great North Pacific Garbage Patch. It is more and more often the case that writers who go looking for nature find it only in whispers. What they find more often is our overwhelming human presence.

Meanwhile, some fiction writers are plunging us into the disasters ahead or taking us to the very precipice of catastrophic loss. In American author Lydia Millet's *How the Dead Dream*, T, a young property developer in Los Angeles, is on a relentless trajectory to success until – more than halfway through the novel – he becomes obsessed by animals on the verge of extinction and starts to break into zoos to observe them. As events beyond his control begin to bring his biography into parallel with theirs, T's loneliness delivers the radical intuition that nature is already dead. He understands that these no-longer-wild captives, deprived of the company of their own kind, their land, and the ability to go about their instinctual business, are experiencing an existential despair. 'It was obvious,' he realises: 'all of them waited and they waited, up until their last day and their last night of sleep. They never gave up waiting, because they had nothing else to do. They waited to go back to the bright land; they wanted to go home.'

In his novel *Clade*, James Bradley follows ten generations of people linked by a common ancestor from the present into an increasingly grim future. It is a terribly sad novel, in which flood and pandemic wreak local – and then global – havoc, opportunistic trees replace familiar landscapes, and bees all but disappear. Yet throughout, there are always small places of refuge, even if this is a tiny beehive tended secretly in the Australian bush or the space of a diary or a young man in the far future able to project his imagination into space. Bradley has said in interviews that it was important to him to preserve his characters' capacity to form bonds and see beauty because, for him, to succumb to the numbing vision of total apocalypse was a cop-out. By imagining a future that we had to survive by connecting with the best parts of our humanity, he hoped to fire our fight to preserve what we can in the present. But for a smaller subset of writers, like Roy Scranton, an ex-US soldier who faced death in Iraq, only acceptance of the catastrophe to come will enable us to salvage anything. 'The biggest problem we face now,' he writes in *Learning to Die in the Anthropocene*, 'is a philosophical one: understanding that this civilization is already dead. The sooner we confront this problem, and the sooner we realize there is nothing we can do to save ourselves, the sooner we can get down to the hard work of adapting, with mortal humility, to our new reality.'

For other writers, the loss of natural abundance has been a prompt to switch from an entirely human point of view to try to imagine how other creatures might see and feel. In academic writing, this is often called the 'post-human' or 'more-than-human' turn, which extends from trying to write human history as part of an ecological history of the earth and its many species to trying to imagine what concepts like justice or goodness might mean if we recognise that other creatures have relationships and agency. At its further edges, this academic writing can feel as wild as the most florid novel, as writers pursue the idea that not only living creatures but 'inanimate' objects, like rocks or paintings, can live their own private lives independent of us. In fiction, Laura Jean McKay's speculative novel *The Animals in That Country* imagines what animal thought might look like. When a pandemic hits Australia, it makes its sufferers hear the silent thoughts and communications of animals, from the charismatic dingo down to pesky bush flies. The dark joke at the centre of its story of a road trip between a woman and a dingo is that even when we can 'hear' them, the animals speak in a haiku-like, associative poetry that we can barely understand. It's also clear that most of them don't like us very much.

Yet popular culture may have been well ahead of the game, as it so often is, in exploring how it feels to be responsible for the deaths of our living companions – and, with them, a significant part of what makes us human. Is it any coincidence that our books and screens over the last decade have been so populated by the undead: by vampires and zombies? Vampires are burdened by their knowledge of themselves as predators and by the dead weight of a future in which they will have outlived all the living things they love. Zombies are even more terrifying metaphors. To be a zombie is to be reduced to having no story at all, and no mission or sense of the future, except to consume the living. If we're really coming to the end of our stories in the Age of Loneliness, there is perhaps no more apt metaphor than an already-dead humanity feeding on itself.

———

The Opposite of Glamour

And yet no matter how hard artists and environmental scientists might work to see the vast changes underway or to urge us stave off disaster, it seems that this type of imaginative labour is over 'here' – and that there is a far more powerful, dominant story about the world over 'there.' That other narrative is glamour.

The fact is that for every book concerned with the fate of the world, there are a hundred, a thousand, films and books and 'lifestyle' television programs, and advertisements, and magazines offering a parallel world of infinite abundance. In this parallel universe, time exists on a different scale. Nothing is permanent, not even ruin, because things can always be 'made over' – properties flipped, ugly ducklings zhoozhed, dream homes located somewhere. In glamour's alternate reality, surfaces always gleam. Decisions are never moral, but only ever aesthetic. Nothing is unobtainable, if you can pay enough. Meanwhile, those who attain glamour are 'winners,' above the ruck in their gilded sphere, while those who don't are 'losers.' In this compelling fantasy version of our planet, long-term catastrophic damage is invisible, hidden by perpetual motion and glossy fluidity.

Glamour, I think, may be our most powerful and fatal fiction, the one that kills us all. I find myself remembering back to *True Blood*, one of those vampire-themed shows of the last decade, in which to 'glamour' someone – drawing on the old Scottish sense of the verb – is to hypnotise them or bend them to your will. For all the finer analysis of his political base, part of Trump's ascent to the American presidency was his ability to channel this kind of enchantment – albeit a debased version, of Mar-a-Lago resorts, model wives, casinos, and $22 Platinum Label Burgers ('Proprietary Blend of Prime Aged Short Rib', caramelized onions, Tarentaise cheese, and Parmigiano-seasoned hand cut fries) at the Trump Grill in his New York Trump Tower.

He trailed into the White House the faux allure of a television show about entrepreneurialism, with its promise that the winner could ascend into a shimmering world of wood-lined boardrooms, private helicopters, and penthouse suites. But Trump's boast that he would make the country 'great again' was only the most egregious embodiment of the intoxicating, globally franchised dream of the 'makeover', with its infinite enticements and bright distractions from our unravelling planet.

Glamour's false abundance is *everywhere*. At the opposite end of the political spectrum, progressive local councils and town planners are often impatient with the local histories of places, which they tell us need to be endlessly 'activated' or 'renewed.' Whenever I pass the newest temporary sculpture or floral pyramid, hot-desking hub, or pop-up store in my inner-city suburb, I can't help wondering if, by habituating us to the endless plasticity of our public spaces, they are softening us up for the great ecological unravelling under way.

In the timeless universe of glamour, things don't evolve or grow; they are simply replaced. Each new object appears to manifest out of thin air, while the world's shadow places, sacrificed to feed our fantasies of plenitude, grow larger. As English author Will Self puts it, the 'Promethean fireball of iPads, Peruvian blooms, farmed salmon and Amazon Prime deliveries,' which those of us with privilege enjoy, requires countless 'Mordors' of indentured workers to ensure its apparently infinite supply. It's all too easy to pick up a travel brochure showing people snorkelling on the unbleached corners of the reef, or to watch couples romance each other in teak-lined resort rooms on dating shows, and reassure ourselves that there is still a surplus of natural bounty somewhere 'out there.' Besides, glamour offers us a vivid array of treats, like the feasts that manifest to enchant people in fairytales, to

The Opposite of Glamour

distract us from us from any longings for a more complicated and complex world that may resist our desires. At the same time, we have to keep looking for the next new thing because we *do* sense that the world is becoming emptier of other living creatures, while each new diversion fails to fully satisfy us.

The challenges seem overwhelming. But perhaps the first step for us writers with a different story to tell is to resist being glamoured ourselves. Over the last few years, I've started to notice grand claims being made for literature: that it has the power to make us better people or offer a 'slow' way of seeing a too-fast world. It's easy to pat ourselves on the back in interviews or at festivals for simply writing, rather than worrying about the specific work our books can do. I suspect that we're much better off conceding that writing doesn't have much power and then getting on with it. Imagination will certainly be part of the challenge of meeting the Anthropocene, though the contribution we make may be, like lyrebirds turning over the leaf litter on the forest floor, of a more modest nature.

Nevertheless, it may be that Australia is the best place for writing about uncertainty and loss. Our colonial history means that our literature is already less comfortable with the land and its creatures than its northern hemisphere counterparts and more tuned to damage and survival. This is especially the case with our writing about nature, which has never established itself as a stable commercial genre but tends to emerge in feral form out of other genres, such as history and memoir. And it almost always engages with the ongoing Indigenous knowledge of Country. Books such as Bruce Pascoe's *Dark Emu*, Kim Mahood's *Position Doubtful*, Deborah Bird-Rose's *Dingo Makes Us Human*, and Saskia Beudel's walking memoir, *A Country in Mind*, are sceptical of any Romantic sense of boundless plenty and adept, in their different ways, at negotiating the rough terrain of broken country. None could be described as 'nature writing' but each is tuned, as Beudel puts it beautifully, to the 'off-key tone of colonised land.' In Australia, the losses are so close that they still ring and echo. Reading Bunurong author Pascoe's galvanising book, in which he digs back into the colonial records to reveal an obscured history of Aboriginal farming and building, is to experience a fantastic kind of double vision, in which he re-sees the damaged land, in terms of what is lost but also what continues.

If we are going to face the terrible losses unfolding around us, Australian writing, with its shaggy self-consciousness, sometimes awkward manners, and unsentimental sense of complexity – the opposite of glamour – may offer the best way forward. Its understanding of abundance as historical, layered, contingent and mutable, is a better place, at least, to start.

Coronavirus Time: Diary

The sense of time-slip begins during the 2019 megafires. Walking my children home from school in Sydney under a red sun I have the nagging feeling, beneath my anxiety, that I've seen this close orange light before. Then I remember. My father made our family nativity set out of pumpkin-coloured cardboard, topped with a skylight of red acrylic. The sideboard lamp cast the same uncanny glow onto baby Jesus and his shadowless entourage.

Three months later, in early March, we are driving with the twins down the New South Wales south coast through green dairy country to isolate from the coronavirus. 'Does the sky seem particularly blue to you?' my partner asks, as we look up the valley. 'I'm having a "severe clear" moment.' A dark joke between us: pilots used the term to describe a sky of perfect visibility on the morning of 9/11. With most planes in Australia cancelled, there are no bright contrails in the usually busy flight path above the escarpment. The air is alert and tender. It occurs to me that we haven't seen a sky like this since our own childhoods.

For this whole first week we feel strangely elated. When we last stood in the back paddock of our Airbnb at Christmas, we had watched a huge plume build above the Currowan fire 40 kilometres to the south as white ash fell onto the brown grass. But over the next months, as the eastern seaboard of the country burned, the fires spared this pocket of rainforest tucked beneath the Barren Grounds reserve. The heavy rains that fell in February, the owner tells me, as she nervously keeps her social distance, overflowed the creek and tumbled huge boulders down its bed. The flowering gums in the bush around us give off a scent of honey while the calls of tiny birds electrify the air.

Stop the World, I Want to Get Off – my mother used to jokingly quote the title of this musical to me when I was little. 'Stop the world,' its hero said, whenever things went wrong. I can't help feeling relieved that the world has at least paused, for now.

Like Melville's Ishmael, I am a natural Isolato. An only child and a writer, I feel as if I've been training for this moment all my life. But it's not just me taking pleasure in a world temporarily stilled. A friend texts me video his brother has filmed in Rome of a man walking naked on an empty bridge across the Tiber. On Twitter, people tweet and retweet images of Venetian canals, water so calm you can see fish in their powdery aqua depths. Video recorded by an unseen man walking its empty *calles* and bridges goes viral: 'Bizarre!' he concludes at its end. I email my publisher. When was the last time the canals were this magically clear – when the Brownings were restoring the Ca' Rezzonico, or in Casanova's time? He replies that he is amazed by the grand scale of its uncrowded public spaces. 'You look at old pictures of Venice and St Mark's Square is almost empty – really, they're different places entirely. The stones of Venice come into their own.'

We give the twins a phone and snake bandages and they explore the paddocks while we work. Their saxophone and flute lessons continue by Skype. At the lip of the cliff at the end of the garden we watch a lyrebird go through its repertoire of other birds' songs with the fixed concentration of a flasher, tail feathers splayed stiffly over its back and head, and I chalk this up as a win for home schooling.

Online, events unfold at a distance. Our neighbourhood Facebook group back home fills with queries about whether it is safe to train in home gyms, if balayage could be considered an essential service, and whether favourite restaurants will deliver. When we learn that a cruise ship has been allowed to disgorge its passengers, without checks, to wander through the city and continue their travel, some untraced, the threat level rises. I search for clips of the plague ship arriving in Delft in Herzog's *Nosferatu*, piloting itself to the strains of Wagner, and instantly regret it. Newspapers report toilet paper hoarding while conspiracies circulate that buses are descending on small town supermarkets to clear the shelves. A German friend says there is a word for this in her language: *Hamsterkaüfe*, rodent purchases.

Back home, in an inner-city apartment with no veranda or yard, life becomes harder. The children need constant help with their Year 3 school assignments, which are distributed across Seesaw and two different versions of Google Classroom. My partner and I work fitfully at our own computers. When a hairy shirtless man in the block next door starts playing guitar to the neighbourhood kids from the outdoor walkway, I feel like putting my head out of my study and yelling, 'This isn't Italy, mate.' In the bathroom, my daughter switches from singing 'Happy birthday' to the Sex Pistols' 'God Save the Queen' as she washes her hands. As the death toll in Italy and Spain rises, I read an interview with a virologist who says he is so attuned to looking at particles of virus that his view of every surface is 'pixelated.'

On the neighbourhood Facebook page, pleas burn and flare out as bargaining turns to acceptance. Where is it possible to still find good charcuterie? Is there a mobile nail service that might do home visits? Does anyone know anything about agencies for fostering dogs? Crowds mass at nearby Bondi in the autumn heat, ignoring restrictions on large groups, and all the beaches in the eastern suburbs are closed. When council fences off the exercise equipment in our park, which has also been busy, heaving joggers take over the paths.

I begin to walk the children to the city instead, to the empty Botanic Gardens, along the least used of the long staircases that plunge down the Woolloomooloo cliff. 'Look,' I say to them, as we stand across from where the foundations for the huge extension of the Art Gallery of New South Wales are being dug. 'You will remember this.' I was their age when we used to pass the seventies blond-brick 'Lego apartments' under construction on the clifftop behind us, on the way to my grandmother's each weekend. As we drove, my father would always repeat the rumour that the missing heiress Juanita Nielsen, who fought the developers trying to destroy the historic Potts Point streetscape and community to build skyscrapers, was buried in the foundations. 'Look,' I say again, as we drive back one afternoon from helping my mother, still living in the family home on the North Shore. 'You will never see the Harbour Bridge as empty again in your lifetimes.' 'Is it really empty? Was it this empty when you were growing up?' my son asks, as we pass only a handful of cars on its ten-lane approach. Yes, I tell him, there were two million fewer people in the city then, which was still in parts a Victorian ruin of abandoned grand department stores, tangled goods lines and waterside warehouses. We fly over the Cahill Expressway, above the Quay where no ferries or charter cruise boats move, and on, through an empty Woolloomooloo, as their childhood melts into mine.

I've written about 'Shifting Baseline Syndrome', in which each new generation takes its reduced world as a starting point for measuring loss. But now, as if in a time machine, we seem to be glimpsing the possibility of an alternative baseline – a world in which we're less intrusive. The viral images of swans and porpoises in the Venetian canals have been debunked but they are still circulating on my feed because the desire to believe in them, or their promise of a different future, is so strong. As if anticipating new freedoms, a long green tree snake is photographed climbing the curved deco brickwork of an apartment in nearby Potts Point. A friend in lockdown in a Spanish village reports, 'There are numerous owls everywhere around us . . . and they have really become gaily, proudly, shamelessly symphonic during humanity's lockdown!'

Throughout April, infections in Australia continue to rise, a significant percentage of them from the cruise ship, the *Ruby Princess*. At least children don't seem to be dying, we say quietly to the godparents on the phone. In the Botanic Gardens, a security guard now moves on people sitting on the grass or squatting by the pond where eels patrol the perimeter in parodic imitation. Police cars drive along the footpaths of our local park and threaten to fine people sitting in the sun but don't stop the joggers. A historian friend gives the children an hour's class on FaceTime and tells them that the first year of Sydney's settlement began with plague. She asks them to imagine how it felt for the Aboriginal people who died in catastrophic numbers from smallpox, an estimated half of their population perishing, within months of the First Fleet's arrival.

On our neighbourhood Facebook page, people post pictures of sunsets from high balconies, rooftop concerts, and video graphics from a Belgian-Dutch study showing that joggers' and cyclists' breaths can infect from a distance of five metres, which they accuse site administrators of deleting. Although I have vowed I would never have one in the house, I panic when the cafes close and have a small coffee pod machine delivered. A group of us who used to meet a decade ago revive our fortnightly games night through Zoom and we find ourselves speculating, over wine, that we are in for a much longer lockdown than we first expected. I text a friend whose mother has just died: 'I'm sitting out the back behind our house looking at a planeless sky,' he texts back. 'It feels like the end of the world.'

Meanwhile, on my feed, images keep appearing of turtles laying eggs on empty Indian beaches and flocks of wild goats besieging a Welsh town. But nature, it seems, is not getting as much respite as I hoped. Airlines are lobbying to loosen their carbon obligations once borders reopen while empty 'ghost flights' track back and forth across the European Union so that they don't lose their allocated airport slots. In Australia, logging continues in the stands of eucalypts that survived the fires and the government announces a review of environmental 'green tape.' I read a study predicting wildlife collapse from climate change will happen suddenly and quickly – a cliff edge rather than a slippery slope – and the future rushes in again.

Over the last years I have been thinking about the way, even as the present accelerates, we are haunted by the deep past, in the form of the fossil carbon we have released into the atmosphere. I have found it unbearable to think too far into my children's future, or to answer their questions about what they might be when they grow up, because I don't believe it will resemble the present in any way. After the fires, I'd been bracing for another disaster, though I can't help feeling that this lockdown is only the grace note, with its moments of beauty and intimations of a different future, which later catastrophes will not give us.

What I didn't expect was that time would become so kaleidoscopic. Since March, friends my age have been joining a Facebook challenge, posting pictures of their younger selves, dressed up at parties or sitting on share house doorsteps.

It's a bittersweet thing to look at them. All those soft young faces.

The Disappearing Paragraph

A new breath. A macro-punctuation mark. A flash of lightning showing the landscape from a different aspect. A collection of sentences with a unity of purpose. A small neighbourhood made up of 'streets' of sentences. These are some of the ways writers have described the work of the paragraph. And yet, among the many unsettling phenomena of our age, I have noticed that paragraphs have been disappearing – at least paragraphs as I once knew them. This may not amount to much amid the greater unravelling of our world but it is a significant disturbance within my own small literary ecotone.

Return. Indent. Return, indent, and onward . . . as you see in these lines before you now. This is how I learned to paragraph on an electric typewriter, and how I would continue to enter text into early word processors as I supported myself with typing work through university. Even before I learned the mechanics, I had absorbed the small visual rhythms of paragraphing by reading everything that came my way as a child, from my Puffin books to the Dickens and Zane Gray novels on my parents' bookshelves, to the yellowing copies of *The Australian Women's Weekly* in the sunroom.

Yet lately, reading recent novels by Jenny Offill, Patricia Lockwood, and Kevin Barry – and many others – I've been struck by how, instead of following on obediently after a tiny indent, each of their paragraphs is separated from its companions by a double-line space. Even in Dominic Smith's story of the invention of cinema, a less 'literary' read for a wide audience, the novel's paragraphs, edges neatly flush with the page margins, shrink away from one another. Every paragraph (or perhaps we should call them text blocks) of *The Electric Hotel* hovers like a small planet in its own atmosphere; though the author breaks the convention, disconcertingly, for lines of dialogue, which follow on in the old way.

In these books, paragraphs are no longer team players. Instead, they've become free agents.

Here is Offill, in one of her perfectly formed paragraphs, which are also distilled scenes, in *Weather*:

Memories are microscopic. Tiny particles that swarm together and apart. Little people, Edison called them. Entities. He had a theory about where they came from and that theory was outer space.

Here is Lockwood, in *No One Is Talking About This*, whose paragraphs hover like the random space-junk of the Twitter stream, which her heroine – a celebrated tweeter – analyses with serio-comic obsessiveness:

'What are you doing?' her husband asked softly, tentatively, repeating his question until she shifted her blank gaze up to him.

The Disappearing Paragraph

What was she doing? Couldn't he see her arms are full of the sapphires of the instant? Didn't he realise that a male feminist had posted a picture of his *nipple* that day?

And here is Barry, in *Night Boat to Tangier*, his novel about two old Irish gangsters, in which the paragraphs seem to hang like speech in the spent air of a Beckett play:

Only the cunten Russians, he said, have less class than us when they get a few pound.

*

To understand a change like the disappearance of the indented paragraph, we need to understand the convention it breaks.

The history of the paragraph stretches back to the ancient Greeks, who laid out their writing in a solid block. The *paragraphos* (a variety of physical marks, including a horizontal line, a line with a forked edge, or with a circle above it) denoted a change in speaker or passage. Scribes in the middle ages standardised this mark into a symbol similar to the pilcrow – a reverse-facing double-stemmed P, with a solid head – which editors still use today to mark up text. It appears in Microsoft Word, in ghostly blue or grey, each time we hit return. (¶).

It was only once the printing press came into use that printers developed the convention – as it has come down to us – of beginning paragraphs on a new line, leaving an indent space for illustrators to fill with an ornament or illuminated capital. When these embellishments were abandoned, the space remained: a little shelf for the eye and mind to get a purchase on, before the new paragraph began. In his *Elements of Typographic Style* (1992),

Robert Bringhurst would standardise this indent space in continuous text as at least one em (an em is a unit equal to the currently specified line height), to mark paragraphs' simple and reassuring consistency. The typographer, he wrote, must articulate paragraphs 'enough to make them clear, yet not so strongly that the form instead of the content steals the show.'

Perhaps no one loved paragraphs as much as the Victorians, who built their long, cadenced sentences into these substantial units of thought, which built in turn into chapters, so that when you look at the dense pages of their novels they seem to bear all the purpose and momentum of an empire. Their paragraphs were like their thick-legged chairs or large shiny jardinières; they furnished a book so that it felt comfortingly solid. (One went to novels, Virginia Woolf observed, not for their sentences but for their chapters; 'for the accumulation,' as critic James Wood puts it, 'of their lustres').

And so, unsurprisingly, it's in Victorian textbooks of prosody that we find the most fulsome analysis of the paragraph. In his 1894 *History of the English Paragraph*, rhetorician and novelist Edwin Herbert Lewis described its double work: it was complete in itself but also 'a unit of composition' in an organic structure. 'Something more than a sentence and less than an essay,' according to his contemporary, A. S. Hill, the paragraph marked the 'natural divisions' of a composition as a whole. Barrett Wendell, author of the bestselling *English Composition* of 1891 was the pithiest: 'A paragraph is to a sentence,' he wrote, 'what a sentence is to a word.'

If the paragraph is a unit of composition, then each tiny indentation at the beginning of a new line – as Lewis puts it most elegantly – 'distinguishes a stadium of thought.' In those long, multi-clausal stretches of Victorian prose the indent offered relief:

a place for the reader to take a quick intake of breath, before (to quote Woolf on the prose of William Hazlitt), 'sentence follows sentence with the healthy ring and chime of the blacksmith's hammer on the anvil.' 'The advantage of at least one paragraph indentation on almost every page of a printed book,' Lewis noted drily, 'is felt by every reader.'

This was our inheritance as readers and writers who went to school in the twentieth century. Our eyes were trained to recognise paragraphs as 'natural' markers of the flows of thought in a reliably progressing and coherent world.

Within this ordered prose universe, Lewis wrote, a double-line space between paragraphs creates a significant interruption in the longer flow of a section.

Its job is to mark 'an unusual break.'

*

Indented paragraphs, following one after the other, are still the convention in printed books and magazines. Even if we have never been taught about them, when we read a novel by Kim Scott or Penelope Fitzgerald, or an essay by Zadie Smith, our eyes will instantly recognise a run of paragraphs as a section – and a double line break as the end of one significant part of a story before we move on to the next.

So what are we to make of a more liberal use of spacing, which puts a line of empty page between each paragraph? Why have some writers, particularly American practitioners of the lyric essay like John D'Agata (who popularised the term) or Eula Biss, decided to suspend their paragraphs between Lewis's 'unusual' breaks? A hybrid of poem and personal essay, the lyric essay tends to segment itself into separate, left- and right-justified bricks of text. (Biss deploys her small sections – each straightened against its left margin as well as right – like stanzas. D'Agata sometimes throws scraps of text onto swathes of empty page.)

In Wayne Koestenbaum's 'My 1980s,' an essay I've loved since I first read it in 2013, the author conjures his youth shadowed by the threat of AIDS in flamboyantly unsentimental text blocks, which move about in time, back and forth, throughout the decade. Each fragment is separated from the next not only by a double line-space but a dinkus (***):

In 1983, I served a friend a veal roast stuffed with pancetta. We agreed that the roast tasted like human baby. We blamed the pancetta.

Or,

I remember a specific homeless woman on the Upper West Side in the 1980s. She smelled predictably of pee or shit and hung out in an ATM parlor near the Seventy-Second Street subway stop. She seemed to rule the space. Large, she epitomized. Did I ever give her money? I blamed Reagan.

There's a great deal going on in the way Koestenbaum, who is also a poet, dispenses with conventional paragraphs for these small prose stanzas. I think he does so to make a point. If readers have come to his essay, trained by standard confessional memoir or storytelling events like The Moth to expect a cheesy epiphany or dewy-eyed 'closure', his form is a rebuff. Koestenbaum's title may flirt with the idea of summing up a whole era but his tiny text blocks refuse to be enrolled in any argument. Instead – floating adamantly in space – each draws us into a narrative cul-de-sac so that we have to contemplate the moment it preserves on its own singular terms, just as the author refuses throughout the essay to judge his younger self. 'When I look back on the 1980s,' he writes, in a rare introspective moment, 'I see myself as a small boat . . . which has no consciousness of the water it moves through . . . Its only business is staying afloat.'

You could say that each text block in Koestenbaum's essay is also a tiny boat, persistently attending, as the author writes of his younger incarnation, to the work of flotation 'which takes precedence over responsible navigation.' While conventional paragraphing infers that the world proceeds with inevitable purpose, every double-line space in 'My 1980s' is intended as an 'unusual break': an elegant refusal turn his life into a story. To witness his body's precise movements and survival through the time of AIDS, when the future seemed radically uncertain, he suggests, is enough.

*

But what does it mean when novelists choose to give their paragraphs freer range on the page? The modernist writers of the last century may have played fast and loose with language and form but they usually held onto the conventional paragraph format – Molly Bloom's famous 22,000-word monologue in James Joyce's *Ulysses* consisted of only eight long, unpunctuated paragraphs, but when she did pause for breath, each followed on, one after the next, after an indent. Instead, it was the novelists of the late twentieth century who would introduce me to the more liberal use of space on the page.

When I read Canadian poet-novelist Michael Ondaatje's novels *The Collected Works of Billy the Kid* and *Coming Through Slaughter* for the first time in the 1990s, it was a revelation – one of the great moments in my writing life of being somehow 'given permission' – to see that it was possible to use space extravagantly around blocks, or even single lines, of prose. Ondaatje's account, published in 1970, of the world through the eyes of Billy the Kid, was laid out like raggedy collage, in which floating blocks of justified text alternated with enigmatic photographs, italicised fragments from letters, and lines of verse as thin and spooky as the workings of the young outlaw's mind. But it was *Coming Through Slaughter*, published the following year, that excited me even more. It told the story of the New Orleans cornet player Buddy Bolden in a combination of images, snatches of invented song, and prose broken into floating paragraphs (sometimes indented, sometimes not), which loomed and receded like illuminated pictures in a slide show. This announced visually that these were glimpses as curated and partial as the photographer Belloq's portraits of Storyville sex workers, which also feature in the novel. Most thrilling of all, Ondaatje would sometimes even throw a single-line riff – like Bolden's loud trumpet blasts as he went mad during a 1907 jazz parade – across the middle of a blank page.

Such as:

Passing wet chicory that lies in the fields like the sky.

To see a writer willing to float a sentence out onto the white page like this gave me a dizzying feeling of potential freedom as a novelist at the start of my own career. We don't have a theory in English prosody that I'm aware of for the effects of such spaciousness. But we can perhaps borrow from Chinese art, which treats empty space as solid space within a painting. In calligraphy, the Chinese speak of 'designing the white.' Empty space is where energy or *qi* dwells. It creates rhythm within the picture. It endows it with the principle of life. Ondaatje's novels seemed to say as much through their use of white page as in their lines of text, which turned mysterious and provisional within its forcefield – as if to suggest that we live in a random and fragile, but ultimately beautiful, universe that we can only glimpse in flux.

Yet what was expressive and irregular in Ondaatje's novels seems to have become a habit for novelists like Lockwood, Barry and Offill. In their books a double-line break between each text block is no longer remarkable but routine.

I'm seeing this shift to systematically placing double-line spaces between paragraphs so often in novels and essays now that it's made me wonder: what if it's crept up unnoticed in literary prose like the rise of carbon dioxide in the atmosphere? Or, to cast about for another metaphor, what if the old internal structures of writing we are used to are like a sea creature's shell, giving shape to the soft creature inside them; and those inner partitions, under some unseen pressure akin to the rise of acids in seawater, have been quietly dissolving and rearranging themselves? Or what if – to take the more positive view – we've been evolving as readers to no longer require runs of indented paragraphs that thread themselves, one after another, into arguments or long sections?

In the online environment, the change has already taken place. Click on an online newspaper like *The Guardian* or *The New*

York Times, or a journal like *Sydney Review of Books* and justified text blocks separated by double-line breaks are the convention – a layout suited to tired or distracted eyes scanning a bright, blue-lit page. They're a natural fit for newspaper prose, which has always been put together like an upside-down Lego pyramid, out of one- or two-sentence paragraphs, which are relatively discrete and contain the least important information (and can thus be cut easily) the further their distance from the opening or 'lede.' The segmented online layout simply makes it more obvious that readers are not necessarily expected to read beyond the opening lines, or may only glance through the body text, in which, classically, the paragraphs will not contain opinion, only facts. In corporate writing, it is a similar story. In a report, an executive summary might have a solid paragraph or two, but all findings and recommendations must be written in point form – to the frustration of my humanities-educated partner, who has to write them, because this makes it difficult to offer analysis or make logical connections.

As the time we spend looking at a webpage dwindles – fifteen seconds on average, according to some estimates – many online journals and websites are slashing article word lengths. And so paragraphs may be going the same way, as journalist Andy Bodle puts it, 'as the harpsichord, the fob watch and the returned phone call.'

And yet, habituated over my reading life, like a koala only able to eat a specific variety of eucalyptus leaf, to printed books and essays organised into runs of indented paragraphs, I have to confess that I'm constantly unnerved by this disarticulated layout and how to read it. As a fellow lecturer explains to his students, every new paragraph introduces a new thought ('New idea . . . new idea . . . new idea!' He jerks his head, like

The Disappearing Paragraph

a spectator at Wimbledon, to demonstrate what he means). If that is the case, then paragraphs separated by emphatic double-line breaks surely jump a train of thought off its tracks with each emphatic break. (To my eye, each gap announces, 'New section . . . new section . . . new section!').

Yet I can't help thinking, even if the decline of the indented paragraph is inevitable, that surely it's worth at least trying to think through what the scattered and vivid energy of disjointed paragraphs, hovering at a discrete distance from each other, might mean. In my more obsessive moments, I've even found myself wondering if they might be setting us up with different expectations of the way information should flow and function. Do prose paragraphs isolated in blank space tell us, at least subliminally, that each separate little 'arena of thought' is more important in itself than any connective tissue between it and the next? Are the double-line breaks between them playing their own small part in our contemporary predisposition to scan writing for 'takeaways' – yes, even in university and literary contexts – rather than valuing it for the way it runs a thought to ground? Are they a cause, or a symptom, of our culture's tendency to fixate on isolated details outside of their context; a driver of those online discussions, especially about fraught subjects, which seem almost inevitably to devolve into the pernickety particularism of tiny 'whatabouts' and 'gotchas?'

Yet the difference between these two ways of paragraphing, cumulative or suspended between double carriage returns, which so often gives me pause (literally) for thought, is one that my students, especially younger ones, find very hard to see – even if I show PowerPoints of the alternate formats next to one another. (Why does this matter so much to her? I see them thinking. And why is she talking about *carriages*?) It is clear that we have come of age as readers within two very distinct spatial regimes.

Nevertheless, surely it does change the way we read, and perhaps even think about the world, if paragraphs have stopped passing meaning in a bucket chain from one to the next; if each now basks between double-line breaks like a Hollywood star wrapped in his or her own spotlight? When I see little text blocks like this, I sometimes find myself thinking of a certain sort of photograph that has become popular in high-end travel and fashion magazines, in which the camera dwells on a singular object – a soft heap of saffron, a hand-shaped doorknob, a cup of freshly whipped matcha – each detached from its surroundings to become singular, glowing and enchanted.

*

Could the truth of the matter be that the older conventions of paragraphing are no longer suited to capturing our present? Jenny Offill writes habitually slim, fragmented novellas, in which her female narrators issue gnomic dispatches in the shape of floating paragraphs separated by double-line spaces – but in *Weather* (2020), she links her scattered narrative explicitly to climate change.

In the third and hottest decade of the twenty-first century, you don't call a book *Weather* without intent. Like so many of the concepts that once formed the stable, taken-for-granted background of our lives, like 'nature' or 'seasons,' this word is now freighted with the worry and instability of our Anthropocene era. While 'weather' refers to the state of the atmosphere in a particular place and time (sunshine, rain, wind, cloudiness, or dryness) and has always been a product of climate (the behaviour of weather over longer periods of time, usually measured in thirty-year increments), it's now eerily tangled up with global climate change, which is increasingly unpredictable.

As *Weather* opens, its narrator Lizzie Benson – a bright woman who has 'squandered' her promising career as a research student – is working in a library, where she often finds her ability to listen empathetically pushes her into in the role of amateur shrink. But soon, on the basis of these skills, she finds herself working a second job for a futurologist and podcaster, answering listeners' emails about looming ecological disaster ('How will the last generation know that it is the last generation?' 'How can we save the bees?'). Lizzie is also the mother of a bright young boy, who she worries about protecting from the horrors on the way. Throughout this short novel, she will struggle to live with the two realities: knowing that we are hastening the world's predictable patterns to their end while, at the same time, her life moves on in all its small, confusing, and often funny detail.

It's difficult to describe the emotional effect of Offill's floating paragraphs, which are loosely corralled into small sections by dinkuses. James Wood wrote of the similarly gnomic writing in *The Department of Speculation* that it 'faces in many directions at the same time,' which is also a superb description of the feeling of *Weather* – except that its fierce undertow of climate terror turns that novel's glittering bittersweetness into nervous blankness. Although Lizzie's story does move forward – she contemplates an affair, her brother struggles with parenthood and unstable mental health – each little prose segment seems frozen in place, as if she can't quite bring herself to describe her life in any lengthy narrative sequence. The reliably curmudgeonly English reviewer Adam Mars-Jones would describe the novel's emotional register as 'unreadable.' But perhaps he wasn't in on the joke. Offill's voice, like Lorrie Moore's, seems aimed at a primarily female audience attuned to the non sequitur and the half-expressed as signals of distress. The closest equivalent I can think of tonally for the novel is French director Claire Denis's film *Let the Sunshine In*, in which the single heroine Isabella (played by Juliette Binoche) encounters one unsuitable partner after the other in loosely connected, inconclusive episodes. When I watched the film, it struck me forcefully that it was unspooling with the suspenseful, hushed hilarity women often adopt when telling stories of awful men, relying on each other to provide the context.

Gertrude Stein I remember, wrote, 'Sentences aren't emotional, paragraphs are.' With no division into chapters to direct its flows of emotion, *Weather* hits us with one intense moment after another (or, as my colleague might say, 'Feeling! . . . Feeling! Feeling!'). To Mars-Jones, this was a precious mannerism, ironic smugness cutting off any possibility of a political reaction to the very real terrors the novel documented. I'm more inclined to read the curious stall of each small segment as a clever fitting of form to function. This is exactly how the present feels, *Weather* suggests: like little bursts of local weather when you're not sure whether they're innocuous or evidence of a more awful story about a climate that's already rushing towards its collapse. Her fragments' remove from the reliable old patterns of the novel – their refusal to sit within longer sections, or to be pressed into the familiar form of chapters – is exactly what makes them addictive and disturbing. How can we commit to the momentum of storytelling, they seem to ask, when the future is so uncertain?

But what of the fact that this pattern is so regular in Offill's novel? The blank spaces between its paragraphs are not the unpredictable swathes of white page that you would find in

The Disappearing Paragraph

Ondaatje's fiction, or even the concentrated lightning in a bottle of the gaps in Koestenbaum's short essay. Instead, they mark out the division between her little pellets of text as regularly as pages from a printer. (Even so, Offill very occasionally clusters lines of dialogue and lists together, without double-line breaks between them, as if she can't quite bear to give up entirely on the possibility of connection.) Perhaps she is trying to alert us to something else about the new climate of feeling that surrounds us. Things loom now with a portentous luminosity, each small prose fragment suggests, but this weird sublimity has become somewhat routine.

Each tiny emergency or moment of beauty or terrifying thought may stop us in our tracks, but then we are swept on to the next. If this happens enough it can feel like a constant suspense; a kind of weightlessness.

*

In our new normal, moments of terror and beauty flash by, one bright and intense thing following the other. Sea slugs that look like David Bowie! University redundancies. Cute animal friendships! The death of a Black man at the hands of Minnesota police. A glockenspiel programmed to play 'Bohemian Rhapsody'! In my darker moments, I find myself wondering if what Mars-Jones identifies as a stylistic tic in Offil's writing is now our general condition.

Is the dwindling of our old ecology of paragraphing, without being noticed or mourned, indicative of a more pervasive loss of executive function, in terms of being able to process long historical sequences or even being able to sit patiently in a moment to see how things unfold; skills that our very survival might depend on? I can't help thinking that our growing taste for short, unmoored paragraphs may point, in the longer term, to a shift in our emotional regulation. After all, Offill's novel isn't unique in its ambiguous, unanchored feelings. Think of television drama, which over the last decade or two has also become emotionally labile and disjointed. From soapy medical dramas punctuated by extreme action – a bomb in the ER! a rapist with Ebola! – to dramedies (*Six Feet Under, Dexter, Breaking Bad, Better Call Saul, Fleabag, Dead to Me, Please Like Me*) which scintillate between tragedy or horror and hilarity ('Drama! Drama! Drama!'), it's hard to know whether to laugh or cry. As we jump from one crisis to the next in this broken world, without the dependable old rhythms of its local climates and seasons to sustain us, is funny-not-funny deadpan becoming our default setting? Perhaps, as the ice sheets melt and the future truncates, our feelings will also only be able to express themselves, like Offill's narrative, in erratic but predictable little meltwater pulses.

Of course novels and essays written in longer, unbroken runs of prose keep being published, and will seem as if they will be with us forever in their quiet insistence on looking forward, until they vanish. But if our paragraphs, like humble ground worms or beetles, disappear entirely, will we even notice they were there?

*

I finished my essay here. And then I worried for days about my pessimism.

Even *Weather*, I remembered, allows itself subdued moments of hope. 'Diminished radiance,' the narrator observes of the day as she heads out for a walk with her son, 'but still some, I'd say.' Maybe, she thinks, as she looks at him, he will be able to have a child when he grows up. ('It will be small and cat-eyed. It will never know the taste of meat.')

The Disappearing Paragraph

There's another way, I realised, of thinking about what the growing fashion for floating paragraphs may have to say to us. As Wayne Koestenbaum points out, silence and blankness can be powerful. When Rimbaud stopped creating poetry at the age of nineteen, he writes, this silence became part of his work; 'a resonance chamber for the lyrics that preceded his deflection from words.'

Perhaps we could see unanchored paragraphs as tiny monuments, given extra resonance and weight by the animal and human silences that seem more and more likely to follow? As we teeter on the brink of an epoch in which birdsong and ice and the lives of an estimated million species may be extinguished from the planet, these little floating blocks may be unconscious metaphors for our future isolation. Might we even listen to their warning, learn to sit with the present for a moment, and think about how to save ourselves from a lonely uniqueness?

Look, they seem to say.

I felt it.

I saw this.

We were here.

Good Neighbours

A man walking home after a night of drinking in Kings Cross was the first to see the humped shape at the top of the steps from the small beach. Assuming it was one of the park's rough sleepers, he continued on his way. The first person to lodge a report was an early jogger, who almost ran into the animal at the corner where the dirt track meets the concrete path along the seawall. By mid-morning, the news had got around. There was a hundred-kilo male fur seal in our neighbourhood.

Over the first few days the seal swam between inner eastern suburbs. He was spotted sunning himself behind the sea wall one bay to the east. He swam laps by the marina café in the bay to the west, closer to the city. But he returned each night to the top of the steps in the park, a few hundred metres behind our apartment.

Our neighbourhood Facebook page lit up:

Just saw him having a swim at Rushcutters Bay. Doing laps! Could be an added attraction when we have coffee.

I'm presuming he's come to see the new marina.

No – he's our official mascot!

OMG, I'm going to rush down to see him after chiro!

By the time I made it down to catch him on land after one of these excursions, police tape was hanging limply between the paperbarks, marking a 50-metre exclusion zone. The seal's dark bulk faded to a dusty paler brown around the neck, like old velvet, or the rubbed nap of a Persian carpet. He didn't move much, sighing once or twice as he flattened like a dog on a flagstone floor in his pungent patch of sea damp on the footpath. A policeman stood outside the barrier. He looked embarrassed to be down here alone.

When I brought the kids down the next day, orange Parks and Wildlife tape had replaced the blue-and-white police tape. It extended around most of the lawn, almost to the park's main footway from Elizabeth Bay, which runs past the tennis court toward the canal and Cruising Yacht Club. A bigger crowd had gathered. A woman in an ORCCA T-shirt, and with a greater sense of resolve, had joined the policeman. A sign hanging from the tape advised there was a 'SEAL RESTING IN THIS AREA.'

The nearest breeding colony for fur seals is at Montague Island, 300 kilometres down the coast from Sydney, off Narooma, but lone seals do haul up in the harbour from time to time, according to the marine mammal expert at Taronga Zoo. There is 'Siri' in Mosman, on the harbour's north shore, and a small colony below the Macquarie Lighthouse at the Heads at Watsons Bay. In 2015 a leopard seal, whose natural habitat is much further south in Antarctica's pack ice, spent several days on the beach at the Spit, which divides lower north shore Mosman from the northern beaches. Other leopard seals have turned up on the ocean side of the city's eastern suburbs, at La Perouse in 2014 and in Bondi in 2019. Juveniles have a habit of venturing north before heading back down to Antarctica when they mature. Since 2014 a long-nosed fur seal named 'Benny' (after Bennelong Point) has been visiting the Opera House, while another smaller seal sometimes joins him on the VIP steps on the building's north side. Benny may have moved here because fish numbers in the harbour have improved in recent years or for some other inscrutable reason. He became such a fixture that he had, until 2017, a Facebook page (Benny the seal) and, until recently, his own page on the official Opera House website. Under each cute photo, he offered trivia and advice on current shows. Visitors were encouraged to 'talk' to Benny via Facebook messenger. 'Let's get chatting,' his avatar said, 'mammal to mammal.'

Australia's fur seals have only returned recently to close to their pre-colonial numbers and this may be why are we seeing them more frequently. Sealing and whaling were the early colony's two major export industries before wool; Captain Philip Gidley King, the third governor, numbered them 'among the very few natural productions of the country that can be esteemed commercial.' Seals were in demand in China and England as furs or leather or as felt in hats while their oil was lighter and less malodorous than whale blubber. And so they were hunted almost to extinction. In 1799 alone, historian Ian Hoskins writes, five thousand skins and 1600 litres of oil were brought back to Port Jackson from Cape Barren Island in Bass Strait, then shipped to China. Between November 1800 and August 1806, this number had risen to 118,721 skins, 98,280 of which were exported. It was little wonder that the unsustainable slaughter and a glutted market caused the seal industry to collapse by the 1820s, though some hunting still continued for a couple of decades into the twentieth century.

And yet, according to some scientists, Australian fur seals are the world's fourth rarest. In 2003, the New South Wales Scientific Committee listed the Australian fur seal as vulnerable, due to bycatch mortality around Montague Island during commercial and recreational fishing, limitation of prey from fishing, and entanglement and ingestion of plastic debris. In 2018, one study suggested that, after recovering between the 1970s and 2007, the pup population appeared to have since declined by 4.2 per cent per year between then and 2013.

So was the seal's appearance in Rushcutters Bay now, in the March of 2018, a warning that the environment was stressed or a sign of life returning to the harbour? Was a century as long as it took, I wondered, to forget pain and human danger?

When I brought the twins down again before school, the seal was back in his patch of damp on the concrete path, propped up on his flippers. From time to time he moved his neck, nose pointed skyward, head shifting slightly from side to side, as if balancing an imaginary ball. As we watched, he lumbered down the small set of steps and into the water. There, he was graceful. At the marina he swam back and forth on his back between the boats. A few people gasped and clapped and filmed him on their phones. So did we. Though I reminded my children that each dusk, just above our heads, tiny wild microbats emerged from their nesting boxes in the paperbarks to flit, like toys on strings, chasing insects in the cool airspace above the water.

'OMG,' someone posted on the neighbourhood Facebook site later that night, 'our 'hood has gone viral (in a cute way!). Let's look after our new neighbour. [Smiley face].'

On its website, ABC Sydney posted clips of the seal 'enjoying the sun.' It was easier to see him in this footage than in real life. As he rolled on his back, his fur gleamed. His darker lower belly looked oily, while a satiny cleavage ran from the fat beneath his neck to his tail. He had a name now: Sealvester.

This was an apt place for an animal out of place to haul up. Rushcutters Bay Park, along with about a fifth of the harbour's perimeter, is 'reclaimed' land; an ironic term in a colonial context, I often find myself thinking, as I take my evening walks. The term means that it was once swampland, which was reclaimed from the sea by a colony certain of its rights to 'take back' even virtual land for its own use. First named on maps as Blackburn Cove, the bay takes its name from the reeds cut by convicts for the colony's thatched roofs, which used to grow around the mouth of the creek running downhill from heavily wooded Barcom Glen; now lined by concrete, the creek is one of the canals that penetrate far into the Sydney suburbs and are haunted, as they fill and empty twice daily, by their old tidal motion. (The tidal creek in next door Double Bay is more unsettling: concreted over by a roadway, it slops and gurgles invisibly and disconcertingly beneath one's feet).

Rushcutters Bay Park was made as part of a great domestication of the harbour, which reached its peak in the early twentieth century, as it deepened its channels for shipping and filled in the 'odorous, unsightly mud flats' at the heads of its bays. To do so, the city built new sea walls between median high and low water marks and dumped 'infill' – a mix of sand, rubbish, gravel, silt, oyster shells and contaminated soil – on top of these estuarine wetlands. The Rushcutters Bay infill came mostly from a nearby and long-gone sandhill. It is strange to think that the old beach still lies below the park's covering of soil and thin grass. This is why the seal had to climb steps from the tiny remaining patch of sand in the park's west corner to reach the path. If you look into the terraced gardens of the apartment block next door, you will see, beneath the hydrangeas and azaleas, a few inches above ground level, the top of an old sandstone rock shelter or *gibber gunya*, which looks, to my eyes, through the fence, to have been darkened by the smoke of past fires. Historian Paul Irish writes that there appear to have been different Aboriginal settlements at different times on either side of the creek that is now the canal. Ceremonies took place here until at least the 1870s, while Aboriginal women, in an act of more authentic reclaiming, used to bail up colonists' carriages near the tollgate on New South Head road, asking for money or gifts for their children.

Much of Sydney's wild history has been infilled. It is, as geographer Denis Byrne has written, a city of spectral beaches. When I was a child, you could feel their pull, in the quiet old city: an eerie bareness about the unpeopled expanses where we went to play school sport or picnic, as if the thin lawn had no wish to grow where a beach should be. These filled-in flatlands turned into parks often feature in the police crime scene photographs of the 1940s. The knowledge that a crime has taken place gives them their frisson but that's not the entire explanation. When I look at them, stark and threatening, pitilessly bare of trees where watery swamp should be, I realise I am looking at a double crime scene. These bleak spaces would become the haunts of the city's disenfranchised and unwanted like homeless eccentric Bea Miles, Shakespeare-quoting scourge of 1950s taxi drivers, and countless other rough sleepers since, who still bed down, in Rushcutters Bay, on the canal edges or in the stands of the nearby cricket oval. The irony is that this area already possesses a whole other layer of historical unease, in that it was, until well into the last ice-melt, the high edge of a deep river valley before becoming inundated swampland. So, before it could be 'reclaimed' a century ago, it had already been taken back by the sea.

But I am atypical, I realise, in dwelling on this history. The park is now part of a neighbourhood so prosperous and so pleasant, with its council signage and plantings of grevillea and kangaroo paw, that any shadows of the past have also been largely 'reclaimed.' It is a magic realist place now, a father at my children's school says. It is hard to believe that anything might ruffle its sunny enchantments.

If a seal turns up in the harbour sick or injured, it will be taken to Taronga Zoo on the north side of the harbour. If it can't be released it may join the fur seals and sea lions in its Seal Bay. Lexie the zoo's Australian sea lion was rescued as an orphan pup; so was Casey, the world's only captive leopard seal until his death in 2014, who was washed up seven years earlier on Wattamolla Beach in the Royal National Park, with a cookie cutter shark bite in his abdomen. Over the years some of these rescue seals have given birth, providing the Zoo with photogenic 'ZooBorns', as one dedicated website (not affiliated with the zoo) calls all new arrivals at zoos around the world.

Some of the zoo's seals perform in the zoo's seal theatre. When my children were tiny their favourite game to play here in the park was 'Seal Show,' in which we recreated the production, having sat through many performances on the stepped bleachers around the pool above the harbour. They were seal babies, each kneeling on an imaginary plinth. It was my job to be MC. Ladies and gentlemen, boys and girls . . . frogs, cats, dogs, and microbes . . . welcome to our famous one and only seal show, I would tell the imaginary audience. Today we have two beautiful baby seals, a fur seal and a leopard seal . . . Each honked and waved. Seals are efficient hunters, I continued, loosely following the scripts we had heard on our visits, so the behaviour each will exhibit draws as closely as possible on the skills they would rely on in the wild.

After each baby seal had jumped through rings and balanced an imaginary ball on its nose, I would conclude with the reminder that seals' natural environment was under threat. Thank you to our seal performers. Wave goodbye! Wave goodbye!

The next time I passed through the park, in the afternoon, quite a crowd had built up. Among the people around the tape I saw faces I recognised; the slim, long-haired Japanese man with two Shiba Inus; a local journalist, pale and intense; parents with children. Two women, university lecturers from the flats above, had come down to keep an eye on things. There were the casual stoppers in active wear with their dogs and people who had come from other neighbourhoods as tourists, leaning with their arms folded against the stone wall. The woman from ORCCA was strict, telling anyone who breached the tape to step back.

A yoga-toned woman in beige and white stopped with her large unleashed brown poodle. It slipped under the barrier and bounded towards the seal, feinted on braced paws, and leapt back. It barked expectantly, repeating this stiff bluff and retreat, as the seal heaved itself up to prop its hefty chest on its flippers. 'Oh, that's a funny looking puppy,' the owner crooned to her dog as it panted and lurched forward, barked and sprang.

'Go on, get out of it!' someone yelled.

The owner laughed. 'She just wants to play – don't you, Darling!'

By this time debate about how the seal should be allowed to interact with the suburb had grown lively. For some, the seal's arrival was an endorsement of our pleasant neighbourhood. For others, including myself, it seemed better that the seal should be allowed to haul up and rest, then encouraged to settle in a less populous position on the harbour. It was only a matter of time, I worried, until someone hurt him or he hurt them. I was not an expert on marine animals so I was content to leave these decisions to the Parks and Wildlife department and their advisors. To others, they were a hostile force, trying to deprive our new neighbour of his liberty.

The next morning, I woke to reports that the NSW National Parks and Wildlife Service had stretched builders' cross-hatched orange polyethylene fencing across the top of what locals referred to as the dog stairs. 'Sealvester has been blocked from his perch in the sun in one of Sydney's most affluent suburbs,' the ABC reported. 'Sealvester has been resting at Rushcutters Bay since the weekend. Authorities have told locals to leave their new neighbour alone.'

By the time I got down there, the seal was trying to shoulder his way through the fluorescent webbing but some part of him was stuck. It was not quite possible to tell which, from a distance. As the tide rose, it pressed him against the sea wall. I watched a council worker in shorts straddle the sagging barrier and gamely pull some of the plastic away to free him. The bulk of the plastic mesh stayed.

By that evening, a rumour had gone around the neighbourhood that dog owners had called the police because their dogs weren't able to play on the small beach behind the steps.

Community Facebook page, 29 March:

Look who's back.
Sealvester has broken through the plastic webbing!
I bet it was someone with opposable thumbs and tools.
Hurrah! Seal 1, Council 0.
The guy knows his real estate.
It's his domain, not the poodles'.

The performers in Taronga Zoo's seal show are a Californian sea lion relocated from another zoo, an Australian sea lion, and a rescue New Zealand fur seal that turned up injured on Sydney's Bondi Beach. According to the scripted commentary, 'Seals for the Wild' is not just for human gratification. Instead of performing circus tricks, these 'ambassadors of the wild' are asked to exhibit behaviours that help their health, such as opening their mouths for examinations, or simulate life in the wild. 'Marley' the endangered sea lion has been trained to emerge from the water with a ring of fishing net around his neck to demonstrate the 'human impact' on seals by pollution and to peer into the water from the pool deck to convey how wild food sources are becoming scarce because of overfishing. During the show's finale one of the seals unfurls the sponsorship banners of the MSC (Maritime Stewardship Council), an organisation which promotes and certifies sustainable fishing, before all three animals dive, leap, balance on their front flippers, and wave.

Was it really worse, I wondered, to jump through hoops and juggle balls, traditional circus tricks, than to recreate, twice daily, the precariousness of life in the open seas?

I was surprised by the hostility I felt toward local self-appointed wildlife experts and by their confidence that they knew what was best for this animal they were claiming as a 'neighbour.' It was clear to me that he should be returned, if possible, to the wild. But was it possible to think of any place or animal as truly 'wild' anymore? Figures had only recently come in that we had reduced the world's wild animal populations by fifty per cent over the previous forty years. The animals and wilderness areas that were left would have to be more carefully 'managed' than ever. I will never forget my disappointment on going to see Connemara's famous 'wild' horses in the Irish county of Galway, only to find a few ponies feeding in a desultory manner behind a fence. You would be hard pressed to call Africa's animal populations in safari parks really wild, now they have become habituated to humans, after being tracked so often: some primates have even been trained to accept close-up pictures or human touch, which puts them at risk of human illnesses. Operators argue that safari tourism helps conserve animal populations, by putting money into local communities and discouraging poaching but it's hard to argue that these animals are truly 'free.' In Australia, our native animals do still range across bush and farmland; yet they are also tagged, studied, treated for mange (in the case of wombats), and culled, while the huge numbers that survive mauling by cats and dogs or being hit by cars are nursed in sanctuaries and released by an army of volunteers.

Wild animals are also under constant virtual surveillance. Often, it is necessary for their survival. Smaller cellular tags can now send more data, more cheaply and quickly, via mobile phone towers, than old satellite tag technologies, providing scientists essential information about animal behaviour. I have on my shelves at home an extraordinary book called *Where the Animals Go*, which shows the journeys, on fifty maps, of tracked wildlife around the world: humpback whales visiting underwater mountains during their Pacific migrations; feral Burmese pythons moving swiftly through Florida's Everglades; the roaming of big crocodiles (christened OzESauce, JK, Big Dunk, Tiny Tim, and Weldon) around northern Australia's Gulf of Carpentaria; vultures sailing on the plumes of thermals; and the vertical migrations of plankton (coated in fluorescing nanoparticles used by surgeons to pinpoint cancer cells) whose traces on a graph resemble elegant trailing tentacles. A wolf christened Slavc undertook an epic 1000-kilometre trek from Trieste to Verona by way of Austria, his journey linking two wild wolf populations. It is a strange experience to read this book, in which each animal traces its autobiography through its movements while also being reduced to a set of data points, its secret life exposed.

Improvements in cheap drone technology – the new-generation drones are essentially 'a fleet of flying smartphones' now, according to one tech writer – means that it's not only scientists who can monitor wild animals. Drone operators are penetrating ever further into animals' territories, which are difficult to access by foot, hoping to film footage that will go viral. Yet studies have shown that even scientifically monitored drones raise the heartbeats and anxious behaviour of some animals – a team from the University of Minnesota observed a black bear's heartbeat increasing 400 per cent, which, as the head of the study put it, is 'well above the heart-beat jump experienced by people riding a double-corkscrew rollercoaster.' In 2014, in America's Zion National Park in Utah, a private drone flying close to a herd of bighorn sheep caused them to scatter, separating calves from mothers. In 2018, the 'life-affirming' video of a brown bear cub scrambling over the lip of a snow-covered mountain to reach its mother in the Magadan region of Russia, attracted 17 million viewers in a single week on the ViralHog YouTube channel. Ecologists pointed out that the mother's attempt to climb such a steep slope was a reaction to the perceived threat of the drone. At one point, the mother even swiped at her cub, making it lose its footing and almost costing it its life, which they interpreted as her pushing it out of the way of an attack.

Geotagged photos embedded with latitude, longitude and altitude data, are also turning animals into unwilling stars, mobbed by crowds, and even alerting poachers – who follow social media postings – to their locations. When images began to spread from a Kenyan photographer's Instagram account of a spotted zebra, nicknamed 'Tira,' in the Maasai Mara National Reserve, a 'stampede' of tourists rushed to the park to take their own photographs, surrounding the scared foal. Meanwhile, national parks around the world face increasing demands to provide visitors with internet access. Geotagging not only threatens animals but the landscapes that sustain them, when they become Instagram 'hotspots,' afflicted by illegal trails, garbage, graffiti and human waste. In Australia, Instagrammers have been flocking to Hyams Beach on the shores of the Jervis Bay Marine Park on the New South Wales south coast since the (spurious) rumour went viral that it has the whitest sand in the world, parking wherever they can in the small village and damaging the sand dunes. In America, so many influencers and advertisers have thronged the tiny Antelope Valley California Poppy Reserve in the Mojave Desert grassland, picking flowers and compacting the fragile soil, that an anonymous saboteur created the Public Lands Hate You Instagram account, exposing those who go off-trail or pick flowers and contacting companies whose products the influencers promote.

With *Where the Animals Go* in mind, I find myself imagining these new human migrations as data points, accelerating and converging: virtual desire lines worn quickly into real ones by car wheels and human feet. Each small migration – for those who have the freedom and money to take it – is a complex story; on the one hand, a Utopian quest for the beautiful or rare but often, at the same time, a rejection of the professional guardians who claim that nature must be regulated, contained, or protected. The fact that we are now able to record our own amateur wildlife footage erodes the privileged knowledge of wildlife experts and documentary makers, whose expertise becomes superfluous and whose imprecations and duty to fact can seem over-serious in a world, for the lucky, of leisure and play. At the same time, these locations, fetishised for a single feature or charismatic animal, become flattened out, thin places, with only the one easily-consumed story to tell before we move on to the next.

Yet there is also a possibility that these types of viral videos ('This Baby Sloth Will Inspire You to Keep Going,' 'Crazy True Stories of Wild Animals Saving People's Lives,' 'Most Amazing Moments of Wild Animal Fights!') may be making us less wild, too, as we watch them at work on our computers or on the devices in our hands. One theorist suggests that cute or inspirational animal videos offer us 'cruel relief': a respite from the corporatisation and commodification of our lives, while ultimately softening us up to endure the uncertainty and injustices of the expanded new world of work, in which the boundaries between labour and play have eroded and we are always expected to be productive and 'on.' We look at a cat video, feel all the 'feels,' and get back to the grindstone.

Do the constantly proliferating videos about beautiful or wild things that move across our screens give us a similarly brief reprieve from our darker knowledge: that we have almost obliterated the lives and territories of wild animals over the last fifty years? I sometimes wonder if there are more 'wild' animals circulating in these multiplying shared videos than there are in the world off-screen. The nature they depict is more fulsome and often kinder than the real thing, borrowing from commercial 'fuzzumentaries' like *Madagascar*, *Happy Feet* and *The Lion King*, which turn wild animals into almost-human characters. (Our neighbourhood 'visual storytellers' were doing their best with 'Sealvester,' posting clips of him swimming and sunning himself to a jazz soundtrack).

The very nature of these sorts of videos is to move us on to the next in a never-ending sequence. They may train us to enjoy the fleeting and relentless flow of an unstable world even as that world is causing us anxiety in real life as we watch our local bushland turn into housing developments and roads – making us feel a little better, for a moment at least, by dampening the background noise of anger or fear. I confess to my own fetish for videos of tough men murmuring gentle words of comfort to trapped animals – an owl tangled in a fence, a drowning sloth – as they rescue them. Happy endings, although another part of me worries about how, or whether, these animals will go on to survive. These videos are substantially different to those provided by the many animal rescue organisations that also fill my feed, which often expatiate on the dangers netting, cars or dogs cause to the animals they rescue. The volunteers, caught up in the daily business of caring for so many displaced and injured wild Australian flying foxes, tree kangaroos, wombats, wallabies, and native birds, show us deaths as well as triumphs.

The point of these feel-good videos may not even be about the animals themselves but – like any other click-bait – to prompt short bursts of feeling. In an era that academic Jodi Dean has christened 'communicative capitalism,' which celebrates speech, opinion and participation, cute videos create pleasant 'hits' of communal emotion that convince us we're exercising our democratic freedoms while replacing genuine political debate or action. In other words, responding emotionally to these videos and sharing them may also be a kind of work, in which we rehearse our role as consumers within the neoliberal market's endless flow, while failing to see real inequality through the warm and 'healing' collective glow.

It's rarely a good thing, if you're a wild animal, to be given a name:

Harriet, the Galapagos tortoise brought on board ship by Darwin, who would die at the age of 175 in captivity in Australia. Frodo, Gombe National Park's 'demonic alpha male' chimpanzee: a fearless killer of monkeys, who would become infamous for beating up primatologist Jane Goodall. Harambe, the seventeen-year-old gorilla shot and killed at Cincinnati Zoo after a toddler fell into his enclosure. Tilikum, the murderous orca imprisoned at Sea World, Florida, who would become the subject of the documentary *Blackfish*.

Martha, the last passenger pigeon.

Benjamin, the last thylacine. Dead of exposure in 1936, at Beaumaris Zoo in Hobart, when he was locked out of his sleeping quarters on a freezing night.

In the past, a lone creature out of its territory would be seen as a 'rogue animal' – today each is a fragile celebrity.

Now that the seal had a name, I observed darkly to my partner when the children were out of earshot, I worried that he was doomed.

Day six. Two temporary galvanised steel and mesh-weld fencing panels had replaced the plastic mesh. Placed on the sand at the bottom of the dog stairs, their bases were weighted with sandbags to stop the tide from moving them.

A seal's face is expressionless. Its chest is more eloquent, a glossy mass of intent. With no access now to his resting place, not even the lowest step, the seal pushed his breast against the fence. When I came to check on him, he had already created or widened a small gap where the mesh-weld panels met.

'Seal ya later!' ran the *Daily Mail*'s headline. 'Residents outraged after Sydney's favourite sea-going mammal Sealvester is locked out of his favourite sun baking spot.' The paper also reported that the seal now had an injured eye and rangers were hoping to relocate it several bays away to Nielsen Park.

On Facebook:

Our neighbourhood efforts to help the seal have not gone unnoticed.

Which moron went to the media?

I blame the entitlement and stupidity of pet owners with unleashed dogs.
Sydney, 2018, no one shall be allowed to have fun.
#takedownthewall
Build a wall!
Time to consult the community for a plan.

The wall had been vandalised, someone reported midway through the thread, and 'our friend' was back on land.

Later in the day, the fence was resurrected at the top of the steps, around the sleeping seal, who was back in his fishy patch of sun.

Good sense prevails!!
Why do the 'authorities' have to get involved?
I can't believe ORCCA and Parks and Wildlife were using webbing made of polluting plastic. #sealgate
I am SO proud that our voices have been heard! And that Sealvester's persistence has been noticed! He looks so happy!

In the early nineties, when I was a student at university in Melbourne, our cultural studies professor gave a paper in which he contemplated, in typically quizzical style, his involvement in a stoush over plans to turn an old quarry opposite his house in a gentrifying neighbourhood into a park. Wild, and with uninterrupted views of the city skyline, it was slated to be cleared up and portioned out into a playground, community gardens, barbeque and picnic sites. As the split between those who were pro- and anti-development grew into a perceived class war, he found himself positioned, in wanting to preserve the area's local charms, as an 'eccentric, spoiling voice.' Yet he couldn't help noticing that the designers – middle-class and flush with federal money – were defining themselves as battlers; and that while they claimed to act on behalf of beleaguered and diverse constituents, such as Vietnamese high-rise residents in need of vegetable gardens, they seemed to be speaking for groups whose needs they had 'imagined in the first place' rather than involving them in actual discussions. Meanwhile local politicians claimed that the community was largely constituted by families, whose 'crying need' for more play areas couldn't be appreciated by residents without children, although it was in fact dominated by childless and single households.

As the professor doorknocked, he discovered that the older residents, workers, and Greek and Italian migrants still living in this gentrifying suburb were the ones most attached, like him, to the way it was. It was the middle-class yuppies, on the other hand, who saw this space as underperforming and in need of refreshment and development. What humbled him most – perhaps naively – was the fact that he found his own arguments for the beautiful, in spite of his academic training, incommunicable in the face of the planners' instrumental understanding of place as amenity. His feeling for the specific local history, complexity and atmosphere of his neighbourhood failed in the face of the soft-left politicians' and designers' commitment to a ready-made template of public value. The paper was so devoid of theoretical flash, and our lecturer's approach so bemused, that we postgraduate students giggled about it for weeks afterwards. Now I think, in all my time at university, that it was one of the most important I attended.

Something similar had happened to our neck of the woods in the two decades since our return to Sydney. It had turned into a community. I had barely heard the word as a child, unless

I was going to ballet lessons in the modest Memorial Community Centre, a low white wooden building on the highway with a library attached to its small hall. Now it was everywhere, in every conversation; but it seemed to mean something different to the philosophy of live and let live that had been the unspoken credo of this waterside suburb's twentieth century incarnation as a low-rent, Bohemian, apartment and entertainment district, in which poor and rich, single and encumbered had rubbed along together. This unstated sense of community was still firm when we had first moved here over twenty years ago. But as our semi-gentrified neighbourhood with its few remaining boarding houses transformed into an 'executive lifestyle' destination, the term seemed to have become as aspirational as the pastel-clad cyclists and coffee-holding couples in an architect's CAD (computer-aided design) mock-up of the latest plans for neighbourhood 'refreshment.' People who used the word, I noticed, often used it in the same breath as words like 'village,' 'wellness,' and 'activation.' It was, I realised, in spite of its fuzzy vibe, the urban planning equivalent of 'reclamation,' assuming that places that had not been tidied up and maximised by as many activities as possible were empty and unused.

To want to hold onto old or local things in all their historical complexity now seemed, as my professor had found, like selfishness: any quibblers were, in Gen-Y speak, 'haters.' 'We're the new demographic, get used to it,' one advocate for an expanded children's playground said to an older resident (and founder of one of the state's first women's and children's refuges), who queried the size of its planned new footprint in a local park. 'There's a war against children!' another wailed online, about objectors to a large new skate park; a claim that might have been true of America's ICE child detention centres or turn-of-the millennium

Rwanda, or even of Australia's neglect of the health of Indigenous children, but perhaps not of a suburb in which families travelled to Bali several times a year and spent weekends on their boats. A friend my own age, a gay academic from Melbourne, was brusque in his assessment. 'For many people, especially straight men,' he said, 'there's no sense of their lives being political or resistant. It's something they possibly wouldn't even think about. But they can invest emotionally in something like riding a bike, and this suddenly makes them feel like an oppressed group, that their lives are politically important.' This wasn't peculiar to my hometown. In England, academic Tom Whyman controversially coined the term 'cupcake fascism' (because the twee, vintagey, little cake is so neat and polite it is not really a cake), to describe the rise of a new kind of infantilised middle-class identity intent on consensus, safety and niceness.

Meanwhile, new street plantings appeared around the old streets, movable planter boxes and bunting celebrating our 'villages' lined the main thoroughfares, and pop-up exhibitions of sculptures came and went on the boardwalk of the industrial-wharf-turned-restaurant-precinct of next-door Woolloomooloo. These were, in fact, rather nice. And yet, I would spend more and more of my time on my solo walks wondering if the 'activation' of spaces was a means of getting us used to neoliberal insecurity and change while convincing us that these investments in infinitely improvable small details were equivalent to real political action. In London, urban wanderer Iain Sinclair was pondering the same thing. He described the sensation of walking through the permanent impermanence of his 'pasteurised' city as a 'ground-zero vertigo.' ('Come back tomorrow and the British Museum will be an ice-rink, a boutique hotel, a fashion hub . . .'). When spaces no longer made sense as themselves but only as ever-changing stage sets, I wondered, were we less likely to worry, or even notice, if we lost a small biome that sustained a particular bat or bird?

A note from the Lord Mayor on our neighbourhood page: 'I'm proud of how considerate residents were to our surprise visitor while he was at Rushcutters Bay'. I remembered the Australian author Patrick White's list of hates prepared before his Nobel Prize portrait sitting in 1973 – among them, 'the overgrown school prefects from whom we never escape' – and experienced a mean little stab of pleasure. But I returned quickly to feeling like an endling, out of step, among all the holders of new economy jobs with their relentless positivity: the brand communicators, event managers, 'visual storytellers' and founders of online consultation platforms.

It was lucky for the seal that he turned up where he did.

If he was a 'rogue' seal in Tasmania – that is, a seal that finds it easiest to fish from the huge salmon farms off the state's southern coast – he would have found himself caught, with around two thousand other seals each year, and transported by road by the Department of Primary Industries, Parks, Water and Environment, to be dumped on the state's north west coast. The relocation program is unpopular not because of the potential to harm seals or the pollution from the salmon farms, or the dwindling of wild fish for them to eat, but because relocated seals become 'aggressive' in their new homes. Referred to by some as 'sea wolves', they shadow fishing vessels, steal catches out of the hands of fisherman as they lean over the boats' sides to grab the fish caught on their rods, and even leap into dinghies. 'If you had some dogs that were killing somebody else's sheep,' one operator said, 'you wouldn't move them and put them on somebody else's farm.' Tasmanian author Richard Flanagan writes that the salmon farms' deterrent methods also include firing 'blunt darts' and 'beanbag rounds' filled with lead pellets, sometimes blinding the long-nosed fur seals, which has made me wonder since what might have happened to this seal on his south-coast fishing grounds.

If 'Sealvester' had hauled up in a protected habitat instead of our inner-city park he might, counterintuitively, have received a harsher welcome. In 2013, journalist Jon Mooallem reported on a spate of Hawaiian monk seal killings. Unlike Australian fur seals, the monk seal population has never recovered from intensive hunting by the Polynesians when they arrived around 1500 years ago. When he wrote his article, around 900 remained in the Leeward Islands, though their numbers were still shrinking and they were among the world's most imperilled marine animals. A handful were spreading to the main islands, where, like Sealvester, they would become celebrities, protected from over-zealous admirers by volunteers. And yet, from 2011, monk seals were turning up shot or bashed to death. This was not an isolated phenomenon. Mooallem recounted other instances in which people were targeting protected creatures; driving through flocks of shore birds, shooting some of the last red wolves in North Carolina, and breaking the wings of hundreds of brown pelicans. (Similar instances are all too easy to find in Australia. In 2018, a Victorian farmer pleaded guilty to poisoning 406 wedge-tailed eagles by injecting an insecticide into lamb carcasses; he was jailed for two weeks and fined $2500, although the maximum penalty under the state's Wildlife Act was $330,000).

In Hawaii, the monk-seal killings seemed to be caused by a number of factors, including competition for fish with a subsistence fishing industry and an inclination to see the animals as an extension of big government infringing on humans' rights. For native Hawaiians, it was galling to find beaches they'd walked for centuries roped off and guarded by monk-seal responders, who were mostly white, wealthy, mainland retirees. Some were sceptical that the seal was actually native to Hawaii, given its absence from traditional chants and art, accusing the government of importing the animals in secret to create jobs for scientists and push an environmental agenda. The widespread feeling was that the animals were receiving more support than people. And the killings kept happening. Mooallem found himself concluding that 'the success of conservation projects relies on a shadow ecology of human emotion and perception, variables that do not operate in any scientifically predictable way.'

While some posters on our neighbourhood Facebook page argued for letting the authorities deal with the situation and others poked fun ('Sealvester! The Musical!!'), a large part of the discussion embraced the seal as a neighbour. He had a right to his patch of sunlight, they wrote. We should feel honoured that he 'chose' us and one of Sydney's best neighbourhoods. Certainly, relocating the fence around the top of the stairs to allow him a small perch seemed to make common sense, though some also saw it as a small victory for local democracy.

To be honest, I came to resent the seal a little, as his presence and the response to it made me confront my ambivalence about my privileged inner-city enclave. And yet – wouldn't the world be a better place if we did accept every wild animal as a neighbour? (Though if one creature could be the cause of so much flurry, and had to be turned into a celebrity to be protected, how long would the goodwill last? Was it only an area so gentrified – so attuned to play-as-work and work-as-play – that could embrace the seal as both a fellow 'sunbaker' and an entertainment?) Besides, who were we – living on stolen land, as the half-buried old rock overhang just outside the exclusion zone reminded me – to extend such an invitation, so confidently? Yet, to be fair, this was a neighbourhood proud of its inclusivity, charitable works and volunteering, even if the goodwill was sometimes dispensed to the homeless in wellness speak in the form of 'blessings bags.' Maybe, as the world's wilder environments were degraded I found myself thinking, we should recognise that our cities were becoming greener refuges for wildlife than traditionally 'wild' places and plan accordingly. Though it was hard to know if the seal had found safe harbour in our bay because industry had been banished from the city's waterfronts to its outer fringes or even offshore, making its waterways an inviting haven, or whether he was a refugee from the pressures of overfishing, or some more mysterious affliction of the oceans that was yet to make itself apparent.

Still, I worried that the attention we were lavishing on one celebrity seal was a distraction from more complex and looming environmental matters. Our national addiction to land clearing beyond our pleasant green inner cities had made Australia responsible for the highest rate of mammal extinctions in the world. Even on the edges of the city, in its south-west, loss of Cumberland Plain woodland corridors to subdivisions and roads was creating enormous risks for vulnerable koala populations. The city centre might be agreeable and green but the city's industrial and poorer western edge was feeling the effects of global heating faster, roasting in temperatures up to ten degrees hotter than my suburb with its sea breezes. In January 2020, the outer suburb of Penrith was, for a few hours, the hottest place on the planet.

And these sorts of patterns were being repeated on a global scale. First-world cities are increasingly nice because we are prepared to turn large tracts of the world into great wastelands where indentured workers eke out a bare life making the clothes we import and assembling our mobile phones.

Now, because of the sea rise threatened by global heating, even the seawall where the seal had come to rest was under threat. Scientists predict that stronger wave action in deep water will increasingly scour out the bases of seawalls and 'overtop' them, causing more erosion from behind. The cost of preparing Sydney's hundreds of kilometres of sea walls is only now becoming apparent, as councils contemplate disassembling them, adding new concrete footings, and rebuilding them, brick by brick. On king tides, when the sea slops over the canal edges and comes close to the top of the sea wall, we were already getting an eerie foretaste of water out of place.

Wave goodbye! Wave goodbye!

The seal, meanwhile, remained inscrutable, propped on his front flippers like a hydrofoil, nose pointed at the sky.

In Coetzee's *The Lives of Animals*, a character observes that wild creatures today have no more power. 'Animals have only their silence left with which to confront us. Generation after generation, historically, our captives refuse to speak to us.'

Two weeks after he first appeared, National Parks and Wildlife, Taronga Zoo and ORCCA monitors noticed the seal – which already had an eye injury and flipper wounds – was declining. His right eyeball had grown opaque so he could no longer see with it and he had continued to lose weight. A vet from Taronga Zoo made the decision to dart him and take him to the zoo's hospital.

As the two white vans left the park, the seal passed away.

A necroscopy would reveal that he was also suffering from a streptococcus bacterial infection to his joints, lymph nodes and right eye. He had no body fat.

I heard the news via Facebook:

So, they spent all that time trying to protect him from us and he's died after this over-protective organisation sedated him. I believe our community was adult and sensible enough for their dogs not to attack him.
He's been staying alone in an unfamiliar place away from a colony and where seals don't usually hang around – I'd have thought that behaviour alone indicates that something might be awry. Strange that some people think their enjoyment of his presence is more important than his wellbeing. Parks and Wildlife are interested in animal welfare. It's their job after all. Why are people so suspicious of their motives?
It's a seal. Get over it!
He's left for Melbourne, where you can get a drink after 10pm.
It's OUR seal and we loved him.
He can go over the rainbow bridge knowing we provided him with a peaceful respite during his last days.
While we didn't learn much about seals, Sealvester taught us about ourselves and what's important in life. [Heart emoji].

A few nights later, at dusk, a handful of residents held a small ceremony for the seal. Someone lit a candle. Someone else placed flowers and a photo where he had rested. Behind them, microbats flitted after insects in swift arcs, through the air, above the water.

The Weight of Things

On 24 September, 2001, *The New Yorker* published its first issue since September 11, the Twin Towers just visible as spectral dark shapes on its all-black cover. In a special longform account of the terror attacks, which would take up almost the whole magazine, editor David Remnick drew together reportage from twenty-two staff writers. 'The day began,' he wrote, 'with what airline pilots call a "severe clear": seemingly infinite visibility.'

It was gripping, watching the magazine's renowned team struggle to find a language commensurate with the event. In one of the smaller colour pieces at the front of the same issue, staff writer Adam Gopnik found comfort in the Adamic act of naming, observing that on the morning of the attack Central Park was filled with autumn birds, 'from the northern flicker to the red-eyed vireo to the rose-breasted grosbeak to the Baltimore oriole.' Still, even in this first account, stunned gravitas began to give way to the magazine's house style of patrician irony. Gopnik would go on to describe the pleasure of being able to still order a meal with a salad in a Washington Square restaurant and, infamously, compare lower Manhattan's smell of lingering death to 'smoked mozzarella.'

What was startlingly apparent in these accounts was the writers' reflexive reaching out for precisely enumerated *things*. Why this appeal to the air, its clarity named and parcelled out? Why the litany of birds? Why, for God's sake, mozzarella?

Lately I've been thinking about the publishing phenomenon of 'books of things,' whose vogue was still in full swing as the millennium ticked over. These popular microhistories – of cod, nutmeg, blood, coal, hearts, umbrellas, cheese, and even the colour mauve – all hoped to emulate the success of Dava Sobel's *Longitude* though it seems astonishing now that the story of a ship's clock could have caused such a sensation. But as I look back, more than twenty years after I first wrote about these books, to try to account for their hold on readers, I find my thoughts returning to *The New Yorker*'s urgent scramble for Things in the wake of disaster, as if the two are intertwined.

Two years before the events of 9/11, we were living in a two-storey converted corner shop on a steep street in North Melbourne. Still semi-industrial in 1999, with one edge extending to a tangle of country and freight rail lines and another to the city's large central market, our suburb boasted a lost cats' and dogs' home, retired wheat silos, red-brick factories, and warehouses that had been turned into storage units but not yet into loft apartments. The wide main street still retained its Victorian street awnings while its bakery, cafes and hot potato shop closed promptly at three each afternoon. Several times a week I would walk the length of the suburb, via a stop at the markets, to my university building next door to 'Dracula's' theatre night club, whose costumed patrons would begin to queue outside in the early evening. When we had arrived in Melbourne at the beginning of the nineties the city had been in recession, its main street a desert of two-dollar shops. The spell of fiscal gloom still hung like a sleeping sickness over our neighbourhood. But now, since the state's economy had begun to recover, small bars were appearing in the city's laneways and shop tops. Meanwhile, an accelerating property market was declaring old suburbs like ours 'hot' and each week more of its wooden workers' cottages, interiors freshly painted and stencilled, were coming onto the market.

Since the middle of the decade, when we lived in another inner Melbourne suburb of such dreamy quietness that I could hear the calls of the gibbons at the zoo a kilometre away, I had been noticing a new genre of book staking its claim on the shelves of the bookshop my partner managed. It typically told the story of a humble thing, for which its author crafted a gripping journey – both physical and historical – whose magnitude was conveyed by a breathless subtitle about how it 'changed the world.'

For my partner, like other booksellers around the world, *Longitude* (subtitle: 'The True Story of a Lone Genius Who Solved the Greatest Scientific Problem of His Time') had been the surprise hit of 1995. This story about John Harrison's eighteenth-century invention of the chronometer, the first clock accurate enough to be used to determine longitude at sea, would sell 350,000 copies worldwide in hard cover alone, followed by paperback and illustrated editions and a two-part television series. In time, professional historians would come to write agonised articles with titles like 'The Sobel Effect: The Amazing Tale of How Multitudes of Popular Writers Pinched All the Best Stories in the History of Science and Became Rich and Famous While Historians Languished in Accustomed Poverty and Obscurity, and How This Transformed the World.' They would observe that these stories were too certain, too neat, and too likely to give readers a false understanding of the messy documentary record on which professional history was based. But the primary feeling in publishing circles in the nineties was excitement. In academic circles too, such books seemed designed, with their 'secret' stories of love and historical detours, to appeal to those of us with newly minted cultural studies degrees.

By 1999, as I began to write about it for a literary magazine, the popular history market was getting hotter by the day as world-changing things were 'discovered'. More and more humble objects seemed suddenly sexy and compelling as new books hit the bestseller lists: Mark Kurlansky's *Cod* ('A Biography of the Fish that Changed the World'); Susan Orlean's *Orchid Fever* ('A Horticultural Tale of Love, Lust and Lunacy'); Anna Pavord's *The Tulip* ('The Story of a Flower that has Made Men Mad'); and Giles Milton's *Nathaniel's Nutmeg* ('Or the True and Incredible Adventures of the Spice Trader who Changed the Course of History').

As I thought about these new nonfiction books, I realised that fiction had also been becoming increasingly thing-centred over the previous decade. This included my own novel, *The Service of Clouds*, which had been published two years earlier in 1997. I had not been conscious as I wrote it of joining any trend: I had simply become obsessed by the panoramic photographs of clouds and mist in the valleys of the Blue Mountains, taken from perilous rock ledges by early twentieth-century photographer Harry Phillips. Collaged into large souvenir booklets he printed himself, they endowed the air with such charisma that it seemed to emanate a yearning that harked back to the Victorian-era writings of John Ruskin, from whose essay 'Modern Painters'

I had taken my title. My heroine Eureka Jones would fall in love with the cloud photographer Harry Kitchings, while he was in love with the fugitive charms of his glass photographic plates, gelatine, fixatives, and emulsions. Nevertheless, readers seemed drawn to fiction about things too and my novel spent a year on the Australian bestseller lists.

Looking back two years later, I recognised that I had been influenced at a subconscious level by earlier bestsellers like Peter Carey's *Oscar and Lucinda* (1989), with its Victorian glass factory, floating glass church and exploding Prince Rupert's drops. And also, I suspected, by Allen Kurzweil's *A Case of Curiosities* (1992), set in eighteenth-century Paris, whose young hero Claude learned the arts of enamelling, watch making, and pornographic publishing before creating a mechanical talking head that squawked '*Vive le roi!*' – unfortunate timing, as the Revolution erupted. I had loved both novels because they tipped the usual balance of background and foreground so that forgotten objects and the knowledge and habit around them acquired a kind of magic, to dictate the human drama. E. Annie Proulx's *The Shipping News* (1993) had been another bestseller; my partner would receive a certificate from Proulx's publishers for selling more than a thousand copies in his shop alone. While I didn't love its bristly descriptions of the workings of a Newfoundland port I was delighted by its layout, in which the dinkuses between sections took the gnarled shapes of illustrations from *The Ashley Book of Knots*. (I also loved the small cherry- and banana-shaped dinkuses in Jeanette Winterson's 1989 *Sexing the Cherry*, in which the arrival of a pineapple at the London docks prompted its heroes' search through time for exotic fruit.)

Reflecting on these global hits, I realised I was more likely to remember their vividly detailed objects than their plots: the winds (*ghibli*, *haboob*, and fragrance-carrying *datoo*) in Michael Ondaatje's *The English Patient* (1992); the minutiae of rooster behaviour and storing turnips in Civil War-era America in Charles Frazier's 1997 *Cold Mountain*; the mysterious ways of ice in Peter Hoeg's *Miss Smilla's Feeling for Snow* (1992); and, most vividly, the ugly chemistry of fragrance-making by a scentless man who kills to preserve his victims' essences in Patrick Süsskind's *Perfume* (1985). This was the earliest book in my personal genealogy, although I could trace its ancestry back, in turn, to Jean des Esseintes' joyfully perverse experiments conjuring landscapes with musks and floral essences in Joris-Karl Huysmans' *Against Nature*. First published in 1884, Huysmans's decadent novel, which I had adored since first reading it in my twenties, featured an aesthete hero who literally locked the door on the smells and noises of fin-de-siècle Paris to commune with his possessions, including precious jewels from Ceylon set into the shell of a tortoise, meals made exclusively of food of one colour, and exotic flowers chosen for their most barbaric and unnatural forms. (I would always think of the table of outrageous and twisted blooms in a Fitzroy flower shop, which arranged its displays by colour, as the '*Against Nature*' corner).

Of course, novelists had been paying close attention to the material world since the Victorian era. A precise eye for furnishings and clothing allowed them to calibrate its grinding moral and class hierarchies. But these books of the nineties brought objects from the background to the foreground and made a fetish of them. The joy of reading them was the almost perverse pleasure they took in enumerating technologies of the past, like the arts of seduction in Arthur Golden's *Memoirs of a Geisha*. ('You may not believe me, when I tell you that this cream was made from nightingale droppings,' says the narrator of the yellow lotion the geisha Hatsumomo puts on her face, 'but it's true.') The details of farm work in *Cold Mountain* were so particular that you could almost use them as an instruction manual. ('Patch shingles on barn roof; do we have a maul and froe? Buy clay crocks for preserving tomatoes and beans. Pick herbs and make from them worm boluses for the horse.') The books frisson went beyond mere elaboration. The attention they lavished on the habits and language around ordinary things that had retreated from most privileged people's lives rendered them not just visible but peculiar, glamorous and exotic. That is perhaps why Huysmans's portrait of des Esseintes in thrall to his porpoise-skin covered books and a bespoke instrument designed to dispense spiritous liquors – a kind of proto-hipster indulging his niche hobbies – feels so much more modern now than its contemporaries.

Each of these books made us see things anew. As each object emerged into the spotlight it revealed itself as both enchanted and enchanting.

The New Yorker very rarely devotes a single edition to a single subject. The earliest occasion was on 31 August, 1946, when it published John Hersey's 'Hiroshima,' the first reconstruction of the nuclear attack and its aftermath. In six third-person strands, based on the eyewitness accounts of two women and four men, Hersey painstakingly recounted the survivors' experiences, from the morning of 6 August, 1945, immediately before the bomb exploded overhead, through to the 'endless parade of misery' over the next hours and days. His article ended twelve days later, as radiated vegetation regrew with eerie vigour and survivors began to experience the symptoms of radiation sickness.

Yet, for all Hersey's forensic detail in describing the horrifying post-blast verdancy of bolting morning glories, day lilies, hairy-fruited beans, panic grass, and sickle-senna, it's hard to imagine him dwelling with rapt attention on the inventory of the rayon manufacturer who was helping citizens evacuate from the city's close-packed residential district on that perfectly clear morning or the minutiae of its residents' dashi-making methods.

Hersey's restraint, as it turns out, was more the exception than the rule in *The New Yorker*, even in the 1940s. The magazine's fetish for things had been in place since 1925, under founding editor Harold Ross, who created its enduring style of informational surfeit. Ross was famous for his relentless margin notes demanding exhaustive detail; 'a thicket of queries and complaints,' in the words of contributor James Thurber. ('Were the Nabokovs a one-nutcracker family?' Ross wrote in the margins of an excerpt from *Speak, Memory*.) The rigorous fact-checking process he established rendered articles clear enough to be read by the least informed reader, but his love of relative clauses did make for chewy, drawn-out writing. While Hersey kept his prose relatively uncluttered, star reporter Joseph Mitchell's portraits of old New York's fading tribes, which many associate with the magazine's mid-century heyday, were chock-full of generous-to-the-point-of surplus detail. In 'Mr Hunter's Grave,' his legendarily fulsome 1956 profile of the Staten Island town founded by free Black oystermen, Mitchell paid lingering attention to the particular, including the images on the gravestones in the cemetery ('death's-heads, angels, hourglasses, hands pointing upward, recumbent lambs, anchors, lilies, weeping willows, and roses on broken stems') and the vegetation in overgrown fields ('sassafras, gray birch, blackjack oak, sumac . . . reed grass, blue-bent grass, and poison ivy').

In the second half of the century (1952–1987), editor William Shawn commissioned writers like John Frazier, Lawrence Weschler, and John McPhee, who consolidated *The New Yorker*'s reputation for exhaustive articles on obscure subjects (fishing, sand mining, chemical tankers, chalk cliffs) that not only paid particular attention to material things but were also prone to long digressions. In one of my favourite pieces, 'LA Glows,' (published under Tina Brown's editorship in 1998), Weschler dissected the light of Los Angeles in probing detail – the stillness caused by the desert's thermal inversion, the whiteness that creates a sense of distance and flatness, the 'billion tiny moons' of particulate matter in suspension that create its mirror-like quality of 'airlight' – to account for its 'egoless bliss.'

These writers' comprehensive articles sometimes extended in two or three parts across several editions, anticipating the 'books of things' with their detours into the historical byways of their chosen objects. In fact, one of the earliest popular microhistories, Susan Orlean's *The Orchid Thief* (1998), had begun as a 1995 *New Yorker* article about a poacher of rare ghost orchids in Florida. (Although it was an international bestseller and would go on to inspire Spike Jonze's eccentric 'comedy-drama metafilm' *Adaptation*, one critic would complain that it 'wilts under the weight of facts and figures.') At the height of thing books' popularity, their *New Yorker*-esque digressions into back story had become such a recognisable stylistic tic that a reviewer of *Phineas Gage* ('A Gruesome but True Story about Brain Science') would express his relief that John Fleishmann's biography of the Vermont rail worker lobotomised by an iron rod had at least spared readers an excursion into the history of the narrow-gauge railway.

But why were things being asked to carry such an increasing load as the century passed its midpoint? One obvious shift was the explosion of sheer stuff into people's lives as manufacturing re-geared after the Second World War, which would kick-start the 'Great Acceleration.' Of all countries, America was surely the champion of exuberant consumption. I have always been impressed on my visits to the US by the unembarrassed human-centred energy of its language compared to more laid-back Australian English: our straws are its 'sippers,' our prams its 'strollers,' our dummies its 'pacifiers,' our Plain-Jane 'milk' its 'creamer'. Those muscular American names cast a small spell on their objects, as if they only become visible when people use them.

By 2001, when Remnick's report on 9/11 appeared, we had learned in the West to understand ourselves as consumers and, as the range of choices available to us grew, more and more objects were turning into *products*. While Joseph Mitchell might have recited a litany of plants and even botanical names, the late-twentieth-century *New Yorker*'s writers had a whole universe of brands to enumerate, as people defined themselves by the tiny discriminations between the products they bought, ate, and wore. (Air Jordans or Nikes, gravlax or smoked salmon?) In 1981, Bret Easton Ellis had published his first novel, *Less Than Zero*, whose characters expressed their disaffected tribal affiliation by wearing Wayfarers and drinking Tab. (Not just the West: in the clubs of Changi, a Singaporean friend told me, if you could only afford to dress in Donna Karan you were a 'factory girl'). As the century came to its end, our relentless consumerism was extending to experiences, which were also being named and transformed, at an astonishing rate, into 'things.' In 2001, the *Oxford English Dictionary* would add new entries for 'channel surfing,' 'cybersex,' 'deejaying,' going the 'full monty,' and 'road rage,' along with 'spamming,' 'media circus,' and 'frequently asked question.'

The term 'severe clear' snagged my attention because it turned the sublime into the slangily familiar. In his history of the air, academic Steven Connor describes how our modern era has reduced the sky from limitless and purposeless space to 'a thin and patchy rind of breathable gas clinging to the surface of the planet,' while in his memoir *Skyfaring*, commercial pilot Mark Vanhoenacker describes the skies he flies through as a 'well-regulated realm', divided into no-fly zones and 'sky-lands' or 'countries of the sky' with names like 'Roberts' and 'Amazonica,' which bear no resemblance to the familiar territories below.

As a word obsessive, I find such language both exciting and appalling for the businesslike efficiency with which it turns the immaterial into a commodity. It gives me the same small thrill I felt in 1997 when I first read Sebastian Junger's *The Perfect Storm* (subtitle: 'A True Story of Men Against the Sea'), another 'thing book,' which offered a forensic account of the extreme weather that hit the north-east coast of America in 1991. I had never come across writing before that anatomised so many phenomena, including the five stages of drowning or the sound of a Force 11 gale, with such assurance. Even 70-foot waves capable of breaking a boat in two or peeling open a shipping container began, Junger wrote, as rough spots or 'cats' paws' on the surface of the sea, when winds found purchase on diamond-shaped ripples called 'capillary waves.' These monsters also had a name that cut their sublime power down to size: 'non-negotiable waves', a term my partner and I still use as jokey shorthand for any life-obstructing problem.

Remnick's choice of expression was a small gesture of control, suggesting that the planes did not fall, like the bomb over Hiroshima, out of an unfathomable sky, but one that derived its meaning from human use and occupation. But the power of things to define our experience had its limits, as the contempt that attached itself to Gopnik's overreaching would show.

As I wrote about the 'books of things' in 1999 in my office above the old shop, I realised that each of their authors offered something more than the story of their chosen objects' discovery or use. They also conjured the strange skeins of thought and emotion which surrounded them. French philosopher Michel Foucault called these ecologies of belief and speech that defined the temperature of an age *epistemes* but we could just as easily call them poles of habit and feeling. Here's Dava Sobel describing her own project in *Longitude*:

> political intrigue, international warfare, academic backbiting, scientific revolution, and economic upheaval. All these threads, and more, entwine in the lines of longitude. To unravel them now – to retrace their story in an age when a network of orbiting satellites can nail down a ship's position within a few feet in just a moment or two – is to see the globe anew.

I was familiar with this approach from my doctoral research in cultural studies, a discipline which also dug back into genres and histories once thought too trivial or lowly for serious regard. In my reading, I had come across histories of private life, which also fed my fiction, like Peter Gay's history of the bourgeois and Alain Corbin's extraordinary history of bells in the pre-revolutionary French countryside, a book of things if there ever was one. I had loved historian Robert Darnton's work on eighteenth-century France, in which he asked why apprentices in a Paris printery could possibly have found a 'great cat massacre' so hilarious. Using their torture and slaughter of the cherished pets of the owner's wife as a starting point, he traced the threads of resentment (the animals were fed better than these young men) and misogyny (they smashed the spine of her favourite grey cat in a mock 'witchcraft' trial) that would fuel the hatred of Marie Antoinette. Here at last, instead of the dull, official school lists of achievement – in Australia, of white explorers, wheat and sheep – were historians bringing neglected material to centre-stage, as evidence of the passions, beliefs and dreams of an age. The objects people cherished or used could be remarkably eloquent about the way they saw the world around them. When the authorities of the First Republic melted down village church bells into coins or cannonballs after the French Revolution, Corbin argued, they not only destroyed a whole 'auditory landscape' but a powerful, non-official way of marking history and time outside the secular rigours of the modern clock. On reflection, my own first novel had probably owed as much to these histories of *mentalités* as to thing-centred novels. To see popular microhistories turn the same spotlight onto the secret life of things – and make hidden scholarly business into the stuff of bestsellers – was thrilling.

Like Süskind's novel *Perfume*, in which a man with no sense of smell became obsessed with concocting a fragrance that would send crowds mad, the popular microhistories – especially the early ones – often focused on things as vectors of obsession and mania. The preoccupations and passions of an epoch found their most florid expression in the worldwide fad for trading tulip bulbs and exotic orchids; the race to dominate the spice and cod markets; or the surgeon of Crowthorne's self-mutilating madness (the contributor to the *Oxford English Dictionary* amputated his own penis in a fit of self-hatred). The books were fresh and exotic because we weren't used to seeing madness taken seriously – except, fairly recently, in academic writing – or reading history that refused narratives of sober progress and achievement. The extraordinary inference that these books led to was that *all* objects were enrolled in human histories that were as halting, partial, haunted, and irrational; this had enormous implications, in turn, for a western civilisation that had always claimed a rational imperative for activities like colonial exploitation. No wonder reviewers and general readers were so excited by these books that 'evoked a vanished world' (*Memoirs of a Geisha*), 'refreshed and invigorated' (*Cod*) and were 'more fabulous than fiction' (*The Perfect Storm*).

But why this great bloom of things now, dragging the luminous threads of thought and belief behind them, and claiming to have changed the world? Perhaps it was a millennial phenomenon; as if, upon reaching the end of this thousand years, the Enlightenment curiosity with which our own modern era began were regarding itself in a mirror; rehearsing its own steps, in these books' pages and revisiting its inventions to see what they meant. In these books we could go back in time and watch the cats' paws of a world in the first phase of becoming more thing-like: tiny ripples, turning into waves.

By 1999, as I worked on my essay, I noticed that things themselves (and not just writing about them) were also acquiring a new charisma. In inner-city Melbourne, old wig makers' stores, milk bars and shop tops were coming back to life as small bars, which sometimes preserved the furniture, signage, or equipment of the former business. In hip inner-city Fitzroy, stores had sprung up specialising in old medical equipment and ephemera: chrome operating tables, pipettes and vials, large plaster models of eyeballs, and formalin-filled jars stained by the dark humours of dissected rats. A student in my novel-writing class had discovered he could make a steady income on a nascent eBay by buying old books on German Shepherds and knitting patterns at garage sales and selling them to northern hemisphere buyers who paid with the stronger American dollar.

As old things were emerging into an eager marketplace, the range of new products in the shops was booming. Supermarket shelves groaned with variations on familiar products: hoi sin sauce 'with added spring onion'; sea salt in addition to the iodised table variety; 'baby' carrots and peas. Visiting London early in 1998, I had been shocked in its hypermarkets to see, beside the shelves of cheap Australian and New Zealand wines, herbs and African mange tout misting in plastic wrappers (uniform, unblemished, and flown in from less economically developed countries like Kenya, where intensive agribusiness had replaced local farmland). Within a few years, I would see these changes in my own supermarket and today it is difficult to avoid produce portioned into plastic to appeal to ever-differentiated market sectors, like Aldi's egregious 'Li'l Snackerz', in which cartoon characters like 'Penny Pear' and 'Bradley Banana' encourage children to eat 'power serves' of smaller-sized fruit. The speed of this proliferation has been staggering. Back in 1950, according to the Our World in Data website, the world was producing 2 million tonnes of plastic a year. By 1999, the cumulative total of plastic in the world was 2.98 billion tonnes. By 2015, the last available figure, the cumulative total was 381 billion.

It was little wonder, then, that alongside the industrial production of more products, bespoke food and craft movements were also stirring. As I was finishing my PhD in the early nineties, I had a part-time job in my department's small library. In the break room a group of women with severe oblong glasses and hand-knitted sweaters would compare notes each lunchtime about their Fowlers Vacola bottling ware, plants grown from Diggers heritage seeds, and the roster for the chicken group at the collectively owned organic farm. Their efficiency terrified me. And yet the global market was already busy converting all these good urges into commercial forms, as the enormous growth of the American Whole Foods company (floated publicly in 1992 and since 2017 an Amazon subsidiary) would attest.

I could see back then that 'books of things' were buying into this newly glamorous phase of things, which seemed ever more eager to tailor themselves to our desires. But I also couldn't help thinking that a melancholy awareness of potential scarcity also dogged at least some of these books; that part of their impulse was a fear that as the range of desirable things grew, something else was lost. *Cod* dealt directly with the mechanics of overfishing, while books about earlier fads, like the hunt for spices or rare orchids, took us back to a time of natural abundance, which the orchid hunters and spice hunters were partly responsible for depleting. Meanwhile, a largely unspoken attraction of books about perfume-making, Civil War-era farming, and glass-plate photography, was the fear that the old ways that sustained them were disappearing. The 'books of things' seemed haunted by a shadow story of disappearance every time they looked for the next object in need of attention.

Were these books trying too hard to distract us, with their busy stories of wonder, from a growing knowledge that the things of our making were displacing nature's riches? Because it's true, we did know. In 1992, in *The Great Deep*, his book of essays about the ocean, English author James Hamilton-Paterson was already pointing to this feeling of loss as our human activities depleted its grandeur. 'The mourning for landscape, this apprehension of death without a proper body to grieve over,' he wrote,

> is one of the century's cruellest legacies. It has often been recorded, but seems to have gone largely unremarked as a likely cause of common forms of despair and depression. For lack of any medically plausible origin these are presumably attributed to the usual domestic disorders, disappointments and jiltings; whereas in reality the sorrow may be far grander, more pervasive and unsolaced, its cause misunderstood by both sufferer and doctor.

I had come to feel that the 'books of things' also came out of an unconscious fear that all the bright new, disposable things with which we outnumbered ourselves were getting the upper hand. Enchanted things came with darker powers that this flurry of books sought, with urgency, to understand. The image that came to mind was the ending of John Carpenter's film, *The Thing*, in which the shape-shifting parasite that is able to take on the forms of other creatures, is killed, and disgorges in a frenzy all the life forms it has absorbed. In my original essay, I found myself wondering if these books of things were in fact books of Last Things, driven by the sense that things had somehow slipped out of our control. Like the possessions of the dead, they demanded satisfaction. What kind of a world did we want to live in? What sort of people would ignore its ongoing desecration?

By 2001, as *The New Yorker* fell back on its reflex of reaching for things, objects struggled to convey the gravity of the moment. In the context of the disaster at hand, Gopnik's enumeration of grosbeaks and Baltimore orioles seemed almost parodic. His smoked mozzarella analogy, meanwhile, was so notoriously off-key that critic James Wolcott would return to its 'hearty flavor' six years later, in his 2007 takedown (titled 'Smugged by Reality') of Gopnik's essay collection, *The Children's Gate*. ('I sometimes wonder,' the review began, 'if Adam Gopnik was put on this earth to annoy. If so, mission accomplished.') So would reviewers in *The Nation* ('New Yorkers may never forgive Adam Gopnik for writing, days after September 11, that the haze drifting north from Ground Zero smelled like an Italian delicacy'); *The New Criterion* ('This unwitting Hannibal Lecter routine is the least of Gopnik's problems'); and *The New Republic*, again ('Gopnik has a skill,' a different reviewer wrote, 'for shrinking everything in the universe to the scale of a bourgeois amenity'). Gopnik had also raised hackles with his perspective on downtown's destruction, noting, as he passed mums and children and hot-dog vendors, that the smoked mozzarella smell was 'not entirely horrible from a reasonable distance.'

The life of a renowned American magazine does not make a world, I know. But in my mind it marks a turn when things – and writers' heavy dependence on them – began to lose their shine. By 2006, in a review of several years of *Best American Stories*, the essayist Elif Batuman would announce her boredom at the endlessly repeated authorly strategy of 'trying to identify as many concrete entities as possible'. She was sick of the 'indiscriminate emphasis on the particular . . . as if literary worth should be calibrated by resemblance to an apple (or, in the lingo of hyperspecficity, a McIntosh).' As I struggled with my second novel,

I also found it difficult to take as much pleasure in the particular. In *The Service of Clouds*, I had dwelled on the odd heaviness of the Victorians' names for things or on the minutiae of processes like photography. It had seemed urgent to show the ways they attached to the dreams and desires of their time: the clouds in my book had, literally, changed shape according to the ideas about the air that were in circulation over the twenty-year span of my novel, growing less magnificent as the twentieth century came of age. Now the technique felt stale, to have exhausted itself. As a reader, I found myself rolling my eyes with impatience at other novels that lingered on the Bakelite of telephones or the tarmacadam surfaces of roads.

With the benefit of two decades' hindsight, I think things lost their magical powers for two reasons. The first was that, rather than being secret or neglected, or needing to be 'rescued,' material objects were, as the century turned, smotheringly ubiquitous. That smoked mozzarella and green salad were part of Gopnik's lexicon as a literary first responder seemed fitting in a Manhattan in the grip of rapid gentrification. A bolting pre-Great Financial Crisis economy meant the newly well-off, financed, and job-secure were moving, often with children, into the once-dangerous inner city and helping turn it from a dynamic ecosystem into real estate. The TV series *Sex and the City* would capture this change, as Manolo Blahnik shoes and Magnolia Bakery cupcakes became the real stars of the show. By 2006, in *The Children's Gate*, Gopnik, writing about life as a parent, would ruminate on the once-pejorative term 'Yuppie.' 'We were called that, derisively,' he crowed, 'before the world was ours.'

This shift wasn't only happening in Manhattan. Beijing was destroying its hutongs (its historical courtyard alleyways), London its old high street shops, as international capital, with its global but rapidly changing list of must-have designer objects, moved into big world cities. When we moved back to Sydney, in late 2001, its old factories and grand post offices and public administrative buildings were now – as they were in Melbourne – beginning new lives as luxury hotels, upmarket shopping arcades, and executive apartments. We would arrive at dinner parties to discover that the hosts had driven across Sydney to 'source' black chickens, or steaks from a popular boutique butchery. The power of things had not quite disappeared. Rather, it had been taken over by the international language of the market. To invoke things now was no longer to capture the pathos of daily life, as Gopnik clearly intended, but to be in their thrall; to enrol oneself in their logic of endless and dizzying succession. Like yuppies in Manhattan, the world now belonged to them.

But it was the internet that changed everything, as my student making a steady living from selling knitting patterns on eBay had discovered. It delivered a shouty cascade of trivial, absurd, ephemeral and ever-multiplying stuff. 'Close-ups of nail art,' as author Patricia Lockwood remembers,

> a pebble from outer space, a tarantula's compound eyes, a storm like canned peaches on the surface of Jupiter, Van Gogh's *Potato Eaters*, a chihuahua perched on a man's erection, a garage door spray-painted with the words 'STOP NOW! DON'T EMAIL MY WIFE!'

The net would drive an insatiable and ever-accelerating desire for things, multiplying and uncovering them until no object was secret or hidden. A straw poll of friends suggests that here in Australia we started buying books on Amazon around the turn of the millennium, followed by eBay and Etsy around 2004 or 2005. We would not really hit our stride until the decade's end, when we would find ourselves going online for everything: fashion, groceries, alcohol, furniture, antique jewellery, and takeaway, which would later soften the sting, for those us who could stay home, of the pandemic. On our first holiday backpacking together in Italy in the early 1990s, my partner and I had painstakingly carried home pretty hand-painted pottery from Assisi rolled up in our clothes. Now I can find such treasures in mere seconds and buy them with a click. The latest unsolicited issue of *Virtuoso Life*, the high-end travel magazine I receive in my mailbox for the sin of having booked a work flight with my local travel agent, informs me that, although cruise travel is at a halt because of Covid-19, I can nevertheless still order 'fun finds from my favourite hideaways': a scarf from Il Pellicano in Porto Ecole or 'ancient Greek sandals' from Le Sirenuse, Positano.

It is also far less difficult these days to find information about things, when so much, even the most niche or unusual, is online. Want to see some Harry Phillips photographs? They're on Flickr and Pinterest, while the viewbooks I sifted through Blue Mountains junk shops to find are for sale on eBay. Recently, surfing the net for the old dial-up modem sound – the hell's gate hissing and warped musical notes that used to accompany internet searches in the nineties – I found it in the Museum of Endangered Sounds, preserved alongside recordings of Tamagotchis, Gameboys, Nokia ringtones and the old Mac Warning, which seemed to protest too much ('*It's not my fault . . . It's not my fault . . . It's not my fault*').

Such instant access to stuff and its history is why more recent 'books of things' are less likely to meet with critical excitement. Besides, their epic claims now seem laughable. Now that things are massed in overwhelming numbers, to the point that even outer space is filled with 'a corona of trash' as author Raffi Khatchadourian puts it, it seems laughably naive to think any single object on its own could change the world.

You will still find 'books of things' on bookshop shelves these days. In fact, there seem to be more than ever. There are microhistories of hearts, the dead human body, cancer, blood, sex toys, oysters, forks, milk, salt, coffee, the colour indigo, cotton, and red hair, but their authors make fewer claims for their worldchanging importance. Over the last decade the genre has also given birth to a small sub-genre of 'thing books' that now openly lament the imminent disappearance of their chosen object, like handwriting, paper, snow, and ice. While they are no doubt still steady sellers, none seems likely to cause the same kind of sensation as those 'thing books' of the nineties. Instead, it's the writers with grand cultural or historical theories, like economist Thomas Piketty, chronicling the history of capital and inequality, or Isabel Wilson, with her analysis of caste systems across civilisations, or, more unfortunately, right-wing pundit Jordan Peterson deriding the undermining of 'Western values,' whose books are today's bestsellers.

Alongside the more familiar popular microhistories, you're now just as likely to find smaller, more modest titles, which explore their chosen objects without conferring gee-whiz stardom upon them. In Reaktion's 'Animal' series, which began in 2005 with *Fly*, writers pitch to write small biographies of single creatures, from bedbugs to bison. Rather than asking writers to track how their animal 'changed the world', the editors ask them instead to explore the 'historical significance and impact' humans have had upon it: a distinct turning of the tables from heroic history to victim impact statement, which recognises our collective impact as a species. Bloomsbury's 'Object Lessons' series, which began in 2015 with *Driver's Licence*, has an even more modest remit: to make 'concise, collectable, beautifully designed books about ordinary things.' Topics pitched by its writers have included the hashtag, blankets, burgers, hotels, rust, bread, eye charts, and the ubiquitous potato. Each book is a small, personal, essay, which is more likely to muse playfully on the different registers through which the object moves than to chart a grand, linear story for it.

These days, literary essay collections about things seem to have replaced thing-centred novels, but they are often modest and home-spun in approach. Amy Leach, Elena Passarello, Melissa Harrison, and Claire-Louise Bennetts' small, finely-observed essays about planets, animals, the weather and the life of a small body of water (*Things That Are, Animals Strike Curious Poses, Rain: Four Walks in English Weather*, and *Pond*) have a bespoke feel, finely-crafted words stitched around their objects like raised embroidery thread. The authors view their chosen objects in such idiosyncratic close-up that they seem to thumb their noses at the vaunting ambition of the older 'thing books.'

These quieter and smaller books about things exist in our new 'after,' in which our pollution and consumption are delivering terrifying consequences – a century sooner than we had been warned to expect them – in part because of our addiction to stuff. As biological life, in all its complexity, falls away, it now looks as if the objects we coveted and traded across continents for centuries made the world smaller, not larger. These more modest books can be thought of as small acts of salvage. Reliquaries for the intricate wonder of things we fear may not survive.

In retrospect, the appearance of 'books of things' in the nineties was, culturally our morning of 'severe clear'. The moment when, for the last time, we saw things in all their ambiguous power and beauty, before they began to overwhelm us.

Covid Walking: Diary

When coronavirus locked down the city, I began to walk every afternoon. Once I had crossed my busy local park, the streets were empty. My walks looped around the Darling Point escarpment and sometimes down the steep steps into Double Bay, as far as its harbour pool. On other afternoons, before dusk, I would walk in the opposite direction through Woolloomooloo and around Mrs Macquarie's Point, pacing the length of the naval yards across the bay. Sometimes I would loop from this walk through the gates of the Botanical Gardens and along its shadowed paths. Less often, instead of turning back home, I would keep going through the gates at the other side and into the deserted city, where it seemed I could see the buildings clearly for the first time since my childhood.

As I walked, I also began to take photographs on my phone. Posting a set online, I gave them a title: 'Covid Walking Moods'.

Without meaning to, I had started a project.

———

Because the square format was difficult to access on my new phone, I reloaded an old app I hadn't used for ten years, with 'lenses' and 'films' I swiped across the back of a virtual retro camera until they settled in place with a satisfying click.

Two settings – one colour, and one black and white – allowed me to recreate winter's subdued milky light.

The black and white photographs had a sensual graphite quality, powdery and shiny at once, like pencil sketches. You will have to take my word for the colour photographs' green shadows, luminous reds, and exaggerated viridescence.

The sprawling arms of an angophora, the scarred limbs and hanging roots of Moreton Bay figs. When my eye was in, things almost seemed to want to fit themselves inside the frame. Wild grasses leaned out from cliff stairways to catch the light. Rowboats, stacked on their ends, lined up attentively.

But what I liked best about this app was that the match between the 'viewfinder' and view was inexact. In order to catch

Covid Walking: Diary

the image I wanted, I had to move the camera into the approximate position, hold my breath, and click. As if I was sneaking up on them, I caught things slightly off-centre.

At dusk the high mansions loomed over the steep streets. On the flat, the marbled car parks beneath apartments stretched like crypts into the hillsides.

On fine days, as the sun sank, it cast rosy shadows across the western sides of the hills. The skies were mauve, peach, pink, and lemon yellow, the water glimpses a flat gold. On inclement days, whole weather fronts rushed through the eastern Heads, or from the west.

Sometimes I would also take short film clips, especially if I arrived at the end of Darling Point at the same time as the small ferry from the city as it described a fast arc through the thin light to briefly pause and take off again. There were so few commuters that often the attendant didn't bother to throw the rope loop around the pylon on the wharf, or set out the gangplank, as the engines churned. At home, I could watch these small videos again and again.

These clips, shot between the trunks of the park's angophoras, were often the most liked online. No matter how empty the ferries were, the recorded message in a male voice still sounded out, the hull of the ferry still clanked and groaned. Watching the footage, a friend wrote, made her want to cry.

These walks had become the highlight of my days. But what was I doing as I took them? It had become fashionable to write about the pleasures of *flâneurie* but I didn't feel like an idle stroller in my half-abandoned city. Always a stopper and starer at peculiar detail, I was looking as I'd never looked before. Perhaps I was more like Gustave Doré's 'New Zealander.' In the final illustration in Thomas Macauley's *London: A Pilgrimage*, this visitor from the future sits on a rock to sketch the ruins of London across the water.

The Victorian critic John Ruskin believed that every person should learn to draw and take a notepad with them. The sketcher's eye becomes:

> accustomed to search into the cause of beauty, and penetrate the minutest parts of loveliness. He looks up, and observes how the showery and subdivided sunshine comes sprinkled down among the gleaming leaves overhead, till the air is filled with the emerald light, and the motes dance in the green,

glittering lines that shoot down upon the thicker masses of clustered foliage that stand out so bright and beautiful from the dark, retiring shadows of the inner tree, where the white light again comes flashing in from behind, like showers of stars . . .

But as I walked, I was doing something between glimpsing and staring. I would catch a mood and study the details of my pictures later.

Each time I passed the Covid-19 testing centre in its tent beside the cruising yacht club, an old slipway behind it, I crossed to the other side of the street.

One evening, on the long, curved street at the back of Darling Point, I came across a man in plastic booties and scrubs, putting his test kit into the boot of his hatchback after a home visit. We pretended we didn't see each other.

I have walked for twenty years around these parks and streets. I have walked with my children and I have walked through two tragedies. I could tell you that a skipping rope on asphalt sounds like the heartbeat on a foetal ultrasound. Yet I have always felt lifted up by my city's melancholy loveliness. And now, as I walked through autumn, and then into winter, it didn't let me down.

In his book about the Aboriginal people who managed to stay in coastal Sydney well into the nineteenth century, Paul Irish describes their movements between different parts of their Country, to see family and remake connections, as 'beats.' A beat can also be the movement of a bird's wings, a rhythm, a pulse, a hesitation, a heartbeat, the action of sailing into the wind or vigorously stirring, or, geographically, an area patrolled by foot; gay men subverted this formal term for a policeman's allocated area into the gloriously informal, to denote an area regularly cruised for sex. In Melbourne, I used to drive a carless friend to the beats in Richmond, Fitzroy, Preston and North Carlton. (I dropped him off. I didn't wait). A beat can even be a stretch of water fished by an angler. Perhaps it's overly romantic to imagine that most of these meanings, of amplitude and rhythm and deep life, defined Indigenous people's traversal and visiting of Country, which was also, I know, philosophy and law.

These were my own – though also, history told me, not my own – areas of special interest, which I needed to see, to feel with the measure of my feet and eyes.

'After-comers cannot guess the beauty been,' wrote Gerard Manley Hopkins in 'Binsey Poplars.' I didn't know if I was recording a strange pause as I took these photographs, or something that had been lost already.

Louis Daguerre, I remembered, announced that he could 'seize the light,' whereas Henry Fox Talbot described his process as 'fixing a shadow.'

Nightfall. The Marathon Stairs – known in their day as the 'break-neck' flight – stretch upward from Double Bay. In the lee of an enormous fig tree, a lone jogger runs up into blackness. At the top of the stairs, where they are cut by the steep angle of a curb, the word MARATHON writes itself out of the darkness in darker shadow.

>Flowering grevillea, its centre a bloom of haze.
>The graffitied trunk of a weeping fig.
>Heart of a cycad, frosted by light.

French philosopher Roland Barthes wrote that the photograph moves us when it contains a wound: some detail that seems to sit outside the photographer's intention, which he called the 'punctum.' The small injury asks us to recognise the singularity of existence. It holds our gaze without condescending to mere beauty.

The picture is bound to the real like those pairs of fish, he writes, which navigate in convoy, as though united by eternal coitus.

The photograph always asks us, why this moment, and not some other?

The golden sunset, photographed through jacaranda branches as I walked west, made silhouettes of the tiny seriffed leaves.

An ibis, on a footpath, tagged by its crooked shadow.

Beyond our borders, the virus spread. In America, as thousands died, one newspaper dedicated a section to those who had been lost to put faces to the numbers, like its portraits after 9/11. But this time, the editors wrote, 'There was no finite number of the dead. No geographical point united them. Their backgrounds were of infinite variety. They did not die all at once on a bright blue morning.'

It was dizzying to scroll down as, beneath each photo of a small-town doctor or tribal judge or student, a life unfolded in all its ordinary and extraordinary detail.

In 1789, fifteen months after invasion, smallpox spread to the Indigenous Sydney people. This landscape of small beaches and rock overhangs in which I walked was already haunted by the trauma of an earlier pandemic. The Eora were found, according to First Fleet sailor Newton Fowell, 'laying Dead on the Beaches and in the Caverns of Rocks,' often with a small fire on either side of them and 'some Water placed within their Reach.'

Judge-Advocate David Collins would record visiting different coves with an unnamed Aboriginal man, who looked around anxiously for his people: 'He lifted his hands and eyes in silent agony for some time,' wrote Collins, until 'at last he exclaimed, "All dead! all dead!" and then hung his head in mournful silence, which he preserved during the remainder of our excursion.'

Out of a hedge of vertical sticks, a single magnolia bud, the shape of a lamb's foot.

In a quiet dead-end street in Darling Point, I remember, I once looked down into the low garden of a block of flats, to see a young lamb tiptoeing along its paths.

Like honeybees and earthworms, the virus travelled ahead of the frontier. The Sydney people, fleeing the rapidly spreading outbreak, took the disease with them, passing it through their complex networks that stretched across the country. Settlers moving into areas it had already swept through assumed they had always been as sparsely peopled.

For Roland Barthes, the second wound photographs contained was our knowledge that everything they depicted would die.

Once, he wrote, he had come across a photograph of Napoleon's brother. He was amazed to be looking at the eyes that had looked upon the emperor, but no one else seemed to share his excitement, or even understand it.

'Life,' he wrote, 'consists of these little touches of solitude.'

In films, it's the establishment and tracking shots that move me, in which time and landscape mark out their presence.

The end of Paul Cox's film, *Man of Flowers*: the lonely misfit looks out from a sunset cliff, as seagulls – innocent of the film's high art ambitions – wheel over the sea in the sunset. At the end of Paolo Sorrentino's *The Great Beauty*, a single, long, tracking shot follows the Tiber in Rome as the grey river goes about its ancient business and I am struck to the heart each time I watch it. In Carlos Reygadas's *Japón*, all the children of a poor Mexican pueblo pass the camera – real children, not child actors – on their way to a drawing lesson. In their faces – shy, gentle, greedy, mean – all of human nature seems to pass by.

Looking at a series of takes by documentary maker Timothy Treadwell before he was killed by a bear – of low Alaskan bush, moving in soft wind – director Werner Herzog was moved to remark on the strange secret beauty of these seemingly empty moments. 'Sometimes images themselves develop their own life, their own mysterious stardom.'

Like Barthes, I had no interest in whether my photographs were art. In fact, I liked the way they weren't. They held the record of my body's movements, along with the blunt will or intention, it seemed to me, of the things they depicted.

Barthes's investigation of photography turned, at a certain point in his book, into the 'rediscovery' of his recently deceased mother. It was being in deep mourning that allowed him to understand the way that photographs repeated a momentary instance to infinity. Looking at a photograph of his adored mother's face when she was five, Roland Barthes wrote in *Camera Lucida*, he was moved by 'the impossible science of the unique being.'

Misty rain, and the ferry closes in on the wharf through flat water. A speedboat passes slowly behind it, its wake a white scratch in a seascape of blues.

In the black and white photographs I took, there was something disconcerting about the way they imitated the old processes: colloidal silver grains suspended in gelatine, from the feet of dead cows and albumen, which is egg white. I still remember the pleasure of taking a photography course in the eighties, of watching the prints develop in their baths, of pegging up the wet paper to dry.

In those processes, which draw on the organic and the elemental, the 'fatality' Barthes perceived in photography was made explicit. Was there more or less deathliness about my photographs, now my phone could do their work, in an instant, in my hand?

Some years ago, walking along a Darling Point footpath in spring, I glanced down to see grey noisy miner chicks looking back expectantly, from their hiding place in a low star jasmine border.

In novels, it's the longueurs I remember.

In Tolstoy's *Anna Karenina*, the grass cutting scene takes up several chapters in the middle of the novel:

> The longer Levin mowed, the oftener he felt the moments of unconsciousness in which it seemed not his hands that swung the scythe, but the scythe moving of itself, a body full of life and consciousness of its own, and as though by magic, without thinking of it, the work turned out regular and well-finished of itself. These were the most blissful moments.

I once read that the photographer Brassaï, famous for his night scenes of Paris, used cigarettes to time his long exposures. A Gauloise for a certain light, a Boyard if it was darker. I believe those slim and beautiful cigarettes are in the photos too, just as Bruce Chatwin maintained that whatever he erased remained as a kind of ghost within his texts.

Today night and interior photos no longer hold these small dramas of breath and time within themselves. And yet, when I look at mine, I seem to see an epoch passing, in all the small and quotidian things that define us.

In *Death Comes for the Archbishop*, Willa Cather records, she aimed to write without accent, to touch moments of her story and pass on. She wanted her novel to be like those lives of the saints in which trivial incidents are treated with the same attention as their martyrdom.

Although I also like novels written in a ravishing recherché, it's this type of book I love most, whose images unroll, untouchably themselves.

How often I've wondered, as a novelist, if my job is less to tell stories than to catch a particular fall of light, the curve of a tree limb, those in-between moments when whole ways of being reveal themselves.

In colour, wisteria tendrils draw fluorescent scribbles above a footpath.

A topiarised tree in a pot corkscrews skyward.

Between buildings, gold light reflects itself across a narrow walkway.

It has always struck me that light itself is a kind of wound, like the punctum that holds the gaze in Barthes's photograph: particular, historical, and poignant.

'Our light was not your light, ours was restrained,' the narrator of one of my aborted novels, which is set in 1899, begins.

> It was just as it appears in our photographs. A dim skein stretched out between a spire and a clockface. A luminous blankness at the end of our wide streets. It was not hard, like your light. It was not full of details. Our shades were pensive, our skies absorbed our feelings. Women, alert and straight-backed, staked out sloping stretches of grey lawn for a picnic. Boats drifted like the thought of sex across the corners of our eyes. There was something flat about the light as we moved through it, as if it had been pressed between the sky and some great reflecting surface, the way the sun jellies in still water just before the dusk.

Covid Walking: Diary

The top of a white garage, a harsh glow from its uplight. Thin winter branches vein the dimming sky above.

These days, writes author David Shields, life 'flies at us in bright splinters' and we are increasingly hungry for the real. We no longer experience it, if we ever did, as a coherent fathomable whole and so it's nonfiction – as personal and flawed and cut-about as possible – which makes more sense than the novel, with its urge for coherence. But I have never read fiction, I realise, for its morals or its stories. It seems to me I have always read it for tone, and for its small, intense bursts of place and time.

The novelist I. Allen Sealey uses light to open his Anglo-Indian chronicle, *The Trotternama*. 'Icelight', he writes, is

> the slippery, spermy light that comes just before dawn. It freezes time, or rather, traps it at the tremulous point just short of freezing, when time is neither solid nor liquid but simply a quality of light ... It allows you to get the past down, to copy it, after it's actually melted away.

We have always loved ruins, in the West. But it may be that we're living now among the ruins of life itself. Scientists speak of 'ghost species': populations of creatures that still live but are functionally extinct. A ghost species, writes English nature writer Robert McFarlane, 'is a species that has been out-evolved by its environment.'

This virus may be a sign of our own foreshortened future. Some scientists suggest that it has come about because we have invaded the last wild places, brought the creatures from their homes into our markets, shaking viruses loose from their natural hosts, to find new hosts in us. They warn that this is the beginning of a new era of pandemics.

What if our cities are already ruins as we live in them, I wondered as I walked? Could a flower be a ruin? A park bench? A Moreton Bay fig? The air? Us?

When my son was three, he turned to me with a mysterious look on his face after he woke up from his nap. 'When the sun burns out,' he said, 'we will all turn into birds.'

As the lockdown eased a little, my mother died. I knew I was fortunate, restrictions having lessened, to be able to sit with her over the long afternoon as she took her last breaths. To be able to watch her face, to touch her hand, as the signs of vital life ticked down.

Is she dying now? I asked the nurse. There is kindness in an honest answer.

In one of my favourite novels, Jim Crace's *Being Dead*, an English couple, middle-aged scientists, are murdered by a stranger as they make love in coastal sand dunes. As the novel traces their decomposition in its forward narrative, its other narrative traces their lives back to the past. It is a book full of life and grace, of tender observation.

A hundred years ago, Crace writes, the pair's family and neighbours would have held a midnight *quivering* for them, where they could be lamented hysterically, without embarrassment. Once they had been laid out, the mourners – women first – would weep 'till their shoulders shook, tapping on the floorboards with their boots and sticks, rattling their bracelets and their cuffs.' When the men arrived, 'all the guests would stand to form a circle round the bed. They'd grip the mattress and the bedboards, a shoal of hands, to *quiver* the murdered couple, winnowing and shaking out their wrongdoings so that they'd enter heaven unopposed.' Then, as dawn approached, they would quietly reminisce, reversing the sands of the couple's lives, from their last few months, back to the wonders of their births; 'how sweet and difficult they'd been, how promising, how loved.'

Maybe that's what I'd been doing, posting these small photographs.

'*Quiverings*,' writes Crace, 'were resurrections of the dead.'

In 1940, the Jewish-German philosopher Max Horkheimer wrote in a letter to a friend: 'In view of what is now threatening to engulf Europe and perhaps the world, our work is essentially designed to pass things down through the night that is approaching: a kind of message in a bottle.'

Now, at the same time as we mourn the dead, there is the question of whether new generations will stretch into the future ahead of us. Of death without an echo.

Of all the words for our moment, writes academic Steve Mentz, the Homogenocene scares him most. The end point of our apparently endless hunger for expansion is that everything will become the same as everything else; every ocean in its heat death a home only to jellyfish. 'I am afraid,' he writes, 'of losing differences and distinctions into sameness.'

In wealthy Darling Point a metal-railed stairway still held on. It stretched behind the paling fences of low units, along a roughly hewn cliff that wept, into a bed of dark monstera deliciosa at the side of an old gatehouse.

These old eastern suburbs plantings, wrote novelist Patrick White, were 'associated with my own private mysteries . . . moss-upholstered steps . . . the monstera deliciosa, a rich mattress of slater-infested humus under the custard apples.'

As the days grew longer, great fronts still passed over the escarpment.

In one colour photo, taken after a storm, the clouds have pulled away from the horizon to reveal a plasma-coloured sky and thin violet clouds. In the foreground, on the lawn outside an apartment block, two magpies watch me alertly.

My photographs, caught on the move, continued to sustain me. If I had set out with the intention of taking them, they would have felt stilted, over-arranged. Instead, each was a small gift, a tiny registration of haphazard life – and a rebuff to my tendency to see the world in grimly overdetermined terms.

It always moved me, when my children were smaller and we walked past the old age home at the end of our street, that they never saw age or time when they looked up into the rooms. That girl is wearing a hat, they said. That boy is watching the soccer.

Covid Walking: Diary

Jon Constable, the painter of clouds over English fields, would spend hours lying on his back observing the sky before heading home to paint. 'I have done a good deal of skying,' he wrote. I was also skying, in my own small way, in my city where the low and humid atmosphere seemed to settle into each image, where sky and sea were particularly bound together.

On the pontoon in the middle of the sea baths, whose splintery boundary I walked, two men sat companionably together, sky and water the same blue.

Now, as I walked by the gallery, there was tight young fruit at the ends of the Moreton Bay figs' dark leaves. The hanging draperies of their roots were tasselled and hairy, like desiccated nervous systems.

By February of 2021, it would be estimated that 20.5 million years of human life had been lost globally to Covid-19.

And yet, for all the sad eeriness of their conception, my photos filled me with joy. The things I passed daily had never seemed so alive or miraculous as they pushed and danced their way into my photographs' square frames.

Our job now, I'd read, was to try to imagine the unimaginable. But there was something to be said, too, for witnessing. If we can't love something, how can we want to save it?

———

On seeing John Gould's display of stuffed hummingbirds at the Great Exhibition in the Crystal Palace, John Ruskin declared that he had made a great mistake in wasting his life on mineralogy rather than devoting himself to studying the life and plumage of birds. If only he could only have seen a hummingbird fly, Ruskin believed, it would have been an 'epoch' in his own existence. 'Just think what a happy life Mr Gould's must have been,' he is reported to have said, '– what a happy life!'

*

After the restrictions on travel ended, in spring, we headed down the south coast. The fire-blackened trunks of the gums were bright green with panic growth. I took a few more photographs – grass trees in flower, the pale trunks of banksias – but these would be among the last.

Covid Walking: Diary

The urge to take these photographs had passed.

In Foxground, I continued to walk each day, this time along the road that runs beneath the escarpment to a dead end, and back.

Why did we have to take the same walk so many times, my daughter asked me, one afternoon, as we crossed the cattle grid into the paddocks of a long-gone property cut into the rainforest, where the road became a track. Because, I said, I liked to try to understand a single, small place better. Each time we walked here I could see what was the same and what had changed – and new things can always surprise us.

As I spoke I caught sight of something large stirring in the high vines by the road's edge, where the forest canopy met the ruins of an old wall. I put my hands on my daughter's shoulders and drew her close, feeling the hot blood beneath her skin, as we peered out of the shadows.

Standing on its hind legs, feet up against the stone as it reached to feed on shoots and berries, was a feral goat: a huge beast with horns and a fleece as hairy and magnificent as the illustrations in my childhood book of Greek myths. As we flattened ourselves back into the lantana, the rest of its flock joined it from the forest, tearing loudly at the foliage. Then a plane, back in its regular flight path, passed overhead and with a pounding of hooves, they took off, into the valley.

Everything is Illuminated

Forget its telegenic cast: the real star of *CSI: Crime Scene Investigation* was Luminol. If beams of neo-noir torchlight defined the look of nineties television shows like *The X-Files*, eerie chemiluminescence was its twenty-first century successor. Luminol is a chemical that makes invisible traces of old blood glow blue, as if registering death's secret neon. Luminous haemoglobin-reactive streaks and blooms became the show's visual signature – bloody shoeprints, mop marks, tentacular splashes around plugholes, the walls of a suburban lounge room transformed into a theatre of struggle. The genius of the series, which ran for the first fifteen years of this century, was to match this aesthetic of deathly illumination with a place that had itself been transformed by neon from a small western town into a gamblers' city of sleepless brilliance. Each episode opened with a sequence of shots of Las Vegas's desert sunsets and shining casinos in hyperreal colour as if the city had also been sprayed with some agent to offer itself up, radiant and eerie, to our gaze.

I never watched *CSI* for the drama, I watched it for the light. For the exaggerated sheen on the roofs of new tract houses on the desert's edge as the camera panned across them; for underlit laboratories as sleek as display kitchens; for the gold of a desert sunset igniting a suburban lounge room. I loved its saturated colours, the waxy polish of black cars, the implacable, even gleam of its cobalt blues and pinky purples. In *CSI*, light inhabited every surface, rendering animate and inanimate equally charismatic. The show's manipulated effects – shot on 35mm film using coloured gels with contrast exaggerated in post-production – were pregnant with portent. Gliding above the city's casinos and empty lots, the camera would sometimes stutter, as if what it recorded was on the edge of flaring into further brightness. Even human flesh appeared to be lit up from within, as the camera plunged through it in the show's ground-breaking 'in-wound' animations. The cinematography was so self-conscious, its slick brilliance so intent on playing out its own technical dramas each week, that it overwhelmed the series' storylines and human cast.

By 2005, *CSI: Las Vegas* had become the most popular program in the world. It was a franchise by then, having spawned spin-offs set in Miami (the second most popular program in the world that same year) and New York. It would be accused of influencing jury verdicts and credited with popularising forensic science as a career.

What was it about this show that meant a global audience couldn't get enough of its brilliant play of blood and chemical light?

*

Luminol makes its first appearance in 'Who Are You?,' the sixth episode of the first series of *CSI*. When a woman's skeletal remains turn up in the foundations of a tract home, fleshy head CSI Grissom (William Petersen) and offsider Stokes (George Eads) suspect she has been murdered by her ex-boyfriend. Finding traces of aquarium sand beneath a carpet, they guess this was the site of a violent altercation and spray the floor with Luminol – but it fails to react. Grissom explains that it only works on surface traces of blood and calls for the Alternative Light Source (ALS). As he kneels and points a thin tubular torch attached to a power unit at the area, its concentrated beam suffuses the floor with a light as blue as a Madonna's robe. As it penetrates the maple floorboards, occult (hidden) blood traces spring to life as electric blue spatters, streaks, and handprints. The failure in this first scene is a marvellous flourish. It draws our attention, like a tightrope walker's feigned wobble, to the wonder of this technology while training us to anticipate the many successful Luminol scenes that will follow. It establishes a deep and addictive aesthetic connection – which infuses all of *CSI*'s light effects – between death, revelation and chemiluminescence.

The following episode, 'Blood Drops,' is one of the most beautiful and baroque in the entire series. Although Luminol is not used, the episode marries blood and glowing light to the 'occult' in its other sense, of something supernatural and mysterious. When the entire forensic team is called to a house where a multiple homicide has occurred, they find the bodies of a father, mother, and two sons: the two daughters, a teenager and a five-year-old, have survived. The spilled blood is still fresh – the house smells strongly of copper, Grissom, the most skilled and sensitive of the CSIs, remarks to a younger police detective. As they climb the stairs it congeals in pools and odd circular patterns on the walls. Part of the team's work will be to correlate the sprays and soakings into a pattern that makes sense. As Grissom begins to work with Sara Sidle (Jorja Fox) on the mother, who has been slain in bed, they stop talking as they become aware of a soft patter. The woman's blood is still dripping onto the floor. That's not all – her soul is still in the room, Sidle observes quietly. Later, the two will note that the killer has also 'left something of himself' in the house.

No episode of *CSI* is more disturbing than 'Blood Drops.' It taps into the odd energy of crime scene photography, which Australian writer and curator Ross Gibson points out can be strangely beautiful in the haphazard aesthetic arrangements it creates and the sense of portent it conveys to objects; for until it is solved a crime scene remains literally 'unfinished'. Crime scene photographs document 'bruised places', Gibson writes. They are sites of a great spiritual force, 'vehemently disturbed and disturbing,' where 'incursions from the other side of supposed decency' have taken place. In 'Blood Drops,' light carries the potent weight of the invisible; it appears almost sentient. Slick highlights render domestic objects sinister. The camera dwells on family photographs in the stairwell, and their china rabbits that proliferate, as kitschy and shiny as Jeff Koons's famous stainless steel 'Rabbit,' on the front lawn beneath their mailbox. This supercharged light plasters itself to the living, too, as if with intent. As he approaches the house, the strobes of emergency vehicles play across Grissom's face and later, as she sits in the police car, they seem attracted in swarms to Dakota Fanning's baby-soft golden hair. 'Normal' colours also seem chemiluminescent – the hyperreal green of the lawn, the aquarium blues of the shadows – as if colour, like blood, is pooling around and beneath things. The lurid light is filled with the threat that every surface harbours latent violence.

This uneasy promise of revelation reaches its high point when Sidle uses an ultra-violet camera on Dakota Fanning's chest to reveal a tracery of bruises beneath her translucent skin.

Throughout the series, but especially in these early episodes, the light of *CSI* is omnipresent, perfuse, and mysterious in provenance. Like chemiluminescence, it appears to have an almost Biblical ability to bring itself forth out of darkness, rather than to emanate from any logical light source. The early theoreticians of optics believed that light wasn't reflected by objects but a quality intrinsic to them; that their radiated beams actually penetrated the eye. The light of *CSI* has a similarly personal quality, seeking people and things out, at the same time as its hyperreal shine makes banal locales uncanny. As lean ex-stripper Willows and Grissom search for body parts in a desert turned yellow by post-production manipulation, they walk through viscous sunlight that seems as pregnant with significance as the gold-leaf background of a Byzantine church mosaic. It is as if – as we watch a car move along a desert road between intense tangerine sky and paler desert, or Grissom, silhouetted on a pedestrian crossing within a dusk of unnaturally even, tender blue – we are being asked to believe in a more ancient notion of the air, infused with divine intent.

Within this glowing enchantment of the everyday, inanimate objects loom large. They frequently occupy the foreground of scenes – the pink heel of a patent leather stiletto glistening in close-up, a jagged fragment of toenail glowing in a pair of tweezers, creamy and translucent. They bask in their own sleek glamour, or flare into brightness. In the opening credits, Brown (Gary Dourdan), his own face shadowed, holds a sandshoe to the light as its unfurled laces fluoresce into whiteness. In another episode, a supermarket is flooded so intensely with white light that spilled bags of peas and broken boxes of washing powder almost vibrate with danger. In the universe of *CSI*, it is as if a revolution has taken place and the material things of this world have emerged from their mute service and now assert dominance over the human.

*

There is another kind of cold light that manifests eerily out of darkness and that is bioluminescence. When I was twelve, I travelled with my parents to the Waitomo Caves in New Zealand's North Island. A guide propelled us in a boat on an underground river via ropes strung along the cave's roof. He asked us to be quiet, turned off his headlamp, and the gallery above us ignited softly into an internal dawn of cool blue light. Each tiny, alert point of brightness hung in a nest of sticky silk threads, some looping like spun sugar and others like filamentous stalactites. *Titiwai*, the Maori name for these glow worms (which are actually not worms but insect larvae) means 'projected over water'. Although each larva possesses a specialised light organ at the posterior end of its body the name captures the arresting sense that the reflections in the dark river and radiant insects were a mysterious whole, a glimmering reef of living light. I would remember them when I visited the indoor pool at Randolph Hearst's Castle in California, its mosaic ceiling and floor a continuous field of gold patterns on dark blue. Swimming there at night, a film star is reported to have said, was like being suspended in a galaxy, unsure of up or down or where water and air ended.

The ability of creatures that live beyond the sun's reach to manifest light has fascinated us since ancient times. Aristotle described the bioluminescence of dinoflagellates in the ocean as 'exhalations of fire from the sea.' Pliny the Elder recommended rubbing the slime of a luminous jellyfish onto a walking stick to make a torch. Indigenous people in Indonesia used bioluminescent fungi as flashlights in thick forests.

The phenomenon is rare in land animals (along with glow worms and fireflies, some earthworms, beetles and millipedes can glow) but many underwater creatures can manufacture light. In the Second World War, the Japanese army harvested ostracods, or sea fireflies, from the ocean. Soldiers added water to their dried bodies to produce a cold blue that was bright enough for them to read maps by without giving away their positions. Photographed in glowing close-up, an ostracod is shaped like a luminous bean that is just beginning to sprout, tiny filaments fringing most of its flat rim, although its insides, pale cyan marbled with aqua, resemble a tiny sea-covered planet. In 1955, the Japanese scientist and future Nobel Prize winner Osamu Shimomura extracted luciferin from ostracods to analyse its molecular structure. He discovered that the luciferase enzyme catalyses a reaction between luciferin and oxygen to produce light, not only in these tiny creatures, but also in jellyfish. (Spare a thought for those jellyfish, *Aequorea Victoria*, which were strained 'like cider apples,' according to one text, for their glowing 'squeezate'). Recently, scientists have learned that ostracods emerge each night, just after sunset, from sea grass beds and coral reefs, to put on their light shows. The males emit blobs of radiant mucus, in strings; a different spacing for each species. The females follow these 'strings of pearls' to find a mate. Deep sea biologist Edith Widder believes marine bioluminescence is 'the most common, most eloquent language on earth.'

Living things that glow are enchanting but disturbing. Their ability to manufacture their own light without fire seems otherworldly. In religious iconography a halo or glowing body often designated divine beings. Less well-intentioned creatures could also be light-bringers, like fairies, or the mythical *alicanto* of Chile's Atacama Desert, whose wings and eyes were said to emit strange lights; miners believed that if they followed the nocturnal bird it might lead them to mineral outcrops or hidden treasure but if it sensed it was being followed it would turn off its luminescence or entice them off a cliff. The Romans associated bioluminescent (or 'burning') seas with premonitions while Italians of the Middle Ages had a dread fear of fireflies, which they believed embodied the spirits of their dead.

The most unnerving example of the eeriniess of bioluminescence comes out of America. In the Civil War, some soldiers' wounds were observed to glow. When taken to hospital, these patients were more likely to survive; a phenomenon that remained a mystery until this century when two schoolboys working on a science project developed the hypothesis that soil-dwelling *Heterorhabditis* nematodes were drawn to hypothermic soldiers' wounds if their body temperatures became low enough to provide a host environment. These parasitic worms were themselves hosts to the *Photorhabdus luminescens* (*P. luminescens*) bacterium. When the nematodes vomited the bioluminescent bacteria onto wounds to begin the digestive process, they fluoresced while killing the competing microorganisms that caused gangrene. This phenomenon came to be known as 'Angel's Glow.'

*

In the normal course of things, humans do not have the ability to bioluminesce – or at least not much. In 2009, scientist Masaki Kobayashi, photographed volunteers with ultra-light-sensitive cameras, which registered small light emissions a thousand times weaker than the human eye is capable of seeing. These followed a 24-hour cycle, with emissions most present in the late afternoon and dimmest late at night. The subjects' cheeks, foreheads and necks emitted the brightest light. Yet it was the *dead* in *CSI* who seemed luminous, to hover between earthly and unearthly. Gilded by light, their faces often peaceful, they acquired an odd and intimate grace – a kind of aura – from the sober attention the investigators conferred upon them. The series' Miami franchise would push this intimacy to an almost parodic level as its chic-but-maternal coroner Alexx Woods (Khandi Alexander) caressed and spoke softly to the bodies on her slab. Even petrified, waterlogged, or burned, they were rarely disgusting, at least to the investigators who worked on them.

This beautification of the dead on our screens was new. Since *Quincy: M.E.* (1976–1983) became the first television series to feature a coroner, forensic television had traded on horror and heroics. In *Quincy*'s opening credits, a beaten-up Jack Klugman pulled the sheet off a corpse in a grim autopsy lab in front of a row of fainting and vomiting police cadets, although the body on the slab remained decorously out of shot. By the nineties films like *The Silence of the Lambs* were dwelling on the abject horror of bloated and mutilated bodies, which were almost invariably female and often the victims of serial killers; a kind of corpse porn that would become a staple in series like *True Detective*. By contrast, *CSI*'s autopsy rooms and laboratories were as glossy as a Bang & Olufsen catalogue, as exquisitely lit as Howard Carter's 1923 photographs of King Tutankhamun's tomb. (In fact, before he joined Howard Carter's expedition, photographer Harry Burton had travelled to Hollywood to learn the craft of cinematographic lighting).

In *CSI: Las Vegas* everything glowed and gleamed, as if the advertisements had leaked from the ad breaks into the program itself. The same highlights that plastered themselves to computers and handbags now gilded the autopsy room and everything within it. The series' baroque colour manipulations were closer to Baz Luhrmann's dreamy, light-soaked advertisements starring Nicole Kidman for Chanel than a gritty police procedural. Meanwhile, *CSI*'s glamorous actors, like Marg Helgenberger – whose sun-ravaged face and strawberry blonde hair the camera dwelt upon – were good-looking enough to be models. As they worked, the slick lustre of the manipulated light effects seemed to want to transform them – with a kind of ruthless appetite – into gorgeous objects. Even the things that dead victims had touched seemed burnished by their desires. They brooded and glowed with the dramas of blood; they might even be imbued with the spirits of the dead. The glossiness stuck to everything like an ersatz 'Angel's Glow.'

The visual language *CSI* deployed was that of glamour: the closest thing we have come up with to satisfy our desire to radiate light ourselves. Glamour transports the people, things and spaces it touches into a shining realm that exceeds the limits of the earthly. It's no coincidence that famous Hollywood actors became known as 'stars.' The world glamour conjures is half-imaginary and half-real, holding us to ideals that can never quite be attained in real life. It coats everything with an aura determined by the market, which, like a rainbow, recedes as quickly as we try to grasp it. Objects endowed with glamour are, in one academic's felicitous description, 'phosphorescent.'

Glossy colours and textures are central to glamour. Academic Nigel Thrift writes that late-twentieth century advertisers quickly worked out that new computer technology could pigment almost any material with shades that reached the limits of human colour perception. Thrift writes that while the materials we associate with glamour have always shone, designers have made them even more alluring and tactile over the last decades: plastics can now reproduce the effects of mother of pearl, diamond, speckled glass, metal and stone. He describes the Los Angeles Prada store, a temple of glamour, which sports black and white marble, aluminium, zebrawood, gel waves, polyester screens, silicone bubbles, and laminated glass that fades from translucent to transparent – along with eighty different kinds of light. Our desire for luminescence only seems to grow. On a recent visit to a Mecca Cosmetica store I was struck by the huge range of makeup products that offered to endow my skin with 'glow' and 'radiance,' along with a dazzling array of facial 'polishes,' 'highlighters,' and 'illuminators.'

It's no coincidence that when *CSI: Las Vegas* first went to air, the city was also undergoing a make-over into a more glamorous destination. A big part of this transformation was the banishment of its famous neon. By the time *CSI* aired, this 'liquid fire' (neon gas captured in tubes of glass and set to scintillate, blink, and shimmer) had come to be associated with seedy casinos, bankrolled by mob money, which were part of a libidinous night-time economy that invited people to forget the daylight world. Urban theorists of the 1960s had been fascinated by the city's brilliant light displays, which made architecture transcend its own limits as buildings disappeared beneath throbbing facades that endlessly drew, erased, and rewrote themselves. But perhaps no homage to its gaudy melancholy was more exuberant than director Franc Roddam's Las Vegas sequence for the 1987 film *Aria*, in which ten directors were invited to create film clips for operatic arias. Roddam chose Wagner's 'Liebestod,' his camera dwelling on a young Brigid Fonda and James Mathers as they drove from the desert, through the strip's enormous crimson-and-orange blooms, to cut their wrists in a hotel bathtub. This was an image Las Vegas was eager to leave behind. The Italianate Bellagio, whose vast frontage featured lit-up fountains that 'danced' to music, and whose lobby roof featured 600 illuminated glass flowers, was typical, when it opened in 1998, of the new generation of 'luxury' casinos intent on replacing seaminess with a more glamorous patina. *CSI*'s slicker and more sophisticated aesthetic mirrored the city's reinvention, in which the old neon-clad casinos, like The Stardust, The Mint, and The Dunes, were exploded into the desert dust while their baroque signage was sent to the city's Neon Graveyard.

But it wasn't just *CSI*, or Las Vegas – as the millennium turned, the whole culture was pivoting towards glamour as its dominant and inescapable aesthetic. Luxuries once associated with the rich were rebranding themselves from aspirational to democratic necessities that could turn us all into 'celebrities.' Cruises were newly glamorous (or at least pretended to be); so were food, couture handbags, plastic surgery and dental veneers; stretch limousines would even become a staple of school formals. In 2005, as *CSI* dominated world ratings, the *Real Housewives of Orange County* premiered, a show about wealthy American women leading 'glamorous lives . . . in a California gated community,' who didn't blink at flying to an exclusive island for a weekend on a private jet; and it would spawn its own franchise (with series in New York, Beverly Hills, Dallas, New Jersey, Atlanta, and even Melbourne and Sydney). Although some social commentators contend that a new 'Gilded Age' had been building since the eighties, it seemed to have gone platinum by the 2000s. The goal was to get as close as possible to the lifestyle of the ultra-rich, for whom life was always predictably clean and shiny – and, once even slightly tarnished, disposable.

Yet *CSI* was a show about *corpses*. Lit like movie stars, they were even treated to their own in-flesh close-ups. Was the show also hinting that there was something queasy about glamour itself, which touched everything with the same glossy aesthetic? That it could be softly squeezing the life out of the world as it pushed everything, human and inhuman, onto the same radiant plane?

*

There was another story about light playing out in *CSI*'s use of Luminol: it offered us illumination in its old-fashioned sense of enlightenment. When applied to a crime scene, the chemical's blue light manifested a spectacular certainty. It fluoresced with knowledge. As Catherine Willows tells a new recruit in the series' pilot episode, the detectives are able to offer closure to the victims. Doing this, she drawled, is guaranteed to 'make you feel like King Kong on cocaine.'

This promise found its most perfect expression in the show's in-wound sequences (or 'CSI-shots'): sped-up CGI-generated tracking shots that swooped, with whooshing sound effects, into a body's hyperreal flesh. These macro-close-up simulations allowed our eyes to follow (or perhaps recreate the force of) the path of a bullet through the tissues of a heart or the tip of an ice pick into a brain. If the program's corpses were beautiful from the outside, they were even more astonishing inside. As if they had undergone their own Luminol transformation, organs and tissues no longer operated mysteriously in darkness beneath the skin, but — as bright red capillaries burst or the alveoli of a dying lung collapsed — they were lit up from within as these sequences took us to the precise threshold between life and death.

While police procedurals usually revolved around action, *CSI* made a fetish of thought – that was another reason why I liked it. The crime scene investigators of the night shift, derided by the cops as the 'nerd squad,' were unusually talented individuals who loved their work. As the camera dwelt upon their faces in the laboratory or the strange silent fishbowl of a crime scene, they brought an almost mystical reverence to forging their private connections with the dead. As they bent over ruined bodies, removed Scrabble letters from a victim's throat, or peered at epithelials under a microscope, their faces, alight with calm concentration, had the absorbed grace of renaissance angels.

This unhurried, methodical, almost meditative pursuit of knowledge formed the narrative structure of the original *CSI: Las Vegas,* especially in its early episodes. 'What does the room say?' Grissom asks one of his staff. 'Concentrate on what cannot lie. The evidence.' When a detective blunders into the kitchen in 'Blood Drops' and tells Grissom there is nothing to see, he replies testily, 'You guys will never get it.' The show brought crime scenes to life with knowledge, as the crew painstakingly reconstructed the angles of bullets or established the place of death through local pollen. Their methodical devotion to method was emphasised by the fact that they often did their work in dark rooms, under the sweep of high-voltage torches or the shorter beams of close torchlight. Real forensic detectives have complained that *CSI*'s plots were thin and that results are rarely obtained so quickly but that was precisely the point. The show held out the possibility of truth. 'We resolve,' Willows tells a raw recruit. 'We restore peace of mind.'

It was quite marvellous to watch as each investigator or small team gave a case their full attention, conducted almost all of the evidence-gathering and lab work, and pursued it to its very end in a chain of evidence as seamless as those 'CSI-shots.' Often they were able to solve a case by consulting an online database: of shoe prints, tyre treads, carpet swatches, marks on bullet casings, or even, in one episode, clown makeup designs. Investigating a fire in a lounge room, Stokes scrolls through a database of furniture, drags the icon of a particular brand of sofa into an on-screen model of the room and, using another database of ignition temperature, recreates the fire, to establish that the 'Curie point' of the sofa is so high that if the fire had begun here the damage should have been much greater. (This ability to divide up and name the world was another of *CSI*'s pleasures). In another episode, Willows uses red tape to trace the angles of blood spatter, graphs these lines into a computer, and we are able to watch the exact sequence of death play out before our eyes.

CSI offered a powerful vision of information technology. Unlike other procedural dramas of the eighties and nineties, their detectives beleaguered by a cheap and uncaring bureaucracy, its crime teams were well-resourced with cutting-edge equipment and focused on each victim as an individual for whom truth must be found (a message driven home by The Who's 'Who Are You,' whose jittery guitar chords would introduce each episode from the second season on). One critic has suggested that this was a consoling fantasy for a country traumatised by 9/11, in which it was proving immensely difficult to identify the missing from their remains. But would it have been so compelling if the public good wasn't also under assault around the world, particularly in highly privatised America? After all, *CSI: Las Vegas* debuted in the same year that the result of the US election, and ultimate victory of George W. Bush, would be determined by 'hanging chads': incompletely punched holes in Florida's antiquated Votomatic-style punched card ballots, which were only one of a ramshackle and diverse range of state-based processes in a country unable or unwilling to put in place a unified federal voting system. It was also ironic that a corpse in one of *CSI*'s labs would receive closer individual attention than an uninsured living body in an American hospital system in which baroque layers of health insurance also meant that quality of treatment, or even its possibility, were determined by the package taken up by a person's employer and by the logarithms of an insurance company. The fictional Las Vegas detectives' investigations moved much faster than the real-life criminal justice system, too. In 2019, *The Atlantic* would report that close to a quarter of a million rape kits, some up to thirty years old, were sitting in police storage untested, due to a lack of funding resources and a reluctance on the part of police to treat rape as an urgent crime. I could contemplate all of this with a certain equanimity from Australia where, in spite of neoliberal 'efficiency dividends,' we still held onto federally funded universal healthcare, nationalised voting, and a degraded-but-functional public service.

And yet, at the same time as the show offered a fantasy of a seamless public good, its Luminol scenes depended for their shop-stopping effect on revealing the hidden violence beneath America's glossy surfaces. I had often wondered, watching the program, what I might have seen revealed if I had sprayed Luminol in the share houses where I had once lived. At the very least, the bathrooms and bedrooms would likely manifest blood drops and jismic sprays – but would Luminol also reveal Van Gogh-like swirls of greater savagery? *CSI* gave us a Las Vegas, and an America whose apparently clean surfaces seethed with an invisible brutality that it constantly brought to light. While this has long been a trope of crime fiction ('Down these mean streets a good man must go who is not himself mean, who is neither tarnished nor afraid,' wrote forties noir master Raymond Chandler), Luminol's eerie glow suggested that violence had acquired an uncanny, almost supernatural, force.

Still the show's conviction that science and facts matter – its insistence on evidence – seems touching from the perspective of 2020, when the most basic facts, such as how viruses multiply or how vaccines work, have been politicised, to the point of causing many thousands of deaths to Covid-19, a diagnosis denied vehemently by some victims even until death. Yet it's possible to also catch sight, in the show's glow, of a massive reconfiguration of knowledge that was already underway. There was something claustrophobic about those 'CSI-shots', in which the camera entered a body that was *already* transparent and lit-up with knowledge to find an answer that was *already there*. Luminol's blood-activated shine offered instant truth in the form of visual confirmation. The detectives followed scientific methodology but they were almost always right. Real-life crime scene investigators have pointed out that there is much more speculation involved in interpreting evidence, which does not lead as inevitably to a conclusion. Even DNA analysis, which has banished the chance of error in identifying a suspect to one in a quadrillion, needs a matching profile to already exist in the CODIS (Combined DNA Index System) database; and it still forms only part of the chain of evidence in a courtroom. (In spite of this, legal professionals have noted a '*CSI*-effect' among juries, who will sometimes reject deductive evidence unsupported by DNA 'proof').

In *CSI*, blood has only one story to tell. Maybe I'm drawing too wide a bow but it feels significant that the show's global popularity grew at the same time as a whole range of fundamentalisms – economic, religious, political, judicial – were on the rise, all seeking an implacable and instantaneous 'truth.'

Alongside them, we've seen a growing impatience for narrative and ambiguity in public discourse, which have been replaced by the demand for the immediately obvious. Even in the arts, where you might expect the most elasticity, there has been a building expectation that they can provide instantaneous 'takeaways'. Why read Proust's *Memories of Time Past*, when Alain de Botton could distil its most important life 'lessons' for you in *How Proust Can Change Your Life*? Why spend years at university learning to master a discipline, when you can now enrol in a 'bespoke' degree, or short course (a 'short offering' in management discourse), and tick off rubrics and 'learning outcomes'?

The enlightenment that *CSI* offered, brilliant and ready-made, was entirely different from the Enlightenment's history as a seventeenth- and eighteenth-century intellectual movement: a revolution in thought that valued reason tied to notions of progress, democracy and freedom from church or state. Real knowledge takes trial and error and one of the few certainties for those who research for a living is that evidence can look entirely different when looked at in a new light within an evolving discipline. It accretes over time – but duration has also dropped out of the public understanding of research. Meanwhile, the widespread belief in the possibility of an absolute proof that speaks for itself makes a large part of the general public increasingly hostile to knowledge that depends on scientific method and interpretation; and more susceptible, at the same time, to those who claim, emphatically, to be in possession of the truth. And so we shouldn't be surprised if a great number of people are prepared to 'decide' whether climate change exists on the basis of whether they instinctively agree or disagree or that vaccines cause autism on the basis of a single outlying academic paper among thousands. Without a sense of the slow hierarchies of a discipline, how could someone looking for 'answers' tell the difference? Why shouldn't they put their faith in the certainty of a charismatic preacher or YouTube pundit? Watching the cinematography of *CSI: Las Vegas* lavish the same patina on everything, dead or alive, in the same way that the constant glossy flow of our internet feeds reduces everything to the same scale, I feel as if I can see another way of understanding the world blooming before my eyes. For a show that was supposedly about thinking, its luminous intensity often made critical distance impossible.

CSI: Miami would make this claustrophobic sense of brightness even more pronounced. In place of the original's Luminol gleam it gave us sticky sunlight in a palette of yellows and golds. The Florida franchise torqued its light effects to such a fever pitch that TV critics fell over themselves trying to describe them. It was if, one wrote, the cinematography had been hijacked by the Teletubbies. The light was Zoroastrian, claimed another, benevolent and malevolent forces fighting it out in every shot. The gestures of its head CSI, played by ginger-headed David Caruso, were so studied that comedian Jim Carrey could have talk show audiences in stitches by delivering the actor's 'scene-buttoning' lines with an exaggerated dryness while clips of Caruso settling his sunglasses back onto his nose after one of his humdingers became viral memes. If the original *CSI* was about eerie glamour, *CSI: Miami*'s greater theme seemed to be repetition: a kind of comic-noir eternal return, in which all the gestures and effects that made the original show fresh and grave had been rendered weightless.

This jadedness seemed appropriate to an era in which cinematic special effects were becoming a do-it-yourself affair. Midway through its run, the series would find itself competing with a growing suite of apps like Hipstamatic (2009) and Instagram (2010), whose colour-enhancing filters could render snapshots in every style from Tintype and Polaroid prints to Kodachrome. For a short time, everyone's feeds looked like overexposed pictures from their parents' shoeboxes, though the filters and combinations would grow more sophisticated, to mimic iconic street photography, propaganda, and stills from video art and indie movies. These retro apps have given way, in turn, to apps that polish images so that Instagrammers can present perfectly curated selves and lives. Top apps of 2020 were Prisma (which turns photos into 'paintings' and 'drawings'); Oberlo (for styling food with a birdseye view and popping colours), and Visage (which whitens teeth, enhances skin shine, and applies makeup in selfies).

But what if nature under duress is becoming as weird as the special effects in *CSI: Las Vegas* and *Miami*? How should we feel about the way the show linked baroque effects and death? After the 2019–2020 Australian bushfires, which turned the sky an eerie orange for weeks, I would never want to see the Miami series or use the exaggerated colour filters in a photo app again.

*

In the end, the most compelling reason for the popularity of the *CSI* franchise may have been that by linking glossy light effects and corpses it articulated something we could feel but not quite see: that glamour is a kind of violence that beautifies the deathly comet tail of endless consumption it trails behind it. I think it's no coincidence that the show's urge to turn everything luminous took hold around the world at the same time as human activity was threatening bioluminescence in nature.

Fireflies (actually beetles from the family Lampyridae) are thought to have been flashing their intermittent blinking patterns or trails of yellow, orange, or electric blue – each unique to its 2000 species – for 100 million years. But reports in 2020 suggested that they are threatened by loss of habitat, pesticides and nocturnal light pollution, which can make them lose track of time or position or fail to recognise important objects. A study of British fireflies showed that the new LED streetlights, which replaced the older sodium models with a bluer light, were more likely to disrupt males seeking a mate, as they homed in on a female's green glow. Commercial exploitation doubles down on these unwitting threats. Last decade, massive 'glow shows' became popular at theme parks and indoor entertainment centres in China; it is estimated that in 2016 alone they collectively purchased around six million fireflies harvested from the countryside. In 2009, vendors on the country's online shopping platform Taobao were selling up to 200,000 live fireflies a day as romantic gifts and party decorations. Although China banned the practice in 2017 and its theme parks are now experimenting with laser lights, the country's rarest fireflies may already be gone.

In the ocean, artificial light from global shipping movement and cities is disrupting the vertical migration of bioluminescent zooplankton from the safe depths of the ocean to their night feeding at the surface. (The nightly ascent of an estimated 5 billion metric tonnes of deep ocean creatures around the globe to feed on microscopic surface plants, which these gleaming creatures are part of, is, incidentally, the world's largest migration). Because the zooplanktons' shine, a defensive mechanism, is comparatively less bright next to human-made light they at greater risk of being eaten by predators. But the causes for some die-offs of the planet's light shows remain unknown. In 2014, 'nature flipped the switch' as one report put it, on the shimmering blue-green dinoflagellate displays in Puerto Rico's Mosquito Bay, which suddenly went dark. In 2010, a study published in *Nature* suggested that rising ocean temperatures had caused the world's phytoplankton population to drop by 40 per cent.

Paradoxically, increased bioluminescent blooms may be distress flares from a beleaguered nature. Bioluminescent algae thrive where oxygen levels are low and nitrogen and phosphorous levels are high, which is 'bad news,' in the words of a marine scientist, for the larger marine food chain. A 2014 study tied three outbreaks of *noctiluca scintillans*, or sea sparkle, in the Arabian sea to oxygen-deficient water. These glowing blooms had displaced tiny diatoms – those single-celled algae the Victorian 'diatomists' loved to arrange into beautiful patterns beneath their microscopes – at the base of the food chain in an ecosystem that supports 120 million people. Since 1994 in Australia, *Noctiluca scintillans* have been lighting up the Derwent River in Hobart, Tasmania, and the south coast of New South Wales with displays of electric blue so spectacular that followers post and follow them on Facebook pages dedicated to sightings. Scientists are inclined to see the Tasmanian blooms as a sign of global warming, which, as one reporter put it, has 'never looked so beautiful.'

While we may not know the exact chain of cause and effect, we can feel the uncanniness now within the beauty of these bioluminescent displays. Like a natural Luminol, they may be registering the deadly traces of our human touch in a world that is now 1 degree Celsius warmer than it was in the late nineteenth century. The phosphorescent blooms we're witnessing may be like the end of a firework display, I think, when the biggest and most beautiful rockets are set off just as the show ends. Dying, as *CSI* intuited, can be very beautiful.

We are in the charismatic phase of environmental collapse, which we might just be able to slow if we take radical action; though the world is currently on a trajectory towards a three to four-degree rise in temperatures by this century's end. What comes next will not be as lovely: more frequently burned, leached of colour and complexity, and increasingly silent. The 2019–2020 fires here in Australia gave us a foretaste of what writer Danielle Celemajer has described as a 'sensory apocalypse.'

At the end of our tour of Waitomo Caves, my parents bought me a souvenir pen. Its end was filled with liquid, on which, when I tilted the pen from side to side, the little flat-bottomed boat would glide backward and forward beneath that living constellation. I wish I could find the pen again, to return to that time, even for a moment. Meanwhile, I continue to hope that Bermuda fireworms mate in an orgy of fluorescent green that lights up the Caribbean. And that, somewhere in the Atlantic Ocean, the Abralia squid is still changing its colours to match the moonlight.

Selected Bibliography

Introduction

In 2004, the IGBP (International Geosphere-Biosphere Program) published the first graphs of the 'Great Acceleration,' showing socio-economic and earth system trends from 1750 to 2000. In 2015, they were updated to 2010.

Ben Strauss, director of Climate Central's program on sea level rise is quoted predicting that the 22nd century would be the 'century of hell' under a high emissions scenario in Brady Dennis and Chris Mooney, 'Scientists nearly double sea rise projections for 2100, because of Antarctica,' *Washington Post* 31 March 2016: https://www.washingtonpost.com/news/energy-environment/wp/2016/03/30/antarctic-loss-could-double-expected-sea-level-rise-by-2100-scientists-say/. Bruno Latour describes the collapse of critical distance in his seminal article 'Agency at the Time of the Anthropocene,' *New Literary History* 45 (1), 2014; for a description of Russia's exploding permafrost, see Andrew E. Kramer, 'Land in Russia's Arctic Blows "Like a Bottle of Champagne",' *The New York Times*, 5 September 2020: https://www.nytimes.com/2020/09/05/world/europe/russia-arctic-eruptions.html. Lyall Watson's description of Earth's atmosphere can be found in his *Heaven's Breath: A Natural History of the Wind* (NY: New York Review Books, 2019). Hopkins praises speckled things in his poem 'Pied Beauty,' *The Poems of Gerard Manley Hopkins* (London: Oxford University Press, 1967). George Saunders's story of sitting in a plane's smoke-filled cabin appears in Joel Lovell, 'George Saunders Has Written the Best Book You'll

Read This Year,' *The New York Times*, 3 January 2013: https://www.nytimes.com/2013/01/06/magazine/george-saunders-just-wrote-the-best-book-youll-read-this-year.html.

Signs and Wonders

The World Wildlife report I refer to is the *Living Planet Report 2014: Species and Spaces, People and Places*, edited by R. McLellan, L. Iyengar, B. Jeffries, and N. Oermerlans which attracted appalled worldwide attention after it made such great losses known for the first time (Gland, Switzerland: WWF, 2014). In 2020 a panel of 125 experts would amend this figure to estimate that we have killed 68 per cent of the world's wild creatures since 1970 (R. E. A. Almond, M. Grooten and T. Petersen eds, *Living Planet Report 2020: Bending the Curve of Biodiversity Loss*, Gland, Switzerland, 2020). For a discussion of the 'worst-case scenario' melting of the world's ice sheets, see Thomas Slater, Anna E. Hogg and Ruth Mottram, 'Ice-sheet losses track high-end sea-level rise projections,' *Nature Climate Change* 10, 2020, pages 879–881. Study author Tom Slater describes the rise as 'faster than we could have imagined' in Chris Baynes, 'Climate crisis: Ice sheets melting at a "worst-case scenario" rate,' *Independent*, 2 September 2020. https://www.independent.co.uk/climate-change/news/climate-crisis-ice-sheets-melting-global-warming-greenland-antarctic-a9699921.html.

Chris Jordan's gallery of photographs of dead seabirds that have ingested plastic, titled 'Midway: Message from the Gyre,' along with a short explanation of his project, can be found at his website: http://www.chrisjordan.com/gallery/midway/#about. The process of kneeling over the birds to take his photographs, Jordan wrote, was 'like looking into a macabre mirror.'

See also, on plastic: Cameron Muir, 'Ghost species and shadow places: Seabirds and plastic pollution on Lord Howe Island,' *Griffith Review* 63, 2019, pp. 201–215; Jennifer L. Lavers, Ian Hutton and Alexander Bond, 'Clinical Pathology of Plastic Ingestion in Marine Birds and Relationships with Blood Chemistry,' *Environmental Science & Technology* 53 (15), 2019, pp. 9224–9231; Rebecca Giggs, *Fathoms: The World in the Whale* (New York: Simon & Schuster, 2020). UNESCO estimates that 8 million tons of plastic pollution are entering our oceans annually, killing 100,000 marine animals a year.

Gretta T. Pecl, Miguel B. Araújo, Johann D. Bell, Julia Blanchard, Timothy C. Bonebrake, et al., discuss changing animal movements in 'Biodiversity redistribution under climate change: Impacts on ecosystems and human wellbeing,'

Selected Bibliography

Science, 31 March 2017, 355 (6332), p. eaai 9214. The German study that set off widespread alarm about an insect 'apocalypse' was Caspar A. Hallmann, M. Sorg, E. Jongejans, H. Siepel, N. Hofland, H. Schwan, et al., 'More than 75 per cent decline over 27 years in total flying insect biomass in protected areas,' *Plos One*, 12 (10) 18 October, 2017, e0185809. Subsequent studies have suggested that insects could be more resilient and the outlook more complicated than this data appeared to suggest initially: Ed Yong, 'Is the Insect Apocalypse Really Upon Us?', *The Atlantic*, 20 February 2019. https://www.theatlantic.com/science/archive/2019/02/insect-apocalypse-really-upon-us/583018/. Richard Kock, a professor of wildlife health and emerging diseases at the Royal Veterinary College in London describes saiga antelope and their fawns dying 'as if a switch had been turned on' in David Derbyshire, 'The terrifying phenomenon that is pushing species towards extinction,' *The Guardian*, 25 February 2018. https://www.theguardian.com/environment/2018/feb/25/mass-mortality-events-animal-conservation-climate-change.

Leading scientists have linked the global Covid-19 pandemic, like MERS, SARS, and bird flu before it, to our continued encroachment on wild places, which allows pathogens to pass from wild animal populations. Covid-19 is described as nature's 'clear warning shot' in Damian Carrington, 'Coronavirus: "Nature is sending us a message," says UN environmental chief,' *The Guardian* 25 March 2020. https://www.theguardian.com/world/2020/mar/25/coronavirus-nature-is-sending-us-a-message-says-un-environment-chief. Ecologist Ken Green describes the disappearance of bogong moths in Graham Readfearn, 'Decline in bogong moth numbers leaves mountain pygmy possums starving,' *The Guardian*, 25 February 2019. https://www.theguardian.com/environment/2019/feb/25/decline-in-bogong-moth-numbers-leaves-pygmy-mountain-possums-starving.

For an example of the many forums in which scientists are openly expressing their shock and grief, see Gaia Vince, 'How scientists are dealing with "ecological grief",' *The Guardian*, 13 January 2020. https://www.theguardian.com/science/2020/jan/12/how-scientists-are-coping-with-environmental-grief. Joëlle Gergis writes of her loss of hope in 'The great unravelling: "'I never thought I'd live to see the horror of planetary collapse,"' *The Guardian*, 15 October 2020. https://www.theguardian.com/australia-news/2020/oct/15/the-great-unravelling-i-never-thought-id-live-to-see-the-horror-of-planetary-collapse.

Sergei Fyodorov, researcher at the Institute of Applied Ecology, Yakutsk, describes the sounds of the Batagaika crater in (no author), 'Disturbing melody of melting permafrost in "crater" called "gateway to hell,"' *The Siberian Times* 10 March 2017. https://siberiantimes.com/other/others/news/n0895-disturbing-melody-of-melting-permafrost-in-crater-called-gateway-to-hell/. UNFCCC spokesperson Nick Nuttall describes melting icebergs as sounding like animals in pain in a report on the United Nations' web page on 14 June, 2016: https://unfccc.int/news/sounds-of-melting-icebergs-inspire-climate-action. Oskar Glowacki, a geophysicist at the Scripps Institution of Oceanography at the University of Carlifornia, San Diego, describes the 'songs' of melting icebergs in Laura Lipuma, 'Sounds of melting glaciers could reveal how fast they shrink,' AGU GeoSpace blog, 10 May 2018. https://blogs.agu.org/geospace/2018/05/10/sounds-of-melting-glaciers-could-reveal-how-fast-they-shrink/. Edgar Allan Poe's story 'A Descent into the Maelstrom' can be found in *The Works of Edgar Allan Poe*, The Raven Edition, Volume II. Project Gutenberg, 2000. https://www.gutenberg.org/files/2148/2148-h/2148-h.htm.

All quotes in this chapter from Freud's hugely influential essay 'The "Uncanny,"' are taken from James Strachey, translator and general editor, in collaboration with Anna Freud, *The Standard Edition of the Complete Psychological Works of Sigmund Freud, Volume XVII (1917–1919), An Infantile Neurosis and Other Works* (London: The Hogarth Press and the Institute of Psycho-analysis, 1925). Bruno Latour writes about the way the world is speaking to us in 'Agency at the Time of the Anthropocene,' *New Literary History* 45 (1), *Winter* 2014, pp. 1–18. Elsewhere, he has spoken of catching a plane from Paris to Calgary, Canada, in 2016, which took him over the melting Baffin ice sheets, where the fissures in the tundra below the window reminded him of the agonised face in Edvard Munch's painting, 'The Scream.' See Ava Kofman, 'Bruno Latour, the Post-Truth Philosopher, Mounts a Defense of Science,' *The New York Times Magazine*, 25 October, 2018. https://www.nytimes.com/2018/10/25/magazine/bruno-latour-post-truth-philosopher-science.html.

The New Yorker's article on parch marks was Sam Knight, 'The British Heatwave and Aerial Archaeology,' 5 March 2018. https://www.newyorker.com/news/letter-from-the-uk/the-british-heat-wave-and-aerial-archeology. The *Daily Mail*'s account mocking Jeremy Buckingham's visceral response to the smell of rotting fish at the Menindee Weir is Laura Withers, 'Bizarre moment former MP VOMITS while holding a dead fish that was one of a million killed "in man-made crisis",' 10 January 2019. https://www.dailymail.co.uk/news/article-6575127/Bizarre-moment-former-MP-VOMITS-holding-dead-fish-one-million-killed-man-crisis.html. Zadie Smith writes about our 'new normal' in 'Elegy for a Country's Seasons,' *The New York Review of Books*, 3 April 2014. 'It's hard to keep apocalypse consistently in mind,' runs the subhead, 'especially if you want to get out of bed in the morning.'

The necessarily brief explanation of the Yarralin's understanding of the Cosmos in this chapter is taken from Deborah Bird Rose, 'Exploring an Aboriginal Land Ethic,' *Meanjin* 43 (3), pp. 378-387. Although this is among Rose's earlier work, I've referred to it because it offers an approachable and user-friendly entry into Rose's writing. So does Deborah Bird Rose and Anna Clarke, eds, *Tracking Knowledge in North Australian Landscapes: Studies in Indigenous and Settler Ecological Knowledge Systems* (Casuarina, NT: North Australia Research Unit, ANU, 1997). Bird Rose explores the possibilities of Indigenous knowledge systems for negotiating the Anthropocene in 'Slowly – writing into the Anthropocene,' *TEXT Special Issue 20: Writing Creates Ecology and Ecology Creates Writing*, October 2013. See also Bruce Pascoe, *Dark Emu* (Broome: Magabala Books, 2014), Victor Steffensen, *Fire Country* (Richmond, Vic.: Hardie Grant, 2020) and Frances Bodkin, *D'harawal Climate and Natural Resources* (Sussex Inlet, NSW: Envirobook, 2013). For information on Indigenous astronomy, see the Australian Indigenous Astronomy site: http://www.aboriginalastronomy.com.au/. For an overview of Indigenous weather knowledge, see Timothy J. Entwhistle, *Sprinter and Sprummer: Australia's Changing Seasons* (Collingwood, Vic.: CSIRO Publishing, 2014).

Roman Fedortsov tweets images of deep sea fish at @rfedortsov, Secrets of the Ice at @brearkeologi, and Lego Lost at Sea as @LegoLostAtSea.

Coal, an Unnatural History

The booklet my children are handed to search for 'Shawn the Prawn' is (no author), *Australian Parliament House: Children's Trail* (Australian Parliament House, undated). Information about the stone used in Parliament House is taken from Wolf Mayer, *Images in Stone: A Guide to the Building Stones of Parliament House* (Canberra: Australian Government Publishing Association, 1996). This essay also owes a large debt to Ann Elias's fascinating 'The Black Diamonds of Sydney Harbour,' *Environment and Planning E: Nature and Space*, 2 (3), 1 September 2019, pp. 645–664.

Other works cited in this essay: James Bradley, 'How Australia's coal madness led to Adani,' *The Monthly*, April 2019. https://www.themonthly.com.au/issue/2019/april/1554037200/james-bradley/how-australia-s-coal-madness-led-adani; Geoffrey R Evans, 'Transformation from "Carbon Valley" to a "Post-Carbon Society" in a Climate Change Hot Spot: the Coalfields of the Hunter Valley, New South Wales, Australia,' *Ecology and Society* 13 (1) Article 39. http://www.ecologyandsociety.org/vol13/iss1/art39/; M Forrest, 'A Piece of Coal,' *Sydney Mail*, Wednesday 20 August 1913, p. 23; Barbara Freese, *Coal: A Human History* (NY: Basic Books, 2003); Alana Grech and Laurence McCook, 'Shipping in the Great Barrier Reef: the miners' highway,' *The Conversation*, 25 May 2015; Richard H Horne, 'The True Story of a Coal Fire. Chapter I,' *Household Words*, 6 April 1850; Richard H Horne, 'The True Story of a Coal Fire. Chapter II,' *Household Words*, 13 April, 1850; and Richard H Horne, 'The True Story of a Coal Fire. Chapter the Last,' *Household Words*, 20 April 1850; Ian Hoskins, *Coast: A History of the New South Wales Edge* (Sydney: New South, 2013); Oliver Milman, 'The "great dying": rapid warming caused largest extinction event ever, says report,' *The Guardian* 7 December 2018. https://www.theguardian.com/environment/2018/dec/06/global-warming-extinction-report-the-great-dying; Dana Nuccitelli, 'Burning coal may have caused Earth's worst mass extinction,' *The Guardian*, 12 March, 2018. https://www.theguardian.com/environment/climate-consensus-97-per-cent/2018/mar/12/burning-coal-may-have-caused-earths-worst-mass-extinction; Ruth Park, *The Companion Guide to Sydney* (Sydney: Collins, 1973); Guy Pearse, David McKnight, Bob Burton, *Big Coal: Australia's Dirtiest Habit* (Sydney: New South, 2013); Eilís Phillips, 'Ghosts, Angels & Death Omens: The Seven Whistlers in Mining Folklore,' Folklore Thursday website. https://folklorethursday.com/halloween/ghosts-angels-death-omens-seven-whistlers-mining-folklore/; Steffan Rhys, 'In darkness for years, the dangerous and harsh life of pit ponies,' *Wales Online*, 9 April 2008. https://www.walesonline.co.uk/news/wales-news/darkness-years-dangerous-harsh-life-2182018; Josh Robertson, 'Adani groundwater plan could permanently drain desert oasis, scientists say,' ABC website. https://www.abc.net.au/news/2018-03-21/adani-groundwater-plan-risks-permanent-damage-to-desert-springs/9569184; Frank Walker, 'Ancient spirits lifted,' *The Sydney Morning Herald* 13 July 2008. https://www.smh.com.au/national/ancient-spirits-lifted-20080713-gdslxe.html; Jeanette Winterson, *Why Be Happy When You Could Be Normal?* (London: Vintage, 2012).

Selected Bibliography

Terror from the Air

Sources include: Anonymous, 'Explosive Fire Activity in Australia,' NASA Earth Observatory website, 6 January 2020; Anonymous, 'Thirsty koala drinks from cyclist's water bottle near Adelaide as heatwave continues," ABC News website, 28 December 2019; Ann Arnold, 'Bushfires devastate rare and enchanting wildlife as "permanently" wet forests burn for the first time,' ABC News website, 27 November 2019 https://www.abc.net.au/news/2019-11-27/bushfires-devastate-ancient-forests-and-rare-wildlife/11733956; Australian Government Bureau of Meteorology, 'When bushfires make their own weather,' AGBM blog, 8 January 2018; Tony Birch, 'Walking and Being,' *Meanjin* Summer 2019; William J. Broad, 'The Hiroshima Mushroom Cloud That Wasn't,' *The New York Times*, 23 May 2016; Tom Griffiths, 'Season of Reckoning,' *Australian Book Review* 419, March 2020; Freya Mathews, 'Koala Makes us Australian: Reflections on the Great Fires,' ABC website, 9 March 2020; Mary Mrad, '"Offering a koala a drink from a bottle isn't without risks": Dr Chris Brown explains the best way to care for the dehydrated animals amid Australia's bushfire crisis,' *Daily Mail Australia*, 9 January 2020; Naomi Parry, 'Suspended in the New Normal,' blog post, January 6 2020. http://www.naomiparry.net/2020/01/06/suspended-in-the-new-normal/; Stephen Pyne, 'California wildfires signal the arrival of a planetary fire age,' *The Conversation*, 2 November 2019; Graham Redfearn and Adam Morton, 'Almost 3 billion animals affected by Australian bushfires,' *The Guardian* 28 July 2020; Gina Rushton, 'Babies Are Being Born Into Smoky Delivery Rooms As Australia Burns,' *Buzzfeed News*, 3 January 2020. https://www.buzzfeed.com/ginarushton/baby-delivery-canberra-bushfire-smoke; Ivan Smith, *The Death of a Wombat*, illustrations by Clifton Pugh (South Melbourne: Sun Books, 1977); Kerrin Thomas, Michael Cavanagh and Kim Honan, 'Beekeepers traumatised and counselled after hearing animals screaming in pain after bushfires,' ABC News website, 20 November 2019. The first written story to imagine the sufferings of a native animal (a kangaroo) was Sarah Porter's *Alfred Dudley; or, The Australian settlers*, published in 1830.

For a brilliant reconstruction of Australia's first mega-blaze, see Kevin Nguyen, Philippa McDonald, and Maryanne Taouk, 'Anatomy of a "mega-blaze,"' ABC News website, 27 July 2020. This diary takes its title from philosopher Peter Sloterdijk's *Terror from the Air* (Boston: MIT Press, 2009).

Birds
Michael Balter, 'Which Came First: the Dinosaur or the Bird?' *Audubon* January–February 2015; Marcia Bjornerud, *Timefulness: How Thinking Like a Geologist Can Help Save the World* (Princeton: Princeton University Press, 2021); Riley Black, 'Why. Birds Survived, and Dinosaurs Went Extinct, After an Asteroid Hit Earth,' *Smithsonian Magazine*, 15 September 2020; Riley Black, 'Dinosaurs Evolved Flight at Least Three Times,' *Smithsonian Magazine*, 7 June 2021; Steve Brusatte, *The Rise and Fall of the Dinosaurs: The Untold Story of a Lost World* (London: Macmillan. 2018); Quanguo Li et. al, 'Plumage Colour Patterns of an Extinct Dinosaur,' *Science* 327, 1369 (2010); Robert McFarlane, *Underland: A Deep Time Journey* (London: Penguin, 2020); John Pickrell, 'Why Did Dino-Era Birds Survive the Asteroid "Apocalypse"?' *National Geographic*, 25 May 2018; John Pickrell, 'This "Wonderchicken" walked the earth with dinosaurs,' *National Geographic* 19 March 2020; John R. Platt, 'I Know Why the Caged Songbird Goes Extinct,' The *Revelator*, 3 March 2021; Verlyn Klinkenberg, 'What Were Dinosaurs For?' *New York Review of Books*, 19 December 2020; Carl Zimmer, 'Evolution of Feathers,' *National Geographic*, February 2011.

How it Feels Now: After 'Hysterical Realism'
Alexandra Alter, 'Don DeLillo Deconstructed' (author interview), *The Wall Street Journal* 29 January 2010; Theodore Adorno, *Minima Moralia: Reflections from Damaged Life* (London: Verso 2020); Claire Armitstead, 'Ali Smith: "This young generation is is showing us that we need to change and we can change",' *The Guardian* 23 March 2019 https://www.theguardian.com/books/2019/mar/23/ali-smith-spring-young-generation-brexit-future; Lauren Berlant, *Cruel Optimism* (Indiana: Duke University Press, 2011); James Bradley, *Clade* (Melbourne: Hamish Hamilton, 2015); Mark Davis, 'The Decline of the Literary Paradigm,' *Ten Years, Heat* 12 new series (Giramondo, 2006); Don DeLillo, *Underworld* (London: Picador, 2011); Don DeLillo, *White Noise* (London: Penguin 25th anniversary edition, 2009); Ceridwen Dovey, *Only the Animals* (Melbourne: Penguin, 2014); Emily Eakin, 'The Author as Science Guy; Richard Powers, Chronicling the Technological Age, Sees Novels, Like Computers, as Based on Codes,' *The New York Times* 18 February 2003; Peter Gay, *Freud: A Life for our Time* (New York: W. W. Norton, 2006); Amitav Ghosh, *The Great Derangement: Climate Change and the Unthinkable* (Illinois:

Selected Bibliography

University of Chicago Press, 2016); Justine Hyde, '"From the Wreck" author Jane Rawson' (profile), *The Saturday Paper* June 23–29 2018; Stuart Jeffries, *Grand Hotel Abyss: The Lives of the Frankfurt School* (London: Verso, 2016); Krissy Kneen, *An Uncertain Grace* (Melbourne: Text, 2018); Wayne Koestenbaum, 'My 1980s,' *Salon* 24 August 2013; Jon McGregor, *Reservoir 13* (London: Fourth Estate, 2017); Phillipa McGuinness, *The Year Everything Changed: 2001* (Melbourne: Vintage, 2018); Jennifer Mills, *Dyschronia* (Sydney: Picador, 2018); Timothy Morton, *Hyperobjects: Philosophy and Ecology after the End of the World* (Minneapolis: University of Minnesota Press, 2013); Mathias Nilges, 'Neoliberalism and the time of the novel,' *Textual Practice* 29 (2) 2015: Jane Rawson, *From the Wreck* (Melbourne: Translit Lounge, 2017); Elizabeth Rush, *Rising: Dispatches from the New American Shore* (Minneapolis: Milkweed, 2018); Ali Smith, *Autumn* (London: Penguin, 2017), *Winter* (London: Penguin, 2018), *Spring* (London: Penguin, 2019), and *Summer* (London: Penguin, 2020); Zadie Smith, 'This is how it feels to me,' *The Guardian*, 13 October 2001: https://www.theguardian.com/books/2001/oct/13/fiction.afghanistan; Patrick White, *The Tree of Man* (Melbourne: Vintage, 2009); James Wood, 'Human, All Too Inhuman' (review of Zadie Smith's *White Teeth*), *The New Republic*, 24 July 2000; James Wood, 'Tell me how does it feel?' *The Guardian*, 5 October 2001: https://www.theguardian.com/books/2001/oct/06/fiction.

The Bureau of Linguistical Reality can be found at: https://bureauoflinguisticalreality.com/. As this book went to press it was still accepting submissions of new words for its 'dictionary of the future.'

Gum Trees
For some of the most recent information on the complex lives of trees, see David George Haskell's *Songs of the Trees: Stories from Nature's Great Connectors* (Melbourne: Black Inc, 2017) and Peter Wohlleben's *The Hidden Life of Trees: What They Feel, How They Communicate—Discoveries from a Secret World* (Melbourne: Black Inc, 2016).

Other works cited in this essay include: Sophie Cunningham, *City of Trees: Essays on Life, Death and the Need for a Forest* (Melbourne: Text, 2019); Karl Gruber, 'Trees that can walk up to 20m per year,' BBC, 16 December 2015: http://www.bbc.com/travel/story/20151207-ecuadors-mysterious-walking-trees; Martin Harrison, 'The Red Gum,' in *The Kangaroo Farm* (Brooklyn, NSW: Paper Bark Press, 1997); Emma Marris, 'Trees in Eastern U.S. Head

West as Climate Changes,' Scientific American 18 May 2017: https://www.scientificamerican.com/article/trees-in-eastern-u-s-head-west-as-climate-changes/; Les Murray, 'The Gum Forest,' Australian Poetry Library. https://www.poetrylibrary.edu.au/poets/murray-les/poems/the-gum-forest-0617017; Ruth Park, *Companion Guide to Sydney* (Sydney: Collins, 1973); Ethel Turner, *Seven Little Australians* (Australia: Penguin Group, 2010); Eric Rolls, *A Million Wild Acres: 200 Years of Man and an Australian Forest* (West Melbourne: Nelson, 1981).

The Opposite of Glamour
Glenn Albrecht, 'The age of solastalgia,' *The Conversation* 7 August 2012; John Berger, 'Why Look at Animals?' from *About Looking* (New York: Pantheon Books, 1980); James Bradley, *Clade* (Melbourne: Hamish Hamilton, 2015); Saskia Beudel, *A Country in Mind: Memoir with Landscape* (Crawley, University of Western Australia Publishing, 2013); Horatio Clare, *Orison for a Curlew* (Wimborne Minster: Little Toller Books, 2016); Christopher T. Filstrup et al., 'Evenness effects mask richness effects on ecosystem functioning at macro-scales in lakes,' *Ecology Letters* 22 (12) 2019; Donovan Hohn, *Moby-Duck: The True Story of 28,800 Bath Toys Lost at Sea and of the Beachcombers, Oceanographers, Environmentalists, and Fools, Including the Author, Who Went in Search of Them* (New York: Penguin Putnam Inc, 2012); Franz Kafka, 'A Cross-Breed (A Sport),' from *The Penguin Complete Stories of Franz Kafka*, Nathum N. Glatzer, Ed. (Harmondsworth: Penguin, 1983); Elizabeth Kolbert, *The Sixth Extinction: An Unnatural History* (New York: Henry Holt & Company, 2014); Kim Mahood, *Position Doubtful: Mapping Landscapes and Memories* (Brunswick: Scribe, 2016); Freya Mathews, 'Planet Beehive,' *Australian Humanities Review* Issue 50, May 2011; John McGregor, *Reservoir 13* (London: HarperCollins, 2017); Lydia Millet, *How the Dead Dream* (Boston: Mariner Books, 2009); Steve Mentz, 'The Neologismscene,' blogpost, Arcade: Literature, Humanities and the World website, no date; John Mooallem, *Wild Ones: A Sometimes Dismaying, Weirdly Reassuring Story about Looking at People Looking at Animals in America* (London: The Penguin Press, 2013); Les Murray, 'The Flying-Fox Dreaming,' from *The New Collected Poems* (Sydney: Duffy & Snellgrove, 2002); Will Self, 'The Frowniest Spot on Earth,' *London Review of Books* 28 April 2011; Roy Scranton, *Learning to Die in the Anthropocene: Reflections*

on the End of a Civilization (Oregon: City Lights Books, 2015); John Steinbeck, *Cannery Row* (London: Penguin Classics, 1994) and *The Log from the Sea of Cortez* (London: Pan Books, 1960); Anna Tsing, 'Feral Biologies,' paper for Anthropological Visions of Sustainable Futures, University College, London, February 2015, quoted by Donna Haraway, 'Anthropocene, Capitalocene, Plantationocene, Chthulucene: Making Kin,' *Environmental Humanities* 6 (1) May 2015.

The Disappearing Paragraph
Richard M. Coe describes the paragraph as a 'macro-punctuation mark' in *Toward a Grammar of Passages* (Carbondale: Southern Illinois University Press, 1988). Isaac Babel describes paragraphs as flashes of lightning in K. Paustovsky, *The Story of a Life: Years of Hope* (New York: Pantheon Books, 1969). Alexander Bain calls them 'a collection of sentences with a unity of purpose' in *English Composition and Rhetoric: A Manual* (New York: D. Appleton and Company, 1867). Australian writer Tony Macris conceives of paragraphs as 'small neighbourhoods' in A. Macris, 'Words and Worlds,' The *And Is* Papers: The Refereed Papers of the 12th [AAWP] Conference, held in Canberra during November 2007: https://www.aawp.org.au/publications/the-is-papers/ (downloaded 15 December, 2007). Gertrude Stein' statement about paragraphs is from *How To Write* (Mineola, NY: Dover Publications, 1975).

The novels mentioned are Jenny Offill, *Weather* (London: Granta, 2010); Patricia Lockwood, *No One Is Talking About This* (NY: Riverhead Books, 2021); Kevin Barry, *Night Boat to Tangier* (Edinburgh: Canongate, 2019); and Dominic Smith, *The Electric Hotel* (Sydney: Allen & Unwin, 2019).

Information on the use of space in Chinese painting is taken from Weimen He's catalogue notes for 'The Mystery of Empty Space: An exhibition of twentieth century Chinese painting', The Ashmolean 26 July–16 October 2001. https://www.heweimin.org/Texts/mystery_of_empty_space.pdf. See also: Andy Bodle, 'Breaking point: is the writing on the wall for the paragraph?' *The Guardian*, 22 May 2015; Virginia Woolf, 'English Prose' and 'William Hazlitt,' in *Delphi Complete Works of Virginia Woolf* (Delphi, 2013). In my discussion of Koestenbaum's 'My 1980s' (from *My 1980s and Other Essays* [NY: Farrar Straus and Giroux, 2013]) I follow the author's lead in using the 1980s-specific term 'AIDS', rather than 'HIV/AIDS', which is now the convention. He writes on Rimbaud's silence in *Figure It Out* (NY: Soft Skull Press, 2020).

Good Neighbours
Chris Anderson, 'Here come the drones!' *Wired*, 26 July 2012; Denis Byrne, 'Remembering the Elizabeth Bay Reclamation and the Holocene Sunset in Sydney Harbour,' *Environmental Humanities* 9 (1) 2017: 40–59; James Cheshire and Oliver Uberti, *Where the Animals Go: Tracking Wildlife with Technology in 50 Maps and Graphics* (London: Penguin, 2018); J. M. Coetzee, *The Lives of Animals* (Princeton: Princeton University Press, 2017); Jodi Dean, 'Communicative capitalism: this is what democracy looks like,' *Journal of Communication and Languages* No. 51 2019; Mark A. Ditmer et. al., 'Bears Show a Physiological but Limited Behavioural Response to Unmanned Aerial Vehicles,' *Current Biology* 13 August 2015; Simon During, 'Clifton Hill: Aesthetics and Local Politics,' *Meanjin* 53 (1) 1994 pp. 61–74; Harmon Ellen, 'Extremely Rare Zebra Causes Stampede at Maasai Mara,' Kenyans.co.ke website, 16 September 2019; Richard Flanagan, *Toxic: The Rotting Underbelly of the Tasmanian Salmon Industry* (Melbourne: Penguin, 2021); Sam Levin, '"Turn it off": how technology is killng the joy of national parks,' *The Guardian* 12 May 2017; Jon Mooallem, 'Who Would Kill a Monk Seal?' *The New York Times Magazine* 8 May 2013; Alison Page, '"This Baby Sloth Will Inspire You to Keep Going": Capital, Labor, and the Affective Power of Cute Animal Videos,' in Joshua Paul Dale et. al., eds, *The Aesthetics and Affects of Cuteness* (New York: Routledge, 2017); Tom Whyman, 'Beware of Cupcake Fascism,' *The Guardian* 8 April 2014.

The Weight of Things
Steven Connor, *The Matter of Air: Science and Art of the Ethereal* (Chicago: University of Chicago Press, 2010); John Gascoigne, '"Getting a Fix": The *Longitude* Phenomenon,' *Isis* 98 (4) 2007; James Hamilton-Paterson, *The Great Deep: The Sea and its Thresholds* (London: Random House, 1992); John Hersey, 'Hiroshima', *The New Yorker* 24 August, 1946; Raffi Khatchadourian, 'The Elusive Peril of Space Junk,' *The New Yorker* 21 September 2020; Patricia Lockwood, 'The Communal Mind,' *London Review of Books* 41 (4) 21 February 2019; David Philip Miller, 'The "Sobel Effect": The Amazing Tale of How Multitudes of Popular Writers Pinched All the Best Stories in the History of Science and Became Rich and Famous While Historians Languished in Accustomed Poverty and Obscurity, and How This Transformed the World.

Selected Bibliography

A Reflection on a Publishing Phenomenon,' *Metascience* 11 2002; James Thurber, *The Years With Ross* (New York: HarperCollins, 2001); David Remnick, 'The New Yorker in the Forties,' *The New Yorker* 28 April 2014; Mark Vanhoenacker, *Skyfaring: A Journey with a Pilot* (New York: Knopf, 2015); James Wolcott, 'Smugged by Reality,' *The New Republic* 11 February 2007.

The essay in which I first tried to account for the popularity of this genre was 'The Books of Last Things,' Peter Craven, ed., *The Best Australian Essays 1999* (Melbourne: Black Inc., 1999).

Covid Walking: Diary
Hector Pifarre I Arolas et al., 'Years of life lost to COVID-19 in 81 countries,' *Scientific Reports*, Article number: 3504 (2021); Roland Barthes, *Camera Lucida* (London: Vintage, 2006); David Collins, *An Account of the English colony in New South Wales: with remarks on the dispositions, customs, manners, etc., of the native inhabitants of that country* [1798] (Hong Kong: A.H. and A. W, Reed, 1975); Newton Fowell, letter to his father John Fowell, 31 July 1790, Mitchell Library of New South Wales transcript http://acms.sl.nsw.gov.au/_transcript/2015/D36453/a619.html; Paul Irish, *Hidden in Plain View: The Aboriginal People of Coastal Sydney* (Sydney: NewSouth, 2017); Robert McFarlane, 'Ghost Species,' *Granta 102: The New Nature Writing*, 2008; Steve Mentz, *Shipwreck Modernity: Ecologies of Globalization, 1550-1719* (Minneapolis: University of Minnesota Press, 2015); John Ruskin, 'An Essay on the Relative Dignity of the Studies of Painting and Music, and the Advantages to be Derived from Their Pursuit' (1838), *The Works of John Ruskin* (Cambridge: Cambridge University Press, 2010); Nakari Thorpe, Olivia Willis, and Carl Smith, '"Devil devil": The sickness that changed Australia,' ABC News website 7 June 2021 https://www.abc.net.au/news/health/2021-06-07/patient-zero-smallpox-outbreak-of-1789/100174988; John Vidal, '"Tip of the iceberg": is our destruction of nature responsible for Covid-19?' *The Guardian* 18 March 2020. *The New York Times* began its Who We've Lost series in March 2019. As this book went into print, it was still running. (See Daniel J. Wakin, 'Faces That Can't Be Forgotten,' *The New York Times*, 16 April 2020). John. Ruskin's remarks on hummingbirds were made in a 'Conversation with M. H. Spielman at Brantwood,' in E. T. Cook and Alexander Wedderburn, eds, *The Works of John Ruskin* (London: George Allen, 1903–12), Vol. 34.

Everything is Illuminated
Candice Gaukel Andrews, 'The Largest Migration on Earth is Vertical,' Good Nature Travel blog, 21 August, 2018 https://www.nathab.com/blog/the-largest-migration-on-earth-is-vertical/; Daniel G. Boyce, Marlon R. Lewis, and Boris Worm, 'Global phytoplankton decline over the past century,' *Nature* 466, pp. 591–596; Danielle Celermajer, *Summertime: Reflections on a Vanishing Future* (Sydney: Hamish Hamilton, 2021); Raymond Chandler, 'The Simple Art of Murder,' in *The Simple Art of Murder* (New York: Vintage Books, 1988); H. Gomes et al., 'Massive outbreaks of *Noctiluca scintillans* blooms in the Arabian Sea due to spread of hypoxia,' *Nature Communications* 5 (4862), 2010; Alexandra Micu, 'Global warming has never looked so beautiful: Glowing plankton in Tasmania,' ZME Science 27 May, 2015 https://www.zmescience.com/ecology/environmental-issues/global-warming-plankton-27052015/; Nigel Thrift, 'The Material Practices of Glamour,' *Journal of Cultural Economy* 1(1) 2008; Abigail Tucker, 'Bioluminescence: Light Is Much Better, Down Where It's Wetter,' Smithsonian Magazine March 2013 https://www.smithsonianmag.com/science-nature/bioluminescence-light-is-much-better-down-where-its-wetter-22988383/; Gaia Vince, 'The heat is on over the climate crisis. Only radical measures will work,' *The Guardian*, 19 May 2019; Ed Yong, 'Photographing the Glow of the Human Body,' *National Geographic* 20 July, 2009: https://www.nationalgeographic.com/science/article/photographing-the-glow-of-the-human-body.

Author's Note

In 2017, then Creative Director Helen Loughlin asked me to deliver the inaugural 'Eleanor Dark' lecture for Varuna: The Writers' House at the Sydney Writers' Festival in the Blue Mountains. This was the beginning of my essay 'The Opposite of Glamour' and also the moment when I thought that I might be able to write this book. Thanks, too, to Professor Ken Gelder, for asking me to speak at the 'Extinction in/and Australia' symposium at the University of Melbourne in 2018, which was also formative in its creation. Also to Catriona Menzies-Pike, editor of *Sydney Review of Books*, for publishing early versions of 'The Opposite of Glamour' and 'Signs and Wonders'; Sophie Cunningham, for asking me to write about time and the Coronavirus for *The Guardian*'s series 'Fire, Flood and Plague – essays about 2020'; Stephen Romei, as literary editor of *The Australian* and *The Australian's Review of Books*, for commissioning review-essays that were formative for thinking about the books mentioned in this collection; and Dr Diana Barnes, at the University of New England, for asking me to give a keynote paper on compassion and writing for the conference 'Compassion: A Timely Feeling,' which formed the germ of my essay on 'hysterical realism' and for her friendship and encouragement.

For reading sections of drafts, thanks to Danielle Clode and Tim Low (any errors that remain are my own). For answering questions and helping with references: Donna West Brett, Ken Gelder, and Naomi Parry. For allowing me to quote from private communications: Anna Funder ('live cremation'), Adrian Martin (on the uninhibited owls of Spain) and Damian Clarke, who forwarded me his brother's footage from Covid-lockdown Rome. Thanks to my colleagues at the University of Technology Sydney – especially Associate Professor Debra Adelaide – for your support. And to my friends on Facebook for responding to my many queries. To our children's four godparents, Ronn, Simeon, Jane, and Brenda, thank you – you are all in this book in more ways than I can count.

Brenda Walker, Deborah Robertson, and Liam Leonard – cherished friends, lifesavers, and the best readers I know – thank you for reading this book in manuscript. Thanks to my Australian agent Jane Novak: for pastoral care as well as agenting. With love for your sustaining friendship: Ronn Morris, Simeon Barlow, Jane McCredie, Sandy Webster and Naomi Parry. Thanks also to James Bradley – who has been writing wonderfully in this space for much longer than I have – for your support, discussions, and friendship. To my copy editor Michelle Swainson. And of course, to Ben Ball, for commissioning me to write this book and your grace about being quoted.

Above all, thank you to Richard, for stepping into the role of single father for the year and a half it took to write this book, and to Sofia and James, for not only understanding that this book took your Mum's time away from you but also throwing your support behind it.